THE SUNDAY TIMES
GUIDE TO
SKI & APRES-SKI

In association with
Harpers & Queen

Alistair Scott
with illustrations by
Nigel Paige

TIMES BOOKS

All hotels which have been classified under the Federation of Automobile Associations are accompanied by their star rating. Those hotels not so classified have no star rating.

The author would like to state that the information contained in this book was checked as rigorously as possible before going to press. Neither the author nor the publisher can take responsibility for any changes which may have occurred since, nor for any other variance of fact from that recorded here in good faith.

Published by Times Books Ltd
16 Golden Square
London
W1R 4BN

First edition published as
Harpers & Queen Ski & Après Ski Guide 1984

Designer: Don Macpherson

Cover Photograph by Mark Shapiro
Typeset in Great Britain by
New Faces, Bedford.
Printed in Great Britain at
Thetford Press Ltd., Thetford.

British Library Cataloguing Data

Scott, Alistair
The Sunday times guide to ski and après-ski.
1. Skis and skiing – Europe – Handbooks, manuals, etc.
I. Title II. Sunday times
796.93'094 GV854.8.E9

ISBN 0-7230-0281-9

ACKNOWLEDGEMENTS

I am grateful to the tourist officers of the individual resorts in this book for all the assistance they gave me when I was doing my research. I am also indebted to the national tourist offices in London who helped in the planning of my trip; particularly Denis Fabri, Pauline Hallam and Rene Bardy from France, Franz Blum from Sitzerland, Luise Oberrieder from Austria, and Italo Somarriello from Italy. Among the British tour operators, Mark Lines, Paul Chase-Gardener, Michael Rumbold, David Lewthwaite, Tessa Morris and Penny Fox were especially helpful in providing contacts and accommodation, as was Caroline Stuart Taylor of the Ski Club of Great Britain.

My greatest debt, however, is to the many workers who so readily showed me round their resorts and passed on so much useful 'inside' information. Thanks to: Carol Shipside, Tim Holmes, Maureen Sale, Chris Brown, Jenny Dixon Smith, Joanna Deakin, Clare Wilson, Tina Merrikin, Cathy Priefer, Alison Grieve, James Rothnie, Sally Dockerill, Marita Van Oldenborgh, Brian Walker, Cathy Batchelor, Emma Walters, Caroline White, Jackie Brown, Vicki Paterson, Janie Ellison, Julie Elkins, Jenny Pickering, Jenny Carlill, Jilly Large, Christabel Hunter, Rose Sheppard, Philippa Kilburn-Toppin, Jenny Solomons, Lizzie Bretherton, Sarah Handley, Julia Waye, Erika King, Colin and Judy McCubbin, Karen Butler, Emma Willis-Fleming, Tessa Rohan, Juliet Heywood, Tracy Clarkson, Ian Barr, Malcolm Scott, Diane Smith, Sue Price, Lindy Brown, Marian Bevan, Andy Gillespie, Sara Colclough, Averil Carr, Charm Eberle, Jo Royle, Linda Harris, Terry Denman, David Lindsay, Jonathan Preston, Clare Creagh-Osborne, Pilla Birkbeck, Tricia Charlton, Sarah Lumley, Debbie Kitchen, Tricia Charlton, Emma Rowan-Hamilton, Amanda Shakespeare, Belinda Boston, Ed Mannix, Claire Dalglish, Sarah Collingridge, Anne Sutcliffe, Kate Harris, Debie Burridge, Jamie Bell, Emma Bonford, Helen Rodgers and anyone whose name I have omitted from this list.

Douglas Rae and Stephen Quinn were instrumental in the production of this book. Rosalie George was another patient editor. Lizzie Norton's help was again invaluable at every stage from piste to proofs.

CONTENTS

THE GUIDE

THE MAPS

INTRODUCTION

The crucial test of a good guide book is its accuracy about places you know. On that score Alistair Scott's Guide to Ski and Après-Ski passes with flying colours: his description of the places I have been to is spot on.

Courmayeur is indeed one of the "happiest, friendliest ski resorts in the alps" and "the two ingredients that blind people to any shortfalls in the skiing are the village (old-fashioned and charming) and the locals (more modern but equally charming)".

St Anton is certainly a bit of a "mish-mash" architecturally and, despite its high-powered skiers, has an après-ski of "sweaty bars" rather than "chic nightclubs".

Nobody who has spent any time in Lech would be the least surprised that the local "sauve Tourist Director, mentioning his fondness for the British, should cite two Lords as close friends".

And, for a purpose-built resort, Les Arcs has indeed "avoided a lot of the mistakes of its predecessors" and despite being the home of ski evolutif, "manages to remain popular with the most chic of French skiers, while still attracting low-budget self-catering skiers from all over Europe."

As well as being accurate, this guide is fun. Each resort is stylishly and humourously described and the skier is given a lively picture of what to expect, on and off the slopes. Nobody should venture to any of these resorts for the first time without consulting it, and the glossary at the back. Who would argue with the definition of a charter flight as "airborne equivalent of cattle truck" or hired equipment as "another useful scapegoat for bad skiers".

The Sunday Times is delighted to be associated with *Harpers & Queen* in expanding and promoting this guide. The British are taking to the slopes in increasing numbers each year and readers of *The Sunday Times* are among them in their thousands.

Though we are still short of world champions, British skiing standards are rising. And, above all, British skiers are now enjoying themselves as never before. This guide captures some of that enjoyment and points you in the right direction for more. I hope you will use it, and benefit from it.

Andrew Neil
Editor, *The Sunday Times*
London, August 1986

FOREWORD

This book does not set out to be a comprehensive compendium of facts and figures on most ski resorts in the world. On the contrary. It is a personal account of 25 resorts in Europe which are the most popular with reasonably good or experienced British skiers and which are, on the whole, served by the leading British ski tour operators.

The problem with existing ski guides, it seemed to me, was that they were so determined to provide every possible statistic on even the smallest resort that they gave up any attempt to be readable or entertaining. Also, because they had to cover so many resorts (the majority of them obscure), in so many countries, they needed several writers, each with his own set of standards and attitudes. Consequently, as resorts are being assessed by different people, it is difficult for the reader to make comparisons. Though I may have prejudices or failings, at least they are consistent throughout this book.

Obviously statistics can have their uses: a resort with five lifts and 15km of runs is clearly inferior to one with 70 lifts and 150km of runs. But in the case of this book, all the resorts featured are fairly major ones and all of them offer sufficient skiing to keep a good skier amused for at least a week and usually a fortnight or longer. In this case, therefore, the statistics seem superfluous. In any case hardly any skiers can understand them. Nobody I asked could tell me how many kilometres of piste or hotel beds there were in their favourite resort, or whether this was more or less than in their second or third favourite resorts. Similarly no real skiers give a damn about how many public jacuzzis there are in each resort or how far away the nearest optician is. (Anybody who is so dependent on his optician as to need to have this information probably should not be going skiing anyway.)

Many resorts in this book have roughly comparable skiing. The reasons why some people will prefer one of these resorts to another will therefore have little to do with the technical quality of the skiing and much more to do with what we might call 'external' factors. These might include the position of the resort relative to airports; the type of accommodation available; the language spoken; the distance from the resort to the lift systems; the tour operators who go there; the number and quality of mountain restaurants; the kind of bars and restaurants in the resort; the other people who go there, etc.

For this reason this book is as much an après-ski guide as a ski guide. It is written, not for demented fanatics, but for people who go on skiing *holidays* and who like to enjoy the evenings almost as much as the days. It treats 'Where shall we have lunch today?' as a question every bit as vital as 'Where shall we ski today?' – indeed it acknowledges that for many skiers the two questions are inextricably intertwined.

I have personally visited each of the resorts in this book, most of them several times in the past few years. In the course of this time I have sampled accommodation ranging from five-star hotels to the floors of chalet girls' laundry rooms. Although I had a lot of assistance from tourist offices and lift companies, I went out of my way to make sure that I did not get simply the tourist director's version of the resort. In fact all resorts sound much the same when you hear them described by tourist directors: 'People think this is an expensive resort but in fact it's amazingly cheap – We've got bigger and better lifts than our neighbours, and more of them too, but by 1990 our lift system will connect with any resort you care to name – The most remarkable thing about this resort is the amazing off-piste – We have one of the best-known ski schools in the Alps – There's an enormous variety of nightlife – you must mention how lovely it is here in the summer.'

For the most part I tried to gauge the resorts I visited through the eyes of British people who were working or on holiday there. I had a lot of help from employees of British tour operators, especially those doing a second or subsequent season in the same resort. Having regular dealings with British visitors, these people are acutely aware of what these visitors liked or disliked and why they came back year after year – or never, as the case may be.

I have skied, eaten and drunk with reps, ski guides, chalet girls, ski bums and seasoned punters in all of these resorts. They have shown me their favourite runs, on and off the piste. They have told me where the queues build up and how best to avoid them. They have taken me to their favourite mountain restaurants and warned me off others. They have forced me to try all the local specialities, no matter how expensive or alcoholic. They have taken me to the key tea shops and bars in each resort. They have taken me out to dinner in all kinds of restaurants (or rather they have chosen the venue and *I* have taken *them*). No matter how tired I looked, they dragged me on to as many discos, nightclubs and late-night bars as possible.

Alas, I have not had time to eat in every restaurant mentioned in this book (the mountain restaurants of Zermatt, for instance, presented a particular problem), but I did eat in an awful lot of them and drank in most of the bars mentioned. In any case, readers should be assured that I accepted culinary recommendations only from people who had proved themselves suitably discerning in this area.

On the whole I have refrained from giving detailed prices. They make boring reading and quickly become out of date. As far as restaurants are concerned I have tried to indicate which are the cheaper and which the more expensive in each resort. All skiing holidays are expensive if you intend to do the thing properly and enjoy yourself to the full. The principal cost factors will be the travel and accommodation: whether a bottle of Coke costs 2FF or 95FF in a given mountain restaurant it is unlikely to make much difference to the overall cost.

In the case of lift passes, on the whole you get what you pay for: the more lifts the more you pay. In any case the difference between a fortnight's pass for the biggest and the smallest resorts in this book is £40 at the most. The only general rules about cost worth bearing in mind relate to countries rather than individual resorts. Italy is cheap (though not as cheap as it once was), Switzerland is expensive, while France and Austria (as far as the resorts in this book are concerned) are roughly comparable. Obviously this rule varies according to the strength of the £ on the foreign exchange market.

In the course of revising the resort entries for this, the second edition of the book, I have tried to include as much topical information as possible. Obviously the mountains have not moved much since the first edition was published but new lifts have been built on them and new runs open.

Many bars and restaurants both on the mountains and in the resorts have changed hands and consequently become more or less popular than before. New chalets, hotels and apartment blocks have been built. The atmosphere of some resorts has changed perceptibly because of, say, new buildings, or a dramatic rise in the number of British visitors. I have tried to reflect all these changes, both blatant and subtle, in the text.

After you have completed the following pages – or even just a particular chapter – you should be able to select and travel to one or more of these resorts armed with the maximum amount of 'inside' information. The kind of information, in other words, that you would get if you had a friend who had worked in each of these resorts for a couple of seasons.

Good skiing!

CHOOSING A SKI HOLIDAY

The most important questions involved in organising a ski holiday are **Where to go?, What type of accommodation?, When to go?, With whom?, For how long? and With which tour operator?**

Where to go?

Consider first of all the skiing. Make sure you choose a resort where it will be suitable for all members of your party. If you have both beginners and experts in the group, then it is important to choose somewhere that caters well for both standards. Do you care more about traditional Alpine charm and atmosphere than being able to ski to and from the front of your accommodation? If so, then choose an old resort with lots of character; if your priorities are the other way round, then look for somewhere offering purpose-built convenience.

How important is après-ski life? If your party consists entirely of people who like nothing more than a quiet drink before dinner and then to flop into bed immediately after it, you can choose a resort without much nightlife – these are often cheaper. If, on the other hand, you all want to burn the candle at both ends while you are on holiday, then make sure you choose a resort with an adequate supply of bars and discos.

Another consideration, particularly for families or the frankly impatient, is the time the transfer from the foreign airport is likely to take. Unfortunately, this cannot always be accurately judged by referring to the estimates given by tour operators in their brochures. On a good day, the journey from Geneva to Val d'Isère, say, really does take three-and-a-half hours. However, on a busy Saturday in February (during the French holidays), it has been known to take ten hours or more because of the severe traffic congestion that occurs around Albertville and Moûtiers. On the other hand, the two-hour transfer to Verbier and the three-and-a-half hour one to Zermatt are seldom much longer, except in very bad weather, simply because the roads in Switzerland are much better.

What type of accommodation?

Essentially, there are three types of accommodation: hotels, self-catering and chalets. Of course, hotels vary enormously in terms of level of comfort and service and price. Generally speaking, they are the best places for groups who want to be well looked after by the locals and have a reasonable degree of comfort, privacy and independence.

Self-catering accommodation is for those who want complete independence. It offers the freedom to come and go, eat and sleep whenever you want. Another attraction of self-catering is that the basic price is relatively cheap. But you must bear in mind the cost of the food you will have to buy, and any meals out you decide to have. Also remember that someone has to do the cooking and washing-up and, unless you have someone prepared to do that on holiday, then you should think about taking another type of holiday.

British people booking self-catering in European resorts would do well to take into account the fact that Continental families seem prepared to put up with much more cramped conditions on holiday than British punters. Therefore, either be prepared to live in very close proximity to the other members of your party, or take an apartment which technically has more beds than you require and spread out a bit.

Nowadays, there are really two types of chalet holiday. The first is the uniquely British chalet party, which has proved so popular since its invention about 25 years ago. A group of between about six and fourteen people stay in a wooden chalet (or large apartment run as a chalet) and are looked after and cooked for by one or two British chalet girls. The chalets are not generally very luxurious (though some are – book early!) and there may not be as many bathrooms and as much hot water as perfectionists might wish. But there is lots of 'atmosphere' and holiday camaraderie. Breakfast, tea and dinner with 'free' cheap wine are included in the price. Cooking standard is Cordon Bleu-ish, but the main course is more likely to be chicken than filet steak. (However, some operators offer gourmet menus when, for a very small supplement, you can get infinitely better food, ditto wine.)

The other type of chalet holiday takes place in the Jumbo Chalet or Chalet Hotel. These are usually small- or medium-sized hotels (usually two-star) which have been taken over by British tour operators and are run by them with a largely British staff. Generally, the rooms are of a decent standard and many have private bathrooms. Meals and wine are included as above, although the atmosphere will be more like a hotel dining room than a private dinner party.

When to go?

When to go depends on when it is convenient for you to take a holiday, how much you can afford, where you want to go and the kind of weather/skiing conditions you prefer.

Christmas/New Year and Easter are both popular periods for skiing holidays and are usually charged at the highest rate. However, from the point of view of snow conditions, these are not always the best dates, even in the higher resorts. At Christmas, the first major snowfall of the winter has not necessarily arrived and at Easter, particularly if it falls in the middle of April or later, the snow on the lower slopes may well have melted. For what it's worth, snow conditions have been better in early April than at Christmas in most of Europe's top resorts for the past three years, but that situation may be reversed over the next few years.

The only way to be certain of getting some skiing at these periods is to choose a very high resort, preferably one with a glacier. Even so, glaciers soon become overcrowded if the lower slopes are bare. The simple rule is that the higher the skiing goes, the greater the likelihood of good snow at either end of the season.

The cheapest (and many would say the best) time to go skiing in Europe is in January, when snow cover is likely to be excellent and the lifts and slopes relatively empty. Prices for holidays departing on 3rd January will be so much cheaper than those for New Year and departure dates in the middle of January are ludicrously cheap. It will generally be quite cold in January and you may not get much of a suntan or be able to have lunch outside, but you are likely to get very good skiing, including powder off-piste.

February is generally quite an expensive month to go skiing, but the weather may well not be much warmer than in January. The other problem with February is that a lot of Continentals take family skiing holidays at this time. French and Swiss resorts are best avoided during the three weeks of the French school holidays in February.

March is, generally speaking, a sunny month when snow conditions are still good. There are often a couple of weeks before Easter when holidays are sold at relatively cheap prices.

April is a good time for those who like skiing on spring snow and those for whom suntans are as important as the quality of the snow, which is generally pretty heavy on piste by this time. If the late-season skiing is good and you have the flexibility to make a last-minute booking, there are often very good deals available for the middle of April. As a rule, however, April is too late to ski in Austrian resorts or in the lower French and Swiss ones.

For how long?

Here again, the answer is dependent on how much time off you can afford to take and how much money you can afford to spend on your skiing holiday. However, if you can afford to take a fortnight rather than a week, then it is advisable to do so. The first four or five days of a skiing holiday are generally spent working yourself up to the standard you were at on your last skiing holiday, so that it is only on the last day of a week's holiday that your skiing is actually improving. In the course of a fortnight, on the other hand, you are likely to make considerable progress. You also have a greater chance of getting good weather and snow conditions. Ten-day holidays are also possible, although the selection is much more limited.

Which tour operator?

Obviously, this depends partly on which is offering the cheapest holiday to the place you want to go, in the type of accommodation you want, on the dates you want. But the price of the holiday should not be the only consideration – paying a little more to another operator could mean getting accommodation conveniently situated in the middle of a resort, rather than on the outskirts. Equally, a slightly higher price may mean flights direct from your local airport rather than from London – though you usually need to book early for flights from regional airports. Some operators tend to have better staff than others – this is particularly important for chalet holidays. It's certainly worth an extra £5 or £10 to be looked after by a really efficient rep and competent, cheerful staff rather than suffer a second-rate holiday, looked after by a rep who scarcely speaks the language and sullen, incompetent staff. Previous experience and personal recommendations should guide you as to which are the best companies in this respect. A good barometer is the standard of service offered by the reservations office of the company. If the staff there are good, then the chances are the staff in the Alps will be, too.

As with all holiday packages, read the small print carefully and note what is and is not included in the price. Also take into account whether you are being given any sort of guarantees against currency surcharges or lack of snow.

Wherever possible, book direct with the tour operator. The staff in the tour operator's own reservations department certainly ought to know much more about the ski resorts served by that company than a travel agent, who may never have skied in his life and for whom skiing is only a small part of his business.

All the tour operators listed in this book have ATOL licences and are fully bonded, which means that any money you have paid in advance is safe, in the event of the tour operator getting into financial difficulties.

GETTING THERE

This is not intended to be a comprehensive list of tour operators, but merely a selection of companies, large and small, that serve resorts listed in this book and have reasonably good reputations for organising skiing holidays. For fuller details, contact these companies for their brochures.

Activity Travel, 19 Castle Street, Edinburgh EH2 3AH (031-225 9457)
Now the largest operator of skiing holidays in Scotland, Activity Travel has diversified into holidays to France and Switzerland. It flies from Edinburgh and Glasgow.

Adventure Holidays, 5 Temple Street, Aylesbury, Bucks. HP20 2RP (0993 831223)
Primarily a schools operator, but does also do useful holidays for unaccompanied children and families.

Beach Villas, 8 Market Passage, Cambridge CB2 3QR (0223 311113)
Principally a summer operator, as the name suggests, but they do have chalet accommodation in resorts like Méribel and Verbier.

Bladon Lines, 56-70 Putney High Street, London SW15 1SF (01-785 2200)
In seven years, Bladon Lines has built itself up from nothing to become one of the largest up-market tour operators. It continues to expand at an alarming rate – in 1986 it bought Ski West. It specialises in chalet holidays, but also does hotels and apartments. Its employees are hideously recognisable in their parrot uniform. The principal backer now is Christopher Needler and the company is run with great style by the flamboyant Mark Lines. They produce two brochures: one up-market, the other down-market, but some accommodation features in both. Sunday transfers to some French resorts are an attraction.

Blue Sky Holidays, Blue Sky House, London Road, East Grinstead, Sussex RH19 1HU (0342 28211)
Formerly part of British Caledonian, this is a middle-market operator dealing mostly in hotels.

Club Mark Warner, 20 Kensington Church Street, London W8 4EP (01-938 1851)
Originally a chalet operator, Mark Warner now specialises in 'club' style chalet holidays in larger hotel-like chalets. Definitely for the more sociable skiers. The programme features some of the best resorts in Europe.

Club Mediterranée, 106-108 Brompton Road, London SW3 1JJ (01-581 4766)
Accommodation in good French and Swiss resorts, but make sure you like the concept of French-run 'club' holidays before booking.

Crystal Holidays, Alexandra House, 138-140 Alexandra Road, Wimbledon, London SW19 7JY (01-879 0555)
Relatively down-market operator with accommodation in French and Austrian resorts.

Enterprise Wintersports, 1 Wardour Street, London W1V 3HE (01-439 7611)
This is the seven-year-old ski section of British Airways' holiday company, Enterprise. It is a reliable operator dealing mostly in hotels and offers accommodation all over Europe, mainly in medium-sized resorts.

French Travel Service, Francis House, Francis Street, London SW1P 1DE (01-828 8131)
Hotels and self-catering in French resorts, obviously.

Global, PO Box 2LS, Eden House, London W1A 2LS (01-637 3333/323 3266)
Although this company has some obscure destinations best suited to beginners on a tight budget, Global offers competitively-priced hotel holidays.

Horizon Holidays, Broadway, Edgbaston, Five Ways, Birmingham B15 1BB (021-632 6282)
This is a middle-market operator with a large number of Austrian resorts and an increasing

number in France. Based in Birmingham, it is particularly popular with skiers in the North of England and offers a good choice of departure airports. Its ski programme has expanded considerably of late.

Inghams, Holiday House, 329 Putney Bridge Road, London SW15 2PL (01-785 7777)
Now 50 years old, Inghams is one of the most famous companies in the skiing business. No longer as up-market as it once was, it is still expert on Austrian resorts and offers an enormous selection. The firm deals mostly in hotels, but also does a bit of self-catering. It has smaller operations in Switzerland, France and Italy. Also produces a separate brochure of luxury Alpine hotels.

Intasun Skiscene, Intasun House, 2 Cromwell Avenue, Bromley, Kent BR2 9AQ (01-290 0511)
A large operator catering for the middle and bottom of the market. Features mostly Austrian resorts, but also some in France and Switzerland.

Kuoni, Kuoni House, Dorking, Surrey RH5 4AZ (0306 855044)
This well-known, up-market tour operator has recently moved into the ski market with an extensive programme of hotel accommodation in top Swiss resorts.

Made to Measure Holidays, P.O. Box 40, Chichester, Sussex PO18 8HA (0243 574333)
This small company is just what it sounds – it will make up packages to suit your precise requirements, including midweek departures and so on. It can also arrange special ski touring expeditions.

John Morgan Travel, Meon House, Petersfield, Hampshire GU32 3JN (0730 68621)
This company is now owned by Meon Travel of Petersfield. Smaller than it once was, it still offers good chalet accommodation in some of the best resorts.

Mountain Lodges, 65 Les Andes, BP37, 73150 Val d'Isère, France (79 06 20 77)
Luxuriously converted old Savoyard houses in Val d'Isère, private ski instructors and five-star service. Run by David McCallum and Patricia Killy.

Neilson Holidays, Holiday House, Domestic Road, Leeds LS12 6HR (0532 434077)
Lately one of the biggest ski tour operators in Britain, Neilsons was taken over by coaching experts, NAT Holidays, in 1986. The company pioneered the ski guide concept. Traditionally popular with skiers in the North of England, it has a good selection of resorts, including hundreds of beds in Les Arcs. Useful choice of departure airports.

Peter Stuyvesant Travel, 7 Percy Street, London W1P 9FB (01-631 3278)
This is a fairly new specialist company, dealing mostly in France and Switzerland. It has retained the services of the bearded sociologist-cum-ski teacher, Ali Ross, and his special instruction weeks have been a success. It offers hotel and self-catering accommodation.

Powder Skiing in North America, 61 Doneraile Street, London SW6 6EW (01-736 8191)
Although North America does not feature in this book, this company is worth a mention since it provides, at considerable cost, fantastic holidays for the fit powder-skiing enthusiast.

Ski an' Do Holidays, 14 Stafford Street, Edinburgh EH3 7AU (031-226 6626)
This is a bright young Scottish company with some chalets and self-catering accommodation. It is run by Alastair Cunningham, who was formerly involved in Ski Snowball.

Ski Club of Great Britain, 118 Eaton Square, London SW1W 9AF (01-235 3011)
The SCGB (or KGB as some people call it) has an extensive programme of holidays, usually organised in conjunction with a tour operator, designed to cater for special interests, both skiing and social.

Ski MacG, 17 Old Court Place, Kensington High Street, London W8 4PD (01-351 5446)
In its independent days, this was one of the finest small chalet operators. It was lately owned by Falcon but has now been bought by Olympic Holidays. Has accommodation in some of the best resorts.

Ski Sunmed, 4-6 Manor Mount, London SE23

3PZ (01-699 5999)
Catering for the younger, cost-conscious end of the market and serving good-ish resorts.

Ski Supertravel, 22 Hans Place, London SW1X 0EP (01-584 5060)
One of the largest and most established chalet operators, it has now survived 22 years in this notoriously volatile market. The company is now run by David Lewthwaite, one of the original founders. This is an up-market operator with a very good selection of chalets in the top European resorts. It also does hotel and self-catering holidays.

Ski-Val, 91 Wembley Park Drive, Wembley, Middlesex HA9 8HF (O1-200 6080)
This is a successful chalet operator specialising in Val d'Isère and Tignes, with several large chalet-hotels in each. It also has a 'club' style residence in Les Arcs.

Ski West, Eternit House, Felsham Road, London SW15 1SF (01-785 9999)
Now owned by Bladon Lines, this company offers competitively-priced holidays in some of Europe's best resorts. It has a great deal of self-catering accommodation and is the leading specialist in direct overland coach travel to the Alps.

Ski Whizz, 170 Ifield Road, London SW10 9AF (01-370 0256)
A small company run by ex-chalet girl, Joanna Deakin and her brother. Good for Chamonix.

Skiworld, 41 North End Road, London W14 8SZ (01-602 4826)
Small company with accommodation in Tignes and other good resorts. Also has a clothing hire shop at its London office.

Small World, Old Stone House, Judge's Terrace, East Grinstead, Sussex RH19 1AQ (0342 27272)
This company started the chalet-party concept about 25 years ago, but it is now rather out of the mainstream of tour operators. It does good chalet holidays in Italy, particularly.

Snowtime, 23 Denmark Street, London WC2H 8NA (01-836 3237)
Specialising solely in Méribel, this company succeeds in being the largest and best-organised in that resort, despite the vulgar pink heart stickers it has put on every ski-lift pylon.

Swiss Travel Service, Bridge House, Ware, Herts SG12 9DE (0920 3971)
Concentrates on hotels in Swiss resorts. Prices are often very competitive.

Tailor-Made Ski Tours, Erlysmead House, Farleigh Wick, Bradford-on-Avon, Wiltshire BA15 2PZ (0225 859598)
A husband and wife team with a great deal of skiing knowledge between them, Colin and Judy McCubbin specialise in Davos, where they give a personal guiding service. Travel arrangements are very flexible.

Thomas Cook Holidays, PO Box 36, Thorpe Wood, Peterborough PE3 6SB (0733 502200)
One of the large middle-market operators, with a good selection of resorts all over Europe. Accommodation is mostly in hotels.

Thomson Holidays, Greater London House, Hampstead Road, London NW1 7SD (01-387 8484)
Currently the largest winter sports operator, Thomsons has an enormous winter sports programme that features nearly 70 resorts. There are lots of small, cheap Austrian villages, but there is an increasing number of Europe's best resorts, like Val d'Isère, although their self-catering accommodation in the best resorts is not always the most desirable. There are hotels of all standards.

HOLIDAY LOCATOR

Ski Solutions, London House, 266 Fulham Road, SW10 9EL.
Once you have given this agency your request in terms of dates, resorts and price they will seek out and book the best package on offer from the many tour operators with whom they deal. There is no extra charge for this service as Ski Solutions make their money through commission from the tour operators. Very useful for last minute bookings.

FLIGHTS

Falcon Snowjet, Astley House, 33 Notting Hill Gate, London W11 3JQ (01-221 0088)
Many shops sell cheap European air tickets, but special mention should be made of Falcon Snowjet, which runs a large number of flights to Geneva and Zurich, as well as to other European cities.

NATIONAL TOURIST OFFICES

Further information and details of accommodation in the resorts listed in this book are available from the relevant offices.
Austrian National Tourist Office, 30 George Street, London W1R 9FA (01-629 0461)
French Government Tourist Office, 178 Piccadilly, London W1B 0AL (01-491 7622)
Italian State Tourist Office, 3rd Floor, 1 Princes Street, London W1R 7RA (01-408 1254)
Swiss National Tourist Office, Swiss Centre, 1 New Coventry Street, London W1V 8EE (01-734 1921)

MODES OF TRANSPORT

By air

Flying is by far the most popular method of getting to the resorts. Most tour operators include a charter flight and onward coach transfer in their holiday prices: you get only a fairly small discount (say £50) for not using this flight. These flights are usually from Gatwick and you pay a supplement if you are flying from further away (Manchester or Edinburgh, for example). You can also pay a supplement and fly from Heathrow if you wish, but this is not really worth it as you often have to wait at the foreign airport for the company's Gatwick flight to arrive.

One disadvantage of these charter flights is that a large number of them have extraordinarily early departure times from Gatwick, requiring you to check in by 5.30am, which means getting up in the middle of the night, wherever you live. For many people, beginning their skiing holidays means stumbling around Victoria station with Moon boots on their feet and skis over their shoulders at 4.30am on a winter's morning looking for the train to Gatwick.

At Gatwick itself, long check-in queues of punters accompanied by skis precariously balanced on luggage trolleys can sometimes bring the departures hall to a standstill. If you are a regular skier, then you are almost certain to meet someone you know at Gatwick, or failing that at Geneva or Munich, on a Saturday during the season. (Transfers are almost always on Saturdays for the simple reason that most hotels will take bookings only on a Saturday-to-Saturday basis.)

Flights for most of the Austrian resorts go to Munich, those for resorts in the Vorarlberg and the north of Switzerland to Zurich, whilst those for most of the French and Swiss resorts go to Geneva. So if you are going to one of the resorts in this book, you are most likely to be travelling to Geneva airport on a Saturday. In a busy week, there can be between 15 and 20 charter flights from Britain to Geneva, some of them enormous Tristars carrying nearly 400 passengers: the airport is swamped by British skiers. You cannot move in the arrivals hall for the crowd of British tour operators' reps, all waving signs and clipboards and trying to identify their new punters.

The head of airport security once tried to move the reps out of the arrivals hall and make them wait outside by the coaches. But the seasoned British reps were not going to wait out in the cold and they won a major victory over the security head.

Once you have got out of the airport building, you board the coach to your resort. Unless the resort is within two hours' drive of Geneva, you will probably have some kind of refreshment stop. This will usually take place somewhere between Annecy and Moûtiers, if you are going to a resort in the Savoie. There are countless restaurants and cafés along this route. They all do very good business in the summer, but during the winter the visits of British transfer coaches on Saturdays are the trading highlights of the week. Naturally, therefore, they are keen to attract the custom of the reps and drivers by whatever means possible. This sometimes means a little profit-share, or otherwise a particularly good free meal in the back room while the punters are being ripped off in the front.

The most popular place is the **Beau Séjour,** which has a car park with room for 12 coaches that is often nearly full. Regular travellers will be relieved to hear that four more loos have been installed here in time for this season. **L'Oasis** is a slightly less popular spot just off the main road beyond Albertville – it never gets too busy here. **Lac Bleu** is well positioned on the main road by Lake Annecy and has the great advantage for self-caterers that there is a supermarket. But the café itself is fairly small and soon becomes packed.

On the return journey, the stop is often in Annecy, where at least there is a choice of shops and restaurants. In fact, Annecy is a very agreeable place to spend an hour or so on a sunny spring Saturday morning. On arrival at Geneva, you will usually be required to unload your luggage from the coach and put it on to large trailers that will be waiting on the pavement. This saves having to check the luggage in and, in fact, with this system very few items have gone missing. The next thing you have to do is join the check-in queue. And there is always a queue because the Geneva airport authorities are reluctant to allocate more than one check-in desk to a charter flight. The most efficient tour operator for getting passengers checked-in and on to their planes is Bladon Lines. Its Geneva operation is ruthlessly managed by John Yates-Smith (brother of the more famous Dick), who shouts and swears at the girls in parrot jackets and occasionally at the punters as well, but usually succeeds in making the planes run on time and sorting out the overbookings. (Incidentally, although all charter flight tickets are valid only for one specified flight, do not worry too much if you miss it. The tour operators have something called a 'mutual aid' understanding and you will usually be put on the next flight that has empty seats available.)

The real social centre of Geneva airport is the bar in the arrivals hall where reps and punters buy each other glasses of Fendant, often paying in French francs, which are accepted at a deeply disadvantageous rate. This is the place to come if you have a one-way flight back to the UK to sell or if you want to buy one. Just ask around the reps until you find a buyer or seller. (The going rate for a one-way ticket varies between £40 and £60.) Be careful not to stay too long in the arrivals bar if you are actually departing, as there is no departures indicator here and you can easily miss your flight. The really rich reps and punters have now forsaken this bar for the cocktail bar in the airport's restaurant complex, where they drink champagne and have a perfect view of the aircraft approaching the runway.

By coach

Coaches are becoming an increasingly popular way of travelling to the resorts, particularly with those on a limited budget. The arguments in favour of going by coach are that it is around £40 cheaper than flying and you get two extra days' (or one-and-a-half days') skiing. The disavantages are that it takes a long time, you probably won't sleep much and you will certainly not be in a fit state to enjoy the first of your extra days.

The coaches leave London (usually Gloucester Road) on Friday afternoon and arrive in the resorts about noon the next day. Most of them are sleeper coaches, in which case the bunks come down at about Paris and are folded up before Moûtiers. These bunks are horizontal seats rather than beds and you will inevitably find yourself on very intimate terms with the people next to, in front of, and behind you. Even if your coach arrives on time, it takes quite a while to get changed into your ski gear, get your lift pass and, if necessary, hire equipment. In fact, you will be doing well if you get up the mountain any more than two hours before the lifts close.

On the return journey, the coaches usually leave the resorts late on the Saturday afternoon. This means you can ski during the day, but remember that you will have to have packed and vacated your apartment or chalet room in the morning and may have difficulty finding somewhere to change in the afternoon. Also remember that ski shops do not like hiring equipment for eight-day periods.

By car

It is a long way from London to the Alpine resorts. If you start early and drive flat out, you can do it in a day, but you will arrive exhausted and will not be on top skiing form the next morning. The alternative is to stay somewhere overnight; this can be pleasant if you find an agreeable little hotel off the autoroute somewhere, but it increases the cost and takes longer. (Remember also that you will have to pay nearly £20 in autoroute tolls.)

If you have three people or more in your car, then you are probably doing the trip cheaper than you would by air, but not if you have an overnight stop. In fact, there are only a few resorts in the Alps where having your own car is a significant advantage. You must also have snow tyres and/or chains. (It's no use deciding you need to buy chains when you get stuck halfway up a mountain. You have to have bought them already, as a precaution.)

By train

Travelling to ski resorts by train is no longer as popular as it once was. It takes nearly as long as the coach, costs nearly as much as the plane and, because of the Channel, is inconvenient. If you are rich, one clever way of having a full day's work in London and being on the slopes the next morning is to take a late flight to Paris and then take the sleeper down to Moûtiers or Bourg St Maurice, for most of the big French resorts, or to Martigny, Sierre or Brig for resorts in the Swiss Valais. But remember that if you want a comfortable sleeper rather than a couchette, you will have to travel first-class.

For Austrian resorts, the Arlberg Express still runs from Unnsbruch to St Anton. There may be quicker ways of getting there nowadays, but they don't have such romantic names.

A LIFT UP THE MOUNTAIN

In many cases, getting up the mountain can be as difficult as skiing down it. Uphill transportation takes many forms, some of them easier than others.

Baby or Rope Tows This is the most primitive form of lift: you hold on to a rope which pulls you uphill. These lifts are usually fairly gentle, although the friction of the rope can wreck expensive leather gloves.

Button or Poma Tows These take one person at a time, so you have only yourself to blame if you fall off. Many of these lifts are now self-service, so you must obey the traffic lights swiftly. They are triggered off by a small trip-bar by your feet. The poles are prone to get tangled up in the starting gate, so you must look carefully to make sure you are grasping the one at the front. Once you have grabbed the pole, be prepared for a forceful jerk – it may even lift you into the air. Bend your knees, but don't try to sit down.

T-Bar, Drag or Anchor Tows These are now rare in France, but there are still quite a few of them in Austria and Switzerland. They are the most difficult lifts to ride successfully. The most important thing is to make sure you have a suitable partner. This does not necessarily mean an experienced skier, as some expert skiers are hopeless on these lifts. The key to success here is to relax rather than stay tense.

Chairlifts These can be for anything from one to four skiers, but are usually for two or three. The more considerate resorts have now fitted foam buffers to soften the blow of the chairs on your calves, but where these are not standard, you have to resign yourself to getting bruises. The experienced passenger moves discreetly forward as the chair approaches, so that his partner(s) take the impact on *their* calves. The safety bar is pretty well essential: it's often a long way to fall.

Telecabines or Gondolas Also known as eggs and bubbles, this form of uphill travel requires very little skill and not much more in the way of nerve. While away the journey by playing psychological games with the stranger(s) opposite you in the cabin. Conversations range from the scintillatingly bizarre to the tiresomely inane. Foot fetishists can have great fun rubbing their ski boots against their neighbour's. The older telecabines take only two people, but the most modern ones accommodate six – often back to back which is not so much fun.

Cable-cars These demand quite a bit of nerve, but spectacular views usually make it worthwhile, unless you suffer from acute vertigo. Try not to look at the 'Charge Maximum: 80 Personnes' sign as you count what you are sure is the hundredth person to get into the car. The archetypal cable-car operator has long greasy hair, a black leather jacket and mirrored sunglasses. He chain-smokes Gauloises and seldom speaks except to mumble monosyllables into the radio. Despite his casual air, he is trained to do pretty daring things on the roof if anything should go wrong. Most cable-cars swing violently as they go over pylons: don't panic.

The Queues Before using these various lifts, the skier will often have to queue for a period. Most British skiers are pathetic about queuing and therefore waste a lot of time. Like it or not, most ski-lift queues are aggressive and the only way to make any progress is to push forward and at the same time take preventive action to stop anyone coming up from behind and overtaking you. Have no sympathy for small children: they are the most aggressive of all. If any argument breaks out, either stay completely silent or start speaking something obscure like Gaelic. Never give away your nationality as this can sometimes lead to racial abuse.

AVORIAZ

'I defy anyone who has ever seen a sore thumb not to recognise the similarities,' one notoriously outspoken tour operator once wrote about Avoriaz in his brochure. Apart from being an extraordinarily negative piece of advertising, the sentiment is unfair on Avoriaz – there are plenty of purpose-built ski resorts that are a lot uglier. The architects of Avoriaz have shown considerable sensitivity towards the Alpine setting by ensuring that all their concrete apartment blocks are covered in wood cladding, mostly pine, although the timber is not weathering as well as might have been hoped when the first buildings were constructed more than twenty years ago.

You get to Avoriaz via Geneva followed by a two-hour journey to the valley town of Morzine, itself an established ski resort and one that has lately become increasingly popular with the British. It was in the news twice in the winter of 1986; once because Princess Anne and her family went there and once because British tourists attacked a local bar owner who subsequently died. Though a pleasant enough town, access to the Portes du Soleil ski area from here is significantly more difficult than from Avoriaz.

To get to Avoriaz from Morzine, you can take a large cable car or drive up to the perimeter of the resort, where there is a large over- and under-ground parking complex. From the car parks, you walk into what seems like an unfinished Western set in which a number of horse-drawn sleighs are waiting. A Tannoy system bellows out newly received sleigh-taxi bookings to the waiting drivers.

Horse-drawn sleighs are indigenous in old-fashioned resorts like Zermatt and Lech, but in Avoriaz they seem contrived and gimmicky. The drivers take no pride in their sleighs or horses and expect passengers to sit on dirty, snow-covered benches while they throw your luggage on top of you with all the finesse of Heathrow baggage handlers. The ride is as nauseating as being on a roller coaster. Even more irritating is the fact that the horses are unwilling to negotiate the short, steep hills that lead to many of the smaller chalets in Avoriaz. (If you think these creatures are truculent, they are a distinct improvement on the reindeer that used to pull the sleighs in the very early days of the resort.)

The alternative method of transport in Avoriaz is the Ratrac. These are noisier and less 'romantic' than the sleighs but considerably more efficient: at least they can go up steep hills. They are run by the omnipotent Pierre et Vacances agency which also operates the sleighs and most other things in Avoriaz (see Accommodation).

Once installed in your hotel, chalet or apartment, your skis or Moon boots will be all you need to get around Avoriaz. The centre of the resort is fairly compact and there's a lift by the top station of the cable car to the shopping centre.

Avoriaz is not an especially good resort for shopping – many of the shops are in unenticing arcades and are rather claustrophobic. Prices are high, even in the supermarkets. This is partly because supplies have to be re-delivered by Ratrac from the main car park. So although this is a good resort for a self-catering holiday, you must be prepared to pay high prices for basic supplies, or bring food with you.

Accommodation

Most of Avoriaz is owned and/or controlled by Pierre et Vacances, an enormous, amorphous property developing company employing rather disorganised staff. Pierre et Vacances also owns two of the four hotels in the resort – the **Ruches**** and the **Snow****, but the best in town, the **Dromonts****** is run independently.

As far as the many apartment blocks are concerned, Fontanes Blanches, Les Alpages, Sassanka, Sassafras and Yucca are all in good condition, while the earlier blocks such as Melezes and Pas du Lac are falling apart and no one is bothering to repair them. There are also a few pleasant, modern chalets, most of which are for about eight people and are in good condition.

Après-ski

The principal early-evening rendezvous point in Avoriaz is the **Piano Bar** of the Hotel Snow, a relatively sophisticated bar with a live pianist most evenings and a lot of plush leather banquettes. However, the prices are remarkably reasonable and several British reps hold their office hours here. Another popular venue for early evening drinking is the **Choucas** – the manager Jacques is great fun. **Le Tavaillon** is a lively bar with good videos; it is much patronised by the French. **Le Bistro** is another key bar with a jolly, cheap restaurant upstairs. For a really quiet drink there is **L'Uby,** which also serves good inexpensive food. **La Tanière,** by the top of the cable car, is a key watering hole for ski instructors and their friends.

Among the better and more expensive restaurants in Avoriaz are **Le Crepy,** which has live jazz played upstairs in the latter part of the evening, **La Grignotte,** and **La Taverne** which is part of the Dromonts Hotel. The standard of restaurant service is generally poor in Avoriaz, as in many purpose-built resorts. The problem is that nobody lives there all year round, so there are no real residents, therefore no enterprising little businessmen who have pride in their standards of service. For the same reason, restaurants and bars change hands more frequently than they do in other resorts.

(Incidentally, all the best restaurants do particularly good trade during the Avoriaz Fantasy Film Festival held in January every year which fills the resort with poseurs for a week. The Festival is of no benefit to skiers since you cannot get into the films unless you are a delegate.)

Other worthwhile restaurants in Avoriaz include the **Mah Jong,** a good but expensive Chinese restaurant, and **Mammaz Pizzeria,** a friendly, even slightly rowdy place that serves very good-value Italian food. For local specialities, the **Brasserie des Fontaines Blanche** and the **Petit Savoyard** are both good.

The nightclub scene revolves around **Le Roc** and **Le Manhattan.** Situated beneath the Dromonts Hotel, Le Roc is actually dug into the mountainside, and has the atmosphere of a furlined Fraggle Rock.

It is expensive – FF80 admission and FF60 for subsequent drinks – and the clientele is suitably chic, and mostly French. People dress up to come here, furs and suede skirts abound and Moon boots must be left in the vestiaire. Mild video nasties are shown on several TV screens and the music is predominantly American.

There is no need to dress up for Le Manhattan. This is a place where you dance in your Moon boots. It is a huge barn of a disco and charges FF50 admission. Its main disadvantage is its popularity with the Swedes, who tend to go overboard on the alcohol and collapse in the middle of the dancefloor. (Swedes and Danes tend to be omnipresent in Avoriaz, as in so many other resorts.)

For a post-disco nightcap, the tiny **Bar Tabac** is the ideal place: it is as narrow as a railway carriage and a third as long, but it has a good atmosphere.

The skiing

The great thing about Avoriaz is that it is effectively the centre of the vast Portes du Soleil

ski area. This means you are ideally placed for expeditions to the 14 or so other ski stations that make up this marvellous Franco-Swiss ski region. These resorts range from small purpose-built places like Champoussin and traditional Alpine resorts like Champèry to towns like Morzine. Torgon, Les Gets, Les Crosets and Morgins are all worthwhile destinations from Avoriaz and are on the main Portes du Soleil circuit.

For obvious reasons it is difficult to depict this whole area very successfully on one piste map (which, inexcusably, has to be bought). So if you are venturing far afield, it is a good idea to go with someone who knows their way around, or at least have the route explained to you before you set off. Remember also to keep an eye on your watch – if the lifts close and you find yourself stuck in Switzerland, the taxi ride back can be very expensive.

Most of the pistes between Avoriaz and the other resorts can be managed by good intermediate skiers, but there is no shortage of challenging black runs, and much of the most difficult skiing is close to Avoriaz itself.

The Chavanette Wall (also known as the Swiss wall) is steep enough to give even the most expert skiers temporary failure of nerve. The World Cup downhill run from the top of Intrets to Morzine-Prodains is a superbly exhilarating black run. On the other side of Avoriaz, the Brochaux chairlift has several good runs underneath it and offers access to a wonderful bowl of powder. Best of all, it is under-used and you seldom have to queue.

Lunches

Les Marmottes, just above Lindarets, is a delightful, informal lunch place serving mostly omelettes, hams and sandwiches. Ordering your food is simple: you just stroll into the kitchen, order your omelette and watch it being cooked for you in under a minute. The terrace outside is a good sun trap.

There is an old barn converted into a snack bar/restaurant at the bottom of **Les Brochaux.** It's best to get there early as they often run out of food before two o'clock and have only Mars Bars left. **Le Refuge du Verard** (close to the bottom of the World Cup run down to Morzine-Prodains) is the perfect *vin chaud* pit-stop – they serve it in half-pint mugs. There's also a limited amount of hot food here. It is run by the charming Tony and Carrie and their dog. (It is also possible to do torchlight descents down to here.) The **Sundance Saloon** at Les Crosets is a Western-style bar.

Le Coquoz, above Planachaux, is the best mountain restaurant in the Portes du Soleil area with appropriately high Swiss prices. (Beware, unless you are feeling very alert it is easy to believe that these prices are in French francs, so avoid ordering the most expensive dish because it seems remarkably good value.)

Le Coquoz is a formal kind of restaurant where it is quite possible for customers to be told to remove their gloves from the table. The waiters are dressed in the uniform of a 1972 North of England stand-up comic with enormous bow ties, dinner jackets and flared trousers. As well as croûtes and all the usual Valasian specialities, there are all kinds of steaks and excellent *magret de canard.* The *soupe de poissons maison* with *rouille* and *croûtons* is really exceptional.

Because it is so high and exposed, Avoriaz is not the ideal place to be in very bad weather as there is not much tree skiing and the resort itself can suffer badly in blizzards. These are the days when the only option is to have a long lunch in the resort itself.

Ski schools

There is one Ecole de Ski Française (ESF) in Avoriaz and the instructors speak reasonable English. Normally, British skiers will be placed in entirely English-speaking classes which will be for half a day, morning or afternoon, depending on level.

Avoriaz is particularly good for children who are learning to ski: the nursery slopes are right in the middle of the village and there is also the Village des Enfants. This is a ski school specially for children run by Isabelle Mir and Annie Famose, both ex-Olympic skiers. About half the instructors in this ski school speak English. It is apparently not suitable for whining or clinging children.

Ski shops

The most popular ski-hire shop with British operators is the one run by Antoine, a friendly moustachioed character whose business is independent of the controlling Mafia. He does not have a particularly large stock, so get there early, but his prices are competitive. Jean Vuarnet, the 1960 Olympic gold medallist who is still promoting sunglasses, has a shop here that has good stock and pleasant service. Superski and Mirafamose are two other shops, both owned by Annie Famose, who owns quite a lot in this resort.

CHAMONIX

Chamonix is an Alpine town rather than a ski resort: in fact, it has more than twice as many visitors during the summer as in winter. But because it is easily reached by autoroute from Geneva and elsewhere, and has all the facilities of a medium-sized town, it makes an ideal centre for a holiday touring round several of the neighbouring resorts. It is probably best visited independently with a car rather than on a package holiday. Simply getting from one side of the town to the other can be difficult without a car, not to mention getting to the satellite resorts of Les Houches and Argentière. (There are a lot of blue and yellow Chamonix buses around but somehow they never seem to be going where you want them to.)

Chamonix is an extraordinarily cosmopolitan town with Swedes, Germans and Americans the most dominant visiting nationalities during the winter season; the British are in fourth place. As only about 20 per cent of these visitors come on organised tours, you are, on the whole, obliged to make your own entertainment, but in a resort as lively as Chamonix this is no problem. Although there are hundreds of tourist-trapping souvenir shops advertising *'Votre photo en vieille costume en 10 minutes'* and so on, Chamonix feels like a real town where people live and work the whole year round.

Accommodation

Hotels are the most popular type of accommodation here and there are nearly a hundred of them in the Chamonix area. At the top of the range there is the **Mont-Blanc****** and the renowned **Albert Premier*****, both in Chamonix itself. Lower down the scale there is an abundance of two-star and one-star hotels, as well as small unclassified bed and breakfast hotels. A central booking agency is run from the Tourist Office, which also covers Argentière and Les Houches.

Several years ago Argentière was a key resort for British chalet operators – Bladon Lines, Supertravel and John Morgan Travel all had chalets here. Today, none of these companies offer chalets on a regular basis. The problem with Argentière is that the skiing is wonderful for experts and good intermediates but is not suitable for lesser skiers and the lifts are some way out of the village itself. Another factor is the limited nightlife. (Most people with cars staying in Argentière drive into Chamonix for nightlife.)

But if you are a party of good skiers who don't have much interest in nightlife, then you can still hire chalets in Argentière: Snow Place have Supertravel's old Chalet Rhodos and Bladon Lines can find chalets on request.

The main British chalet operator in Chamonix is Ski Whizz, a bright young company that has chalets in Chamonix itself and also in Les Houches. They overcome transport problems by having their own fleet of minibuses.

Most of the apartments in the Chamonix area are concentrated in the newish suburb of Chamonix Sud, which consists of a lot of apartment blocks well served with supermarkets.

Après-ski

Simply because of its size, Chamonix offers an enormous amount of nightlife. The following selection of places is therefore representative rather than comprehensive – part of the fun of being in a town like this is discovering interesting new bars.

The **Choucas Bar** is a lively, café-style establishment popular with both English-speaking visitors (though Swedes have lately been banned) and locals. There are enormous video screens and most people drink with one eye on the skiing films. Conversation is frequently suspended as the clientele gasp in unison at a particularly amazing skiing feat. This bar has recently changed hands but its atmosphere is not expected to change radically. The **Driver Bar** (so called because of its owner's obsession with motor racing) is a dark, high-ceilinged drinking place made to appear much larger than it is by strategic use of a vast wall mirror. It is run along British lines, which means you have to fight at the bar to get drinks. It tends to be packed full during the latter part of the evening but there is normally a lively atmosphere.

The most renowned eating place in Chamonix is the restaurant of the **Albert Premier Hotel,** a distinctly up-market Michelin-recommended establishment that is on every skiing foodie's list of shrines. **L'Impossible** is a restaurant opened by the Skieur de L'Impossible, Sylvain Saudan, the man who can ski down any kind of mountain, whether or not there is snow on it. This is a reasonably priced French restaurant with all the usual regional specialities and is particularly suitable if you are going out to eat in a large group. The adjacent bar, **Base Camp,** is also worth visiting. Sylvain himself is not often here because he spends his winter touring top resorts showing films of himself.

In the centre of town, next to the main Post Office, is the **Restaurant Atmosphere** which overlooks the river and has a large sun terrace. It is owned by British ski video expert Janie Power and a couple of Dutchmen, but the kitchen is very French, specialising in high quality fresh seafood. Close to here is the **Brasserie Nationale,** a cheap, spartan (Formica tables, etc.) place with a typical brasserie menu, run by a substantial patron and his even fatter cat. **L'Oustaou** is a good pizzeria in Chamonix, while **Le Crochon** is an expensive, rustic kind of restaurant serving enormous wholesome dishes like charcoal-grilled steaks. **Le Dru** does good set menus, (FF80 for four courses) and is a good place for groups.

Le Pèle of which Le Crochon forms a part, is a vast three-storey chalet-style nightclub with three separate dancefloors, all playing the same music. It's a lively place but the disadvantages are that it is full of Swedes overdosing on alcohol, and the sex ratio is uneven – far more men than women.

Just by the river is the **Casino,** one of the oldest buildings in Chamonix which features in many old prints. As vou might expect, the place is run by Italians and scarcely a word of French is spoken. As well as gambling, the Casino offers floorshows starring topless Caribbean dancers and any other cabaret act it can persuade to winter in Chamonix. The **Chambre Neuf** by the station is a trendy young place for late-night drinking, while the **Jeans Bar** in Chamonix Sud is small but fun.

Les Houches itself is fairly quiet at night: the **Piste Noire** is a small, friendly but unsophisticated disco, the **Relax** bar has an atmosphere to match its name and the **Dent du Géant** is an above-average restaurant.

Argentière is a bit livelier at night but 'unpretentious' and 'unsophisticated' are the key words for nightlife here. The **Bar Savoy** is a jolly, sociable place and is a popular rendezvous point after skiing. Although the name is a cliché, **Chez Luigi** is a decent pizzeria, the **Grenier** and the **Samoyède** are crêperies, the **Rusticana** and the **Marmottons** are other worthwhile restaurants and the **Pat-à-Ski** is the disco.

The skiing

To ski this area properly it is worth getting a Mont Blanc lift pass which covers not only Chamonix, Les Houches and Argentière, but also St Gervais, Megève, Les Contamines and a number of other smaller resorts in the area. The skiing in the Les Houches area is not particularly demanding and is most suitable for beginners and intermediate skiers.

The slopes of Les Grands Montets at Argentière, however, are some of the most challenging in Europe, especially when there's good powder. The price to be paid for this superb skiing, however, is often a long time spent queuing for the two cable cars needed to take you up to the top of the mountain. However, the irritation of queuing can be minimised if you know how to work the system. One person can go early to the ticket office with the lift passes of all the people in his party and reserve places for them in a certain cable car. Meanwhile, everyone else in the party can enjoy a leisurely breakfast. The **Viking Bar** has a sound system which announces the imminent departures of the cable cars, so this a safe place to have a coffee.

Access to the skiing at Argentière has improved with the construction of a new chairlift from Lognan to Petit Lavancher. The disadvantage of this is that the easier access will mean more skiers and therefore the off-piste will be skied out much more quickly.

In Chamonix itself there are two main ski areas. The easier of the two is Flegère, where there are several lifts up above the top station of the cable car, all of them offering good intermediate skiing. The big disadvantage is that, because the mountains rise so steeply out of the valley round here, the only run down to the bottom cable car is a black one and even this is not skiable when snow cover is poor. The other area, Brévent, goes up higher and offers some better skiing, especially around the chairlift up the Col Cornu. Here again the runs down to the bottom are difficult.

There is one other important lift system rising out of Chamonix and this is the cable car up to the Aiguille du Midi. There is some very difficult off-piste skiing down the front of the Aiguille, but the real reason for this lift is that it connects with a telecabine, which in turn gives access to the famous Vallée Blanche. This 12-kilometre off-piste run is in danger of becoming one of the most boring in Europe and has unfortunately become something of a cliché in British skiing circles. Because the skiing is not that difficult (though you must take a guide), thousands of skiers do the run every season and the Vallée Blanche bores are now a feature of skiing society. The run is so busy nowadays that you often have to queue to get down it. The major hazard is the long and treacherous walk down the mountain from the top of the lift to the point where you can put your skis on.

The Vallée Blanche is normally open only from February onwards and even in March you can wait a long time for suitable weather conditions for a descent. For more enterprising skiers with a good guide, there are various other long off-piste routes departing from the Aiguille du Midi.

The possibilities for one-day excursions to resorts on the Mont Blanc lift pass are considerable. You can drive to Megève in three-quarters of an hour and have some difficult skiing on the steep mogul-ridden slopes of Mont Joly. You don't even need to drive into Megève itself: you can get into the lift system a couple of miles outside at Demi-Quartier.

St Gervais does not have particularly good skiing, but it is a very pretty 19th-century spa town which has wonderful decorations at Christmas. Bettex is just outside St Gervais and gives access to Megève's lift system. Further up the valley from St Gervais is Les Contamines, a newish, expanding ski station with lifts up Mont Joly. If visibility is bad

Megève is often the best place to ski in the Mont Blanc area since it is relatively low and has plenty of trees.

Outside the Mont Blanc lift pass is Courmayeur, just half an hour away through the Mont Blanc Tunnel. The weather can often be quite different on the Italian side and the friendly Italian atmosphere of Courmayeur is always worth experiencing. The Mont Blanc Tunnel is not cheap and it is worth going in a group in one car or minibus to keep costs down. Lunch will invariably be good and cheap, however.

Avoriaz and Flaine are both within easy day-trip distance of Chamonix, as is Verbier when the Col de Montets is open. The drive to Verbier takes less than an hour and a half – you park at Le Chable and get into the lift system from there. If the Col de Montets is closed (it often is in mid-winter), you can always take the very efficient train which runs through a tunnel and so functions almost all the time. You join the train at Chamonix or Argentière and change at Martigny for Le Chable.

Lunches

The mountain restaurants in this area are mostly unexceptional, which is one reason why day trips to Courmayeur are so popular. The best restaurant in Les Houches is **La Hutte** at the top of the Bellevue cable car. It does wonderful made-to-order *vin chaud* and equally good *chocolat chaud*. The atmosphere is very relaxed: there is an open fire with armchairs around it.

The **Altitude 2000** at Brévent is a self-service place where you can look straight into the kitchen. They do good hot or cold pizzas and have a wonderful selection of mustards. The most enterprising catering operation in the Brévent area, however, is the little hut at the bottom of the chairlift from Les Vioz to 2000, where an enterprising man heats up *pain au chocolat* and croissants and walks along the lift queue selling them from his basket. A service like this could make a lot of the worst queues in the Alps more tolerable.

Up at Argentière, the **Dahu** hotel does a very good value set lunch – an ideal place to go if the weather makes skiing impossible, as it often does in Argentière.

Ski schools

There are Ecole de Ski Français schools at Les Houches, Chamonix and Argentière but they all have different directors so standards vary. On the whole, the quality of ESF teaching appears to be quite good but as this is such a cosmopolitan area it is usually difficult to find classes conducted solely in English, and English-speaking instructors are generally at a premium. The Ecole de Ski Internationale at Les Houches and Chamonix tend to have more English-speaking instructors.

For off-piste guides you can go to Patrick Vallencant's Ecole de Ski Hors Piste at Argentière which is now managed by Vallencant's former partners rather than the man himself. Gilles Gaby is one highly recommended guide at this school. There is also a Bureau des Guides at Chamonix. D-Tours is a guiding company run by Dean (an American) and Andy (an Englishman). They employ guides of all nationalities, including Scots and Australians, and have a pre-planned itinerary of resorts they will be visiting throughout the week. They have several yellow minibuses so transport is no problem. A guided day in a group of five or six skiers will cost around FF150. Some British operators have special arrangements with D-Tours.

Ski shops

There are masses of ski shops in this area and free enterprise flourishes so prices are generally competitive. One particularly good shop is Ski Extrème in the middle of Chamonix. It is run by an Englishman, Julian Mills, and offers a very good fast ski repair service.

COURCHEVEL

Part of Les Trois Vallées area – see also Méribel and Val Thorens

Courchevel is easily the biggest of the resorts in the famous Trois Vallées area and is without question the most fashionable ski resort in France. It is also popular with the British, although they are markedly less chic than the natives.

Situated in the Savoie above the traffic-jammed valley town of Moûtiers, about three hours' drive from either Lyons or Geneva, Courchevel 1850 is a post-war development and is one of the oldest of France's new resorts. Architecturally it is neither distinguished nor offensive: it has several rather square hotels and a lot of very pretty chalets.

The resort itself is intelligently planned around a lift system based on the Tourist Office complex in the centre. None of the hotels or chalets is more than a few minutes' walk from the piste and you can actually ski to and from many of them.

Courchevel 1850 is the main resort but there are three satellite villages, known by their height – 1300, 1550 and 1650. These are worth visiting on skis, perhaps for lunch, but as places to stay they are poor substitutes for Courchevel 1850. None of them has much in the way of nightlife and communications with 1850 are not particularly good after dark. If you want a quiet holiday with friends or family and do not mind limited après-ski and shopping facilities, the relatively modern 1650 is probably the place to choose. It is significant that several British tour operators who have had accommodation in these satellites have now relinquished it and deal only in Courchevel 1850.

Courchevel is an ideal place to come with a party of mixed-ability skiers since the skiing suits all standards. It is also a good place to bring non-skiers as the resort itself is lively during the day and there are plenty of interesting, if expensive, shops and boutiques. Also it is relatively convenient for skiers to come back to the resort at lunchtime to eat with their non-skiing friends.

The rich should note that there is an Altiport above Courchevel 1850. The runway is kept clear most of the winter and light aircraft take off and land with some frequency. If, however, the Altiport is closed by bad weather then aircraft face a tedious diversion to Chambèry.

Accommodation

This has always been a popular place for chalet holidays, and although on the whole the chalets are luxurious and consequently expensive, most of them book up pretty well in advance. Supertravel is the biggest British tour operator here and the company has the jumbo chalet Bon Séjour as well as several smaller chalets.

There are a number of good hotels in Courchevel, the best of which is probably the **Hotel des Neiges****.** This is a beautiful, luxurious hotel situated in pinewoods just on the edge of the piste. Although it is undeniably expensive (approx FF1000 per person per day full board), it is almost always full – often with the British who can comprise as many as 75 per cent of the guests here during peak British holidays.

There are several very comfortable, good value two-star hotels in Courchevel: these include the **Olympic**, La Potinière**,** the **Tournier***** and the **Courchneige**,** which is right on the edge of the piste. Perhaps the best two-star hotel is the **Dahu**** which is situated right in the middle of the resort, has agreeable, luxurious modern décor, obliging staff and a good reputation for its food.

British operators do not have much in the

way of self-catering accommodation in Courchevel, but you can be fairly certain that what there is will be of a reasonably high standard.

Après-ski

The most popular meeting place for all Brits in Courchevel used to be the Supertravel-owned **Jump Bar,** centrally situated just by the Tourist Office. However the Jump Hotel has now reverted to French ownership and it remains to be seen whether the bar will continue to be a focal point for the British, or whether they will adopt somewhere else.

In any case, there is no shortage of bars in Courchevel 1850. One popular place for early evening drinking is **Le Tremplin,** especially in spring, when you can sit outside. They do very good cocktails here, including a lethal concoction known as the Colossus designed for three or four people, but the service can be snail-like. Piano bars seem to do well here, the best two being the **Mangeoire** and the **Equipe,** which is part of the Tournier Hotel. The brasserie bar of the **Potinière Hotel** is a good-value, unpretentious drinking place.

The best restaurant in Courchevel is **Le Chabichou,** where nouvelle cuisine food is served in an elegant but not-too-formal dining room. There is a good *menu gastronomique* at around FF250, but that is a lot of food and for about FF200 you can choose between the meat course and the fish course. Otherwise, there is an enormous à la carte choice. Good wines can be fairly cheap here and they are served by enthusiastic young staff. There are lots of nice extra touches, such as hot canapés with your aperitifs, a plate of half a dozen mussels before the first course, and a delicious red-wine sorbet before the main course. Le Chabichou is highly rated both by Michelin and Gault Millau and puts Courchevel on the Alpine gastronomic map. (In the summer the chef/owner can be found in the kitchens of the Byblos Hotel in St Tropez.)

Le Bergerie is an old shepherds' hut with a reputation for good food. It can be expensive, but has the advantage that you can dance downstairs after your meal. **Le Fromagerie** is a jolly little cheese restaurant with a very good menu for FF80. The only drawback is that the service is painfully slow. **Le Chouca** is on three floors, with a different type of restaurant on each. The top floor is smart and expensive, while the basement specialises in fondues and so forth for low-budget groups. The middle floor provides middling cuisine at middling prices. If you want a really cheap meal, you can do a lot worse than go to the restaurant at the **Patinoire.** This is the Alpine equivalent of the restaurant at the late lamented White City Greyhound Stadium. You sit among locals and watch the skaters down below you. A popular event at the Patinoire is *ballon balai* – a game rather like ice-hockey except that the players do not wear skates and use brooms rather than hockey-sticks. Occasionally during the season, there are *ballon balai* championships between teams from the different British tour operators in Courchevel.

La Saulire, otherwise known as **Jack's Bar,** is a jolly place for drinks either before or after dinner or for a good, simple French dinner. It is run with great style by Jacques, who genuinely likes the British and so attracts quite a few of the more discerning ones to his bar.

After dinner there is no shortage of entertaining, if expensive, nightlife in Courchevel. **La Grange** is no longer as fashionable as it was five years ago, but it plays good British music from time to time – nobody dances to the French music. They tend to put on rather tacky nude floor shows here.

Les Caves de la Loze is a particularly chic nightclub and very popular with the French. It is run by a glamorous mutton-dressed-up-as-lamb proprietress. The entrance fee is around FF100, including your first drink. People tend to dress very expensively to come here and a lot of people spend their time up in the gallery eyeing the talent on the dance-floor. There is no floor show.

The new **St Nicolas** is famous for

occasionally staging transvestite floor shows. On the whole, though, they have good videos and music more suited to British tastes than at any of the other nightclubs.

For young, fun-loving après-skiers, the cheapest and most informal nightclub in Courchevel is the **Club 73,** where many of the resort's devastatingly pretty chalet girls are to be found usually in the company of good-looking male ski-bums.

The skiing

The skiing in Courchevel and the adjoining two valleys is so copious and so varied in standard that it is guaranteed to keep almost any skier happy for at least a fortnight. What makes this area particularly appealing is that it is possible for skiers of different standards to ski happily in the same vicinity and meet up fairly frequently. On most of the mountains round here there is always an easy and a difficult way down.

If people criticise the skiing in Courchevel, it is usually on the grounds that 'it's all motorway'. There is some truth in this as there are a lot of long, broad pistes, but some of the motorways are considerably more difficult to negotiate than others. In skiing as in driving, motorways are not always the easiest and safest roads. In any case, most people are grateful for a bit of flattering skiing now and again.

One of the most striking things about the pistes in Courchevel, and indeed throughout the Trois Vallées, is the extraordinarily high standard of maintenance. Pistes are well-marked and regular grooming means that you are almost never troubled by rocks, pebbles or patches of grass, even quite late in the season. For good skiers, the couloirs down from La Saulire are a particularly interesting feature of Courchevel. These are steep narrow runs, just wide enough for good, as well as expert, skiers to cope with. In most resorts they would be considered off-piste but in Courchevel they are marked, patrolled runs so you do not need to feel you are taking your life in your hands when skiing them.

Access to the Saulire area has greatly improved recently with the construction of a new 160-person cable car (yet another one vying for the Largest Cable Car in the World Title) from Les Verdons to the top of Saulire, the point where the ski area joins with Méribel. This cable car is very fast and there are seldom queues, even in high season.

There are several long challenging pistes in the area: the Jean Blanc and Jockeys both go right down to Courchevel 1300, as well as Les Suisses, and Combe de la Saulire which is a lovely long run with steep sections and some taxing mogul fields. There is also some testing skiing over at 1650.

From Courchevel, it is easy to take advantage of the skiing in neighbouring Méribel, but if you want to get much skiing at Val Thorens at the other end of the Trois Vallées complex, you need to set off early in the morning. (Equally, you have to remember to leave the Val Thorens area in good time to catch all the connecting lifts back to Courchevel.)

You do not need a guide as such to do the Trois Vallées circuit, but it is advisable to go with someone who knows the area. This is particularly necessary because it is a difficult area to map. The piste maps have improved greatly in recent years, but they still require quite a bit of concentration.

Three lift passes are available to you in Courchevel. There's a pass for the immediate Courchevel area, a pass for the Courchevel valley, taking in all the satellite villages, and the Trois Vallées pass. You can pay a daily supplement to either of the Courchevel passes to ski in the whole Trois Vallées area, but if you plan to ski in the Trois Vallées system more than twice a week, it makes financial sense to buy a Trois Vallées pass to begin with. Beware visiting this area late in the season because, although the snow may still be good, the lift system closes down in stages and skiing starts to become restricted from early April onwards.

Lunches

For some time the most popular mountain restaurant among the British skiers here has been Altitude 2100, known simply as **Altitude 21.** It is a squat, unattractive building but inside it has great charm. There are lots of cosy tables and benches covered in animal skins – amazing protrusions of rock from floor and wall make the dining area more irregular and interesting. The star chef performs in a recess in the middle of the restaurant where he cooks entrecôte steaks and côte d'agneau on a charcoal grill. These are then served with roast potatoes on wooden platters.

The system here is that you order and pay for your food at the bar and you are then given a meal ticket which you negotiate with the chef. This is not a cheap restaurant but it is good value and is colonised particularly by the middle-aged Guernsey-clad Sloane contingent who come to Courchevel in such large numbers. In fine weather there is a large sun terrace outside.

Down below Altitude 21 is the Courchevel Altiport, where the true jet-setters arrive and depart in their helicopters or light aircraft. Just next to the Altiport is the **Altibar.** This is a self-service place which lacks the atmosphere of Altitude 21 but is a good deal cheaper. There is a large sun terrace from which you can watch the aircraft taking off and landing. Occasionally, your meal here may be marred by music from a live, but not very good, guitarist.

The **Soucoupe Restaurant** at the top of La Loze is a self-service place but offers excellent

At 1300, the lowest part of the Courchevel complex, the **Bistrot du Praz** is an ideal place for a long lunch. It is run by Charlie, possibly the most popular character with the British in Courchevel. He is particularly tolerant of crowds of Hooray Henrys. The more outrageous you are, the more he likes it. He charges for destruction, but accepts it with

good grace. It is no coincidence that the Lloyds Ski Team have left their ties hanging up here. The food is very good though rather rich. From the bar, the Brandy Alexanders are particularly recommended. Not surprisingly, a lunch here can often turn into a taxi-home-at-7pm job.

Also in 1300 is **Les Peupliers.** This place does not have much atmosphere, but it does serve excellent nouvelle cuisine food, either in the bar or in the more expensive restaurant.
value for money. It is also a marvellous place for sunbathing in the spring. The **Chenus** at the end of the Chenus run is rather a characterless self-service restaurant but it sells chips on their own. This is the only place in Courchevel that does good chips in decent-sized portions. The **Panoramic Restaurant** at La Saulire is a good place to arrange to meet friends from Méribel but the food is not wonderful and the loos are dreadfully primitive.

In Courchevel 1850, **La Chouca** is a good place for a long lunch on a bad day. They do excellent steak tartare with *gratin dauphinois* and also have a good selection of pâtisseries. It is right in the middle of town, so if you're staying in 1850 you will not need your skis to get there. **La Bergerie** on the Bellecôte piste is another good place for lunch on a snowy day. The **Telepralong Hotel** at the bottom of the 1850 nursery slopes is likewise good for a mega-lunch. Down at 1650, **Bel Air** is a good but expensive restaurant in a part of this satellite which the French consider very chic. Going down further, **Les Flocons** at 1500 is a useful place for lunch.

For a really lavish lunch, choose a fine day and go to the terrace of the **Des Neiges Hotel,** which is just beside the piste. Here you can enjoy one of the best cooked lunches in the Alps in attractive tranquil surroundings with views of pine forests. But be sure to fill your wallet with French francs before you arrive.

Ski schools

There is one enormous Ecole de Ski Français in Courchevel with about 300 instructors. However, the service it provides for British skiers is astonishingly poor for a resort of this size and standing. Almost all the best instructors spend their time giving lucrative private lessons to rich French, leaving the less experienced instructors to teach the classes. Although there are usually plenty of classes in English, the standard of English spoken by the instructors can be low. As the ESF has a monopoly here, there seems little immediate hope of improvement.

Ski shops

There are plenty of ski shops in Courchevel but the most centrally situated is Jean Blanc Sports, which has earned the praise of many punters. Chalet girls complain about this shop occasionally but, as in many other resorts, the real reason for workers complaining about a particular ski shop is that they are not happy with the quality of the skis they have been lent free for the season. No sensible ski shop lends more expensive equipment to workers than it has to.

COURMAYEUR

Situated a couple of miles beyond the end of the Mont Blanc Tunnel, Courmayeur is a distinctly Italian resort easily accessible from Geneva and the French autoroute system. Although the skiing area here is not exceptional, it is hard to find any skier – even an expert – who has not enjoyed his holiday in Courmayeur. The two ingredients that blind people to any shortfalls in the skiing are the village (old-fashioned and charming) and the locals (more modern, but equally charming).

Courmayeur is arguably the happiest, friendliest ski resort in the Alps. Contrary to what some brochures claim, the French influence is no longer very strong here except in a culinary context; the locals speak only Italian and want to be paid in lire. This can pose problems since the banks keep extraordinarily inconvenient hours – the best time to go to the bank is probably in the morning before you go skiing. Sunday closing is more common here than in most resorts.

Accommodation

A clamp-down on British chalet operators by the Italian authorities in the past couple of years means that there are now fewer chalets (or at least fewer legal chalets) than there used to be in Courmayeur. However, this is really no great loss as chalet holidays are not the best form of accommodation in this resort since they simply don't allow you to sample the restaurants.

Although there are expensive and luxurious hotels such as the **Royal****** in Courmayeur, the best way to live here is a simple bed and breakfast arrangement with a modest hotel. The **Bouton d'Or***** is good value for this sort of deal (they give you clean sheets every other day), while places like the **Pension Roma*** and the **Laurent** are even cheaper and perfectly acceptable in terms of comfort. With the kind of hotel and restaurant prices they have here, self-catering is not an option that you need to consider. Many of the hotels and pensions here have special arrangements (often through relatives) with restaurants and can offer you special deals.

Après-ski

The key après-ski drinking place is the **American Bar,** where Steve, the genial English barman, mixes excellent cheap cocktails – try the Paradiso. Most drinks are served with delicious hot canapés. The payment system here is typically Italian: you pay at the till as you leave, but as no chits are issued, it is up to you to remember what you have drunk.

Next door is the **Caffè della Posta,** a quieter, slightly more refined alternative to the American Bar. This is a place to experiment with one of the best Italian drinks – *latte caldo con uovo* – which is a kind of liquid zabaglione.

Opposite these two bars is the **Red Lion,** an authentic small English pub serving Mackeson's and Courage on draught. This pub apparently did great trade at the peak of the British invasion of Courmayeur some years ago, but now that the proportion of British visitors has been reduced it is rather lacking in atmosphere. Indeed, those Brits who come to Courmayeur seem to prefer more ethnic establishments. Other Italian bars worth sampling include the **Bar Roma, Ziggy's** with its large selection of beers and videos and the **Bar des Guides.**

Try as you might, it is difficult to make your dinner bill come to more than £12 a head including wine in Courmayeur; in fact, the bill will often be nearer to half of that. For this money, you can sample a range of restaurants not normally found in a ski resort. **Le Vieux Pommier** is famous for having an apple tree growing through its middle, but it also does excellent antipasta and *carbonella* – a kind of braserade with several types of meat. The **Turistica** and the **Terrazza** are both good-quality cheap restaurants offering good-value, set-menu dinners.

Ino Cosson, who used to own the renowned K2 restaurant, now runs the **Pierre Alexis** in the cellar of his family home. It has a good atmosphere and both the pasta and the anti-pasta are recommended.

If you have the use of a car, **La Palud** at Entrèves, just before the mouth of the Mont Blanc Tunnel, is worth a visit. Here again, the set menu offers such variety, quality and value that you are unlikely to want to deviate. The **Maison di Filippo** is also up here: it has a considerable reputation, but the quality of the cooking has been inconsistent in recent years. In the other direction, but also requiring a car or a taxi, is the **Pizzeria** in the middle of Verrand, a quaint village with incredibly narrow streets.

After dinner, the **Abat-Jour** and the **Clochard** at Dolonne (full of smooth Italians)

are the liveliest of the discos, though there is also plenty of life in the American Bar and elsewhere. The mayor has decreed that all bars in Courmayeur must now close at 1.00am, so the only opportunity for really late-night après-ski is out of town at the **Va Cherie,** run by the legendary Giorgio, whose stomach is smaller than it once was. This is a nightclub-cum-restaurant with no fixed closing time.

The skiing

Courmayeur is unusual in that the skiing area is actually on the opposite side of the valley from the village. The principal access to this area is by an ugly, brown 130-person cable car with doors that roll down like blinds, making you feel as though you are in a cattle truck. This takes you to Plan Checrouit which is effectively the start of the pistes. Here there is something called the Ski-In which is a depository where you can leave your skis and ski boots overnight, enabling you to come up and go home in your Moon boots.

From Plan Checrouit, you can either take the new six-man telecabine to Bar 2000', or the telecabine up to Lago Checrouit or take one of the two chairlifts that will eventually get you up to Courba Dzeleuna. Most of the skiing is intermediate, although, if you go up from Lago Checrouit you can then take a couple of cable cars up to Cresta d'Arp, from where there is a good long off-piste run right down to the bottom of the valley. Although the skiing is not too demanding, most of the pistes are very pretty, there are lots of trees about and there is something very exhilarating about skiing in the shadow (or rather not in the shadow since the pistes are really very sunny) of Mont Blanc.

The run down from Courba Dzeleuna to Val Veny is not very taxing – it's mostly paths – but it is pretty and you do get a wonderful feeling of being alone in the middle of the mountains.

You can ski the Vallée Blanche from here, returning by bus from Chamonix or, alternatively, you can try the Toula run down the front of Mont Blanc – you need a guide for both of these.

Lunches

Just beyond the cluster of Plan Checrouit buildings, you come to **Château Branlant,** which is just that bit quieter and more exclusive than the other restaurants in the area. Up above here is **Da Livio's** where they do the best spaghetti carbonara on the mountain.

At the top of Courba Dzeleuna there is an amazing four-storey wooden bar/café called **The Australian:** you only need to hear the staff's accents – even when they are speaking Italian – to realise why. This is an enormously popular, informal place and on warm days every available inch of wooden step in this conglomeration is sat upon. The speciality here is *prosciutto panina* – a hot roll filled with prosciutto ham.

Down at Zerotta in Val Veny, there are two sun-trap resturants, of which the **Petit Mont Blanc** is much the better for food and service. On hot days both restaurants set up stalls selling snacks to people queuing for the chairlift out of Zerotta.

Ski schools

There is one ski school here with about 80 instructors. Usually there are about eight English classes a week, each group comprising no more than eight people. The instructors speak reasonable English. You can hire guides to take you down the Vallée Blanche from the ski school.

Ski shops

All ski hire is relatively cheap here so there is not much need to shop around. For sheer convenience, the Ski-In at Plan Checrouit is hard to beat.

CRANS MONTANA

Situated on a south-facing plateau above Sierre in the Rhône Valley, Crans Montana (the scene of the 1987 World Ski Championships) enjoys more sunshine than any other resort in Switzerland. In fact, Crans Montana is really two resorts that share the same skiing. Although they sprawl into each other nowadays, they retain different atmospheres. Crans is by far the more expensive of the two resorts, being highly fashionable for the Swiss and the French particularly. It has lots of chic little boutiques – how many other ski resorts have a Davidoff cigar shop? – and is full of promenading people in large fur coats. Montana, on the other hand, is by no means a cheap resort, but is much more down to earth. It is very popular for self-catering holidays, with a particularly good selection of food shops.

Apart from having an inordinate amount of sunshine, Crans Montana also has the most superb view over the whole of the Rhône Valley. The resorts themselves are not especially pretty, but most of the large apartment blocks and hotels have been built in chalet style and blend in fairly well.

Crans Montana is easily reached from Geneva by train or autoroute along the Rhône Valley. You take the train to Sierre and then the funicular to Montana or a bus to Crans or Montana. If you are travelling by car, there are several winding roads up the side of the valley to the sunny plateau.

Accommodation

Although there are some very good hotels,this resort is really a development of apartment blocks. Almost all apartments are privately owned, usually by rich Swiss or Germans, and are consequently furnished to a fairly high standard. The apartment blocks in the satellite village of Aminona are convenient for the ski lifts but not particularly well situated for nightlife unless you have a car.

Several apartment blocks are situated below the main plateau at Marigny (Montana), but there is quite a steep walk back up to the village itself. If you are staying here, it is worth noting that there are lockers at the bottom station of the Cry d'Err telecabine where you can leave your skis and boots.

The majority of the smart hotels in this complex are located, as one would expect, in Crans. The **Beau Sejour****** and the **Eden***** in Crans are both recommended. If you want to be really flash, you can always stay at the **Crans Ambassador*******, which is between Crans and Montana. The **Hotel Curling***** in Montana is run by Nicholas Barras, who is an extremely genial host and no mean drinker. He happily lays on extra events for British guests and will take them skiing or even heli-skiing. As far as nightlife is concerned, it is best to avoid the inconvenient satellite village of Vermala which is up the hill and rather out of the way. (Two settlements further along the plateau – Les Barzettes and Aminona – should be avoided for the same reason.)

British chalet operators have recently rediscovered Crans Montana and now both Bladon Lines and John Morgan have a large number of beds here. Because most of the chalets tend to have rich owners, the standard of accommodation is well above average. The Bladon Lines chalet Hendrica is particularly well placed for the ski lifts and for the nightlife in both Crans and Montana.

This resort is becoming very popular with the British and the number of British visitors is doubling every winter. This is partly due to the not altogether welcome influx of tour operators dealing with parties of school-children. These crowds of unruly children affect Montana particularly and their general standard of behaviour tends to give the British a rather bad name. It is actually surprising that a resort of the quality of Crans Montana tolerates these parties and it is probably unlikely to do so for much longer.

Après-ski

For afternoon tea, **Gerber's** in Montana just opposite the ice-rink has masses of tables outside in good weather, while in Crans the **Constellation** is the best place.

The key early-evening drinking place in Montana is **La Grange,** a lively cosmopolitan bar. The **Bistrot** at the east end of the town is a quieter place with a lot of rustic furnishings. The most bizarre place for an early evening drink is undoubtedly **Des Vignettes,** a small restaurant/café just opposite the ice-rink. It is a pretty place with flowers on the tables and rather kitsch décor of plastic fruit and vegetables. It is run by a rather intimidating elderly Swiss-German woman who makes one of the best Glühweins in the Alps. The brew is prepared ceremoniously behind the bar in a silver teapot with lots of fruit, bayleaves, cinnamon, etc. and you are given strict instructions to let it stand before serving. This is also an unusual place to have a fondue or raclette. In Crans, the most popular place for pre-prandial drinks is **Le Pub,** also known as the George and Dragon. This is one of the more successful fake British pubs in the Alps – mainly because it is run along Swiss lines.

For dinner, **Au Greni,** beside the golf course in Montana, does all sorts of Valaisian specialities and also very good brochettes. The **Cervin** also offers good Valaisian food. For a cheap meal, **Au Vieux Moulin** is a fine pizzeria. Between Crans and Montana, **Le Santal** offers Chinese and Vietnamese food. In

Crans, **Le Cave** is the best place for a fondue or raclette. **Au Robinson** and **La Channe** are also good. Most of the hotels here do very good food and many of them post their menus outside the doors daily so it's worth keeping an eye on these in case you spot something you particularly enjoy.

The best local disco in Crans is **La Pacha.** The DJ here is known as Disco Dougie from Dundee. He was once immortalised in a Bladon Lines' brochure which said, 'Women and children will be amazed at his wardrobe of clinging all-in-ones and tasteful shirts decorated with palm trees. La Pacha is actually quite a good disco despite this!' Disco Dougie (he's not from Dundee but from Bishopbriggs) was not best pleased with this publicity and he's been taking his revenge on Bladon Lines' punters and staff ever since.

The **Whisky-a-GoGo** in Crans is a rather down-market nightclub which specialises in all kinds of preposterous beauty contests. In Montana, the **Number One Club** is the smartest place, while at the **Mazot** there is a live band. Bands here change several times during the season, so the quality varies enormously. None of the nightclubs is cheap and most of them charge an admission fee which includes your first drink.

The skiing

There is a tendency for good British skiers to be slightly condescending when talking about Crans Montana but people who talk in such a way have invariably not skied here. Good skiers who come here for the first time always find that the resort exceeds their expectations. Although many of the runs are south-facing, the pistes are quite high (1500-3000m) and the snow cover lasts pretty well.

There are three interconnecting ski areas. These are Grand Signal/Cry d'Err/Bella Lui, Les Violettes/Plaine Morte, and Aminona. All the bottom stations of these areas are linked

during the day by an efficient bus service along the plateau which is included on the ski pass.

Between Grand Signal and Cry d'Err there is plenty of skiing for beginners on the Chetseron and Verdets runs, as well as some more challenging skiing on the Pas du Loup run. There is a good mogul run from Bella Lui down to Cry d'Err and over the top of Bella Lui there is (snow conditions permitting) a marvellous bowl of powder with one draglift in it. There is an off-piste run from the back of Bella Lui to Les Violettes, or alternatively you can connect with the neighbouring lift system by taking the famous Piste Nationale downhill run from the back of Cry d'Err all the way down to Les Barzettes. From Barzettes you can then take a telecabine up to Violettes.

From Violettes, there is a cable car up to the Plaine Morte glacier at 3000m. Queuing can be bad here at peak times in high season. Because of the problems of blasting potential avalanches, the Plaine Morte can be closed for days at a time during heavy snowfalls, so skiers are naturally very keen to get up here as soon as it is open. There are a couple of draglifts on the Plaine Morte but these are mostly for summer skiing. The main reason for coming up here is the fantastic long run down to the bottom of La Toula and possibly on down to the bottom of either Cabane du Bois or Plumachit. This is an interesting broad run with some steep sections. The views of the Rhône Valley are particularly impressive.

Over at Aminona, there is some pretty easy skiing around Petit Bonvin but further east the new La Toula chairlift serves a steep black mogul slope. Lower down, there is amusing skiing through the trees round about the Plumachit chairlift.

These three areas interconnect very well and it is easily possible to ski from one end of the system to the other in a day: in fact, you would also have time to take in quite a few other runs. When queuing for the telecabines out of Crans or Montana gets particularly bad, as it does in high season, the solution is usually to take the bus along the plateau to either Les Barzettes or Aminona.

Lunches

This area is particularly well served with mountain restaurants, most of them having south-facing sun terraces with excellent views. The best restaurant in the area is **Merbé,** which is slightly off the beaten track just above Grand Signal. They do marvellous fondues and *croûtes au fromage* here, as well as excellent pâtisseries. (Finding a mountain restaurant prepared to do fondues for small numbers of people at lunchtime is no mean achievement.) The service here is particularly pleasant. Up at **Cry d'Err,** there is a large self-service restaurant which is pretty good value, and upstairs there is a much smarter restaurant with good waiter service.

At **Les Violettes** there is a smart restaurant which has more character than you would expect, considering the modern building it occupies. Service here is erratic and attracting the attention of the waiter, particularly outside, is difficult. The horseshoe-shaped restaurant around the cable car station at **Plaine Morte** is run by the same family. The food here is equally good and prices pretty reasonable, considering the fact that you are 10,000 feet above sea level. The *plat du jour* at both these restaurants is almost always worth having and is very reasonably priced. The system for ordering at Plaine Morte is rather complicated. First you sit down at your table and study the menu. Having decided what you want, you go to the cash desk where you place your order and pay for it. In return you are given receipts. You return to your table and exchange the receipts with the waiter for your food and drink. This all sounds complicated but it works well.

On the Aminona side, the restaurant at **Petit Bonvin** has been improved and enlarged and now has a very good selection of food, while the little restaurant below the bottom of the **Plumachit** chairlift has a limited menu but does very good Valaisian dishes.

Ski schools

There are two ski schools here, one in Crans and one in Montana. They both have large numbers of English-speaking instructors and the standard of teaching is high. The instructors make a special effort to make class lessons fun and the ski school organises various kinds of parties and outings, including a torchlit descent from Merbé.

Ski shops

In Crans, Bouby Sports is the best ski shop, although it is not cheap. In Montana, the choice is really between Zermatten Sports, which has a lot of smart clothing, and Rinaldo, which is slightly better for equipment.

DAVOS

Links with Klosters

Davos is more than 5000 feet above sea level and has the distinction of being the highest town in Europe. And a town it certainly is, with 18,000 guests' beds and a daunting one-way traffic system. Like Klosters, it comprises two areas, Platz and Dorf, but the two have long since become united, although each retains a railway station. Road and rail communications from here to Zurich are good, and the journey takes between two and three hours.

Davos is not an attractive town, but then it never has been. There were just as many flat roofs and ugly square buildings at the beginning of the century as there are today. However, it has an extremely pretty situation and the views up to the mountains can make you oblivious of the buildings that surround you.

Davos is not just a ski resort these days: it is a major European conference centre, much used for international political and financial conferences. When you get on the local bus, you are quite likely to find more people in suits carrying briefcases than in anoraks carrying skis. As many as a third of the tourist beds are filled by non-skiers, and at peak conference times the proportion is even higher.

The major conference event in Davos is the International Management Symposium, which takes place around the end of January or the beginning of February. The town is completely packed at this time, and parking is a nightmare. You cannot get a bed for love or money and some people are delighted if they manage to bribe a hotelier to allow them to stay in a bathroom for a night.

Like most conference towns which need to have 'something for the wives to do', Davos has good, fashionable shops and these are as useful to the skier as to the conference wife.

Davos is too cosmopolitan and expensive to become a major destination for British tour operators. However, there are a large number – judging by their cars – of wealthy British visitors who come here independently.

Undoubtedly the best operator is Tailor-

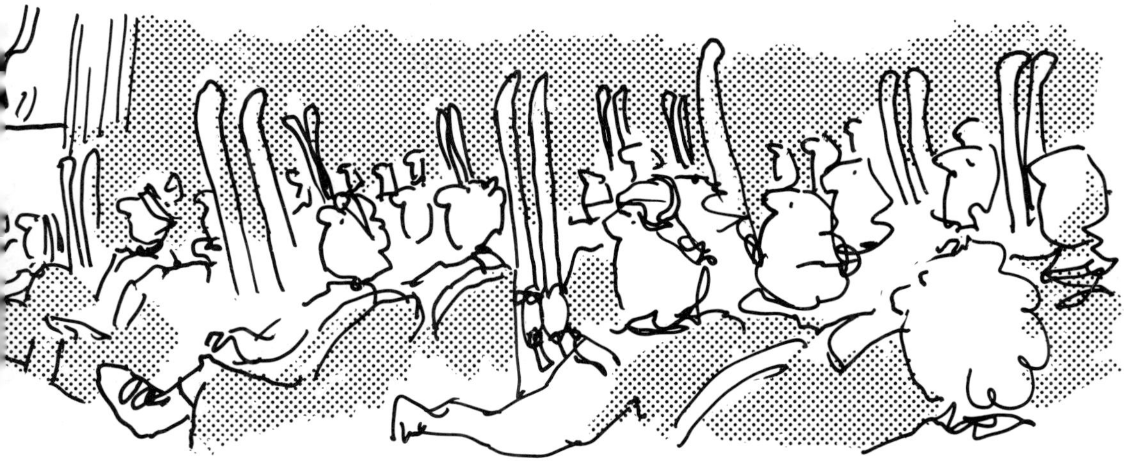

Made Ski Tours, which is run by Colin and Judy McCubbin. They both spend the winter season in the town and offer an expert guiding service as well as all types of accommodation.

Accommodation

Most of the accommodation here is in medium-class hotels, but there are also quite a few modern apartment blocks.

Many of the hotels have English names, and most of them are in Dorf, where the early British visitors gathered. (The British, in fact, started the Davos Ski Club and there is still an English church and parsonage – St Luke's – with services in English every week.) Many of these hotels are now in slight decline but both the **Montana****** and the **Hermann**** remain popular with the elderly British market. The **Parsenn Hotel** is Tyrolean in style and permanently full.

The **Fluella******* and the **Derby****** are probably the smartest hotels in Dorf and both do good trade. In between Dorf and Platz is the **Belvedere Hotel*******, a vast place with 243 bedrooms, which is now owned by the Steinberger hotel group. It has very little in the way of atmosphere. Most of these hotels have their own bars and nightclubs, but they are used mostly by the residents.

Après-ski

There are so many bars, restaurants and clubs in Davos that the most sensible thing is to use the ones geographically convenient, rather than wasting your time getting from one end of the town to the other. The **Postli Corner Bar** at the Post Hotel in Davos Platz is very popular after skiing and there's often some impromptu tea-dancing to a live band. The **Chami Bar** (Chami is Swiss-German for chimney sweep and, hence, good luck) in the centre of town is popular. The décor is surreal with bicycles, milk churns and all kinds of other objects suspended from the ceiling. It has a cosmopolitan clientele which includes lots of locals, and goes on very late into the night. **Trixie's Pub** is a pseudo-British place that must be one of the least successful of the many 'British' pubs in the Alps.

At dinnertime in Davos, you can eat almost any kind of food, except Indian. There is an excellent Chinese restaurant **Zum Goldenen Drachen** in the recently-renovated Sport Hotel terminus opposite the station in Davos Platz. The **Paluda Grill** in the Derby Hotel provides just about the best haute cuisine in the resort, although nowadays it has a serious rival in the restaurant of the **Davoserhof.** The **Gentiana** on the main street in Davos Platz does excellent fondues. About four minutes' drive out of town towards Glaris is the **Islen,** an old farmhouse by the side of the railway tracks where they do excellent grills and liver steaks. For very cheap meals, **Padrino's Pizzeria** is a friendly cosmopolitan place with very fast service. The **National Restaurant** has a very limited menu but its dishes are extremely good value – try the *Geshnetzeletes mit Rösti.* This is a bizarre place and you must not be surprised if the local choir arrives to give an impromptu recital.

There is no shortage of nightclubs and discos in Davos, but one of the best value is the **Postli Club** in the basement of the Post Hotel where they have a very professional band playing disco-type music. There is no admission charge and the wine is reasonably priced. The **Cabana Club** in the Hotel Europe is a trendier sort of disco and here admission is SF10 and the same again for a drink.

The **Jackobshorn Bar** is an intimate little bar/ disco with a good atmosphere. It has a youngish clientele and, unlike some clubs, the music is not so loud that it drowns conversation. Another good place with the young is the very smooth **Carlo's American Bar,** often just known as Carlo's.

The skiing

The major part of skiing in Davos is to be found on the predominantly south-facing

slopes of the Schatzalp and Strelagrat, which in turn give access to the Weissfluhjoch and the Parsenn area. This vast wide open area is always enormously popular with good intermediate skiers. In fact, the Schatzalp part is relatively quiet as most people go past it to ski up at Strelagrat or the Parsenn. Schatzalp itself does not get pisted very much so there are plenty of natural moguls, as well as some very pretty narrow paths through the trees down to Davos.

The Jakobshorn ski area is mostly north-facing and virtually rises up from the centre of Davos Platz. There are some excellent mogul runs here and the area is always popular with ski bums. There are also some good off-piste possibilities, especially for long runs round the back of the mountain. Rinerhorn is a smallish, north-facing mountain reached by a 10-minute train ride from the centre of Davos. This area is particularly good for powder snow and all kinds of off-piste skiing. Because it is some way out of town it's a good place to go when the main resort is very crowded. (Davos gets quite a few weekend visitors.)

The other Davos ski area is at Pischa, which is a short, free bus ride from the Parsenn lift station. This is a relatively unexciting area best suited to not-so-good intermediates. There are, however, great off-piste possibilities if you have a guide.

All these ski areas are included in the REGA pass, as are all the areas in Klosters. At last this pass has been changed to include all the buses running through Davos, for which formerly one had to pay.

One of the more unusual skiing attractions in Davos is a 2½-mile floodlit langlaufing track. If you haven't had enough exercise during the day, you can langlauf for a few hours at night. The cross-country skiing facilities generally are rather good at Davos.

Lunches

The restaurant at **Strela Alp** is a pretty little wooden chalet with cow bells hanging from the roof. They do excellent *Rösti,* generously topped with two *Speigelei.*

The **Strella Pass** restaurant is also a fairly rustic place with lots of big tables outside in good weather. At the **Jatzmeder Restaurant** at the top of Rinerhorn you can grill your own kebabs, sausages, chops and so forth and sit by a big log fire.

On the Jakobshorn, the **Panorama Restaurant** has good views but is otherwise fairly unexceptional. The **Ischalp Restaurant** at the middle station is very trendy with disco music blaring out of the loudspeakers. It tends to attract all the young poseurs of Davos.

Over towards Klosters, the **Parsennhutte** is a barn-like self-service restaurant that is best avoided.

Ski schools

The ski school here is fairly good, although there are not many English-speaking classes. If you can get by in German, then you'll find the ski classes tremendously sociable – everybody has lunch together and goes drinking together after skiing.

There are good touring classes and many of the instructors are experts on the local off-piste skiing. They are also keenly aware of the dangers of avalanches since the Swiss Federal Avalanche Research Institute is situated on the Weissfluhjoch at the top of the Parsenn railway. Lots of people live up there (probably quite a few more than we actually know about), and it is not hard to spot the fibreglass rocks with ventilators and aerials poking out of them. As in many Swiss resorts, the Swiss Army and Air Force maintain a surreptitious presence. Ugly black hornets may zoom out at any moment.

Ski shops

The best ski shop in town is Angerers in Davos Platz. It has very good quality hire equipment and the staff are pleasant and speak good English. The three large Ettinger shops are best avoided – the staff there tend to be off-hand. There is a fixed hire tariff throughout Davos although Ettinger charges even more.

If your skis need any sort of work doing to them, you would be wise to use Helmi Ski Service. This is run by Helmi, who prepares a lot of skis for racers. They are incredibly careful and efficient and will come and pick up your skis from you in the evening and return them the next morning.

FLAINE

Flaine is unusual as a ski resort in that you have to drive down into the middle of the vast snowy bowl that surrounds it. The initial impression, as you look down at the squarish, all-concrete buildings, is that the place has all the architectural charm of a top security gaol. But if you are a keen skier with a young family, you are likely to find this a perfectly agreeable prison in which to be incarcerated for a couple of weeks – and it's only two hours from Geneva. The cells are mostly south-facing, they don't have bars on the windows and complaints of over-crowding are no more common than anywhere else. It is quite possible, though, that some top-security gaols have more nightlife than Flaine: there is a virtual curfew at nine o'clock at night. It is a concrete, functional village that is well sited and well designed for those who are interested simply in skiing. It does not have much in the way of shops, nightclubs or general atmosphere.

Flaine consists of two interconnecting complexes – Flaine Forum and Flaine Forêt. Flaine Forum is the heart of the village where the shops and so on are situated. Flaine Forêt is the newer development above Forum and is mostly apartment blocks, although there is a ski shop and a supermarket.

The principal connection between Forum and Forêt is a bright-orange lift which carries about 20 people at a time. This lift breaks down frequently and there are queues for up to half an hour at peak times in high season. The only alternatives to this are a long, hard scramble up or down the steep gradient between the two complexes or a half-hour walk along the winding road.

Accommodation

This is an apartment-orientated station, the nicest of which are to be found in Flaine Forêt. The Bellier, Capricorne, Castar and Grand Vent blocks are all of very good quality and face south with a view of the mountains. However, most of these apartments are privately owned and are not easily available to holidaymakers.

The Forêt Résidence is a vast apartment block with hotel facilities – bar, supermarket, service and self-service restaurant. The apartments themselves are functional rather than luxurious but represent pretty good value. Some groups of apartments in the Résidence are run as chalets by Supertravel.

The apartments in Flaine Forum are conveniently situated but, being the oldest, the décor is now beginning to look a little tacky – this is especially true of the Vega block where the furnishings are very basic. Beware the Front de Neige block, which is at the bottom of the resort and a long walk away from the Forum.

By far the most pleasant hotel in the resort is the **Gradins Gris***.** It has a gastronomic restaurant and the general standard of service is superb. **Le Totem***** next door has larger bedrooms and a sun terrace but the service can be rather off-hand. The **Lindars**** has a good central lounge with a relaxed atmosphere and is said to be the best hotel in Flaine for children, with its own kindergarten and babysitting service. The **Aujon**** is the only hotel in Flaine that does just bed and breakfast. It has an enormous lounge bar which is a popular meeting place for young people and ski instructors.

Most of the good hotels in Flaine insist on guests taking full board. They offer vouchers for lunch up the mountain but for such a derisory sum that you are virtually forced to come back to the hotel to eat unless you are prepared to spend extra money. The hotel lunches are perfectly acceptable but it is irritating for good skiers to feel they have to return to Flaine Forum in the middle of the day.

Après-ski

The centre of après-ski life for the thousands of British skiers who visit Flaine every season is the legendary **White Grouse Pub.** Opened in 1975 and rumoured to be the biggest money-spinner in the resort, it is owned by the Lees-Jones family of Lees Brewery and is run by Alan and Sue, a Newcastle couple. It has draught lager and bitter, bottled Guinness, a dartboard, horse brasses and counter service only. The beer comes out by lorry from Manchester at least once a month during the season. (The pub itself was designed in Britain and shipped out in two container lorries.)

The White Grouse quickly becomes a home from home for many dedicated British beer drinkers on holiday in Flaine – not for nothing is this resort known as 'Punters' Paradise'. The majority of British reps hold their office hours here every evening. You don't tend to find many French drinking in the White Grouse, but at least the manager has the sensitivity to employ French staff.

The **Snowbub** is an amusing bar in the centre of the station. It is run by Serge, who has been in Flaine for 14 years, assisted by his speedy barman, Pierre. There is a good range of cocktails as well as delicious home-made tarts which makes it a popular tea-time meeting-place. It is also a good rendezvous for pre-ski breakfasts, as it has a south-facing terrace which is especially pleasant later in the season. **L'Éloge** wine bar (next door to Les Chalets) is a recent addition to Flaine nightlife. It is a big, noisy wine bar – no soft furnishings – so not the place to go for an intimate drink. But it is fun later in the evening when it becomes an informal kind of disco.

Les Chalets is the only restaurant with any character in Flaine. A 60-year-old chalet, it was rebuilt in 1972. It serves straightforward French food and regional specialities, but the quality of the cooking is somewhat unpredictable.

A British punter staying in Flaine has to be pretty resilient to avoid a Tuesday or Thursday visit to the **Chalet Bissac,** a restaurant situated on the piste at Flaine Forêt level. It is not normally open in the evenings but British reps arrange special evening events there twice a week.

The menu is timeless – salad followed by fondue bourguignon and chips followed by ice cream. The reps marshall their punters like sergeant-majors: the punters, on the other hand, behave like spoilt children, summoning their rep whenever they need to order more wine or more chips. As soon as the ice-cream is finished, the disco music begins and the tables empty as everyone dashes on to the makeshift dancefloor. You expect to hear a chorus of *Y Viva España* at any moment. What you actually see is a snow conga: a Moon-booted conga will leave the dancefloor, go out of the front door and then conga round the piste for a few minutes before returning. After that, dancing usually takes place on the beams above the dancefloor and an impromptu strip-tease is not uncommon. There is one nightclub-cum-disco in Flaine – called the **Shelby.**

The skiing

Flaine is the principal resort in the Grand Massif ski area which also takes in the neighbouring resorts of Les Carroz and Morillon. It does not seem an enormous area and some of the liaisons between different areas could be better, but it offers enough skiing to keep most good intermediates happy for a fortnight. (In fact, the Grand Massif now claims to be the third largest ski area in France.) The Grand Massif lift pass is worth getting, unless you are an inexperienced skier or obliged to remain close to Flaine because of children. It enables you to get away from the concrete mass of Flaine to some of the older and prettier villages near by. (Occasional rows between the participating resorts mean that this pass is not always available.)

In Flaine itself, the most difficult and dramatic run is the intimidatingly-named Diamant Noir, which runs underneath the new, improved Grandes Platières lift, which now carries 2000 skiers per hour and for which queues are rare. The Tête des Lindars chairlift above the Lindars bubble also gives access to a couple of fairly challenging runs.

Most of the lifts in Flaine are chairlifts or draglifts so you are fairly exposed when travelling uphill in bad weather. In any case, this is not a good place for skiing in bad conditions as much of the skiing is above the tree line. The exception to this is the Aujon area, which offers attractive skiing between the trees. The delineation between piste and off-piste within the Flaine bowl is minimal and this is a good safe resort for skiers venturing off-piste for the first time.

Lunches

At peak holiday times the pistes of Flaine can be insufferably British, but it is easy to escape into a more cosmopolitan atmosphere by skiing over to Plateau les Saix above Morillon. Here, there are three jolly mountain restaurants where lunch is likely to cost a third less than in a mountain restaurant in Flaine itself. **Le Tourbillon** and **Au Rendez-vous des Skieurs** are both pleasant but the most amusing of the three is **Le Chariande** which, although built as recently as 1977, at least looks old. You can sit on the terrace here and eat good cheap lunches of steak frites, etc, while listening to the elaborate Tannoy system which gives constant warning that you must not picnic and advertises the *plat du jour.* The system is also used for relaying the music of Richard Clayderman – who else?

The mountain restaurants in the Flaine Bowl are not particularly inspiring and are fairly expensive. The best of them is **Blanchot.** In Flaine Forum, the **Trattoria** is open all day and does good-value lunches; it has plenty of tables outside in good weather, with views up the valley.

Ski schools

There are two ski schools in Flaine: the Ecole de Ski Français (wearing red) and the International Ski School (wearing green). The ISS is more popular with British skiers.

It was started by a breakaway group of ESF instructors who felt the needs of foreign visitors were not being catered for adequately. Their instructors speak pretty good English and are renowned for their patience with beginners. Both schools use the *ski évolutif* technique for teaching beginners.

If you want private lessons, there is one independent instructor, Yann, who is very highly thought of by former pupils.

Ski shops

Flaine Sport is the best shop in the station. It is situated up in Flaine Forêt close to most of the tour operators' apartment accommodation and is used by most of them. Emile Allais is the main shop in Flaine Forum with a good range of Killy clothing. Snow Ski in the Forum is also good.

GSTAAD

Gstaad and St Moritz are often mentioned in the same breath, but the two resorts could hardly be more different. All that they have in common is a tendency to attract rich jet-setters and be mentioned in gossip columns.

Whereas St Moritz is now a large, sophisticated resort, Gstaad (a third its size) is still a small, pretty alpine village. Apart from the vast folly that is the Palace Hotel, there is really nothing remarkable about Gstaad: you could drive through it without thinking it anywhere special. (The exception to this is at Christmas, when the largesse of Julie Andrews is used to decorate the whole place with fairy lights.)

The jet-set season here is actually fairly short – January and February essentially – so the rest of the time the village is not only quiet but also relatively cheap.

Gstaad is about two hours away from Geneva and has its own railway station.

Accommodation

The ideal way to come to Gstaad is as the guest of one of the wealthy (mostly film-star) owners of a large private chalet. There are lots of luxurious chalets, most of them situated on a south-facing hill behind the village with wonderful views over the mountains. Roger Moore, Yehudi Menuhin, Gunter Sachs, Audrey Hepburn and Prince Rainier of Monaco all have chalets here, but one of the most lavish is that belonging to Vivien Duffield (Clore), who has installed an indoor swimming pool.

In the absence of a private invitation, you can stay at the **Palace Hotel*******, which is not pretty to look at but has excellent service, food and facilities. There are only 1000 hotel beds in Gstaad and there is nothing below three-star standard. If you don't want to go to the Palace, then you can try the **Alpina** just above it, which has been described as 'Browns with Alpine views'. Another excellent hotel is the **Olden*****, a beautiful old building right in the middle of the village.

Après-ski

During the short Gstaad season there is masses of nightlife, although it is never cheap; outside the season things are not so expensive but many places are closed. The bar of the

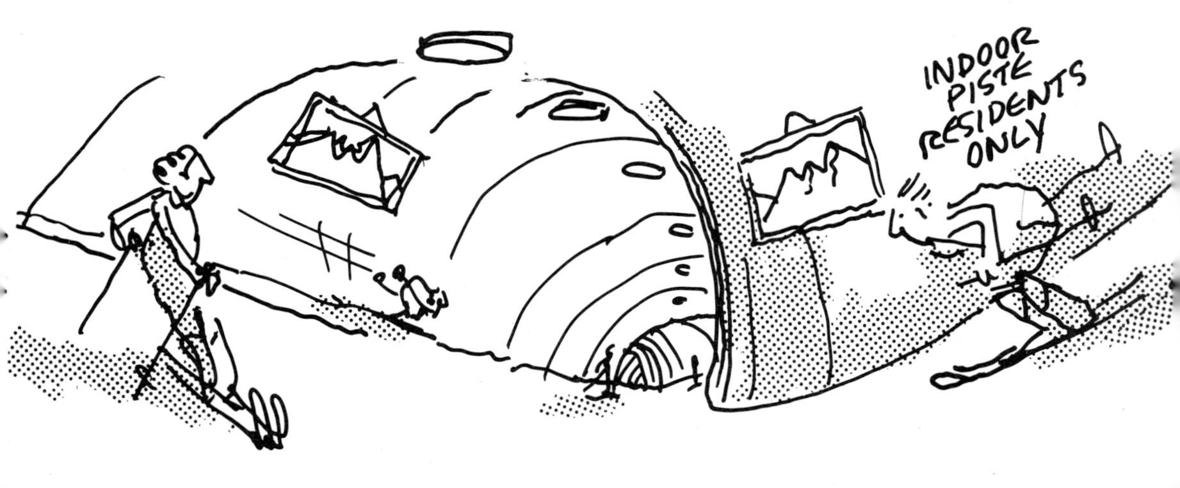

Olden is the most popular place at around six o'clock, when it attracts an intriguing mixture of jet-setters and locals.

For dinner, the **Rôtisserie,** the **Fromagerie** and the **Sans Crevatte Grill Room** at the Palace are probably the most fashionable places, although the *Bellevue Hotel* provides nouvelle cuisine-style cooking that is said to be the best in the resort. The **La Cave** restaurant in the Olden also has a good reputation for its steaks and its *menu gastronomique*. There's a piano here and the owner's wife will sometimes give an impromptu recital of Swiss songs.

A few minutes drive out of the old village is the **Chlösterli,** a beautifully converted old stable block on the site of a monastery. There is a good-value restaurant here (they also do an enormous salad buffet at lunchtimes) and a large dancefloor.

The most sophisticated nightclub is the famous **Greengo** at the Palace Hotel. Entry is around SF30 and does not even include a drink – but there is a live band. As an annexe to the main disco, a floor is erected over the swimming pool. This floor used to cover only part of the pool but there were problems with sub-aqua orgies and it now covers the whole pool. (The atmosphere at the Palace is particularly good on New Year's Eve, as you would expect, with at least three live bands.) The **Chesery** is another key nightspot, but the dancing is only to records. Admission to the disco here is expensive, but admission to the bar is free. The **Taburi** in the **Sporthotel Victoria** has live bands playing alpine jazz and rock and roll.

But there are one or two cheap places to go in Gstaad in the evenings: at **L'Arc-en-Ciel** you can get a pizza for as little as SF10, while the **Post Hotel Rossli** serves good Swiss food for slightly more.

The skiing

Gstaad is part of a ski area little known in Britain – the Weisse Hochland. It comprises nine resorts which are all on the same lift pass and as much as 20 miles apart. Annoyingly, the best skiing in the region is on the Diablerets Glacier which is not covered by the Weisse Hochland pass.

Three main ski areas emanate from Gstaad itself. They all start at different points and to get from one to the other you really need a car. The Eggli system has some good long intermediate runs and connects with the neighbouring village of Rougemont, where they speak French (Gstaad is German-speaking). From Rougemont, you can either get a telecabine back and ski down to Eggli or take the train back to Gstaad, since it is included in the lift pass. The Wispile area is the smallest of the three and offers mainly intermediate runs.

The Wasserngrat is the most famous mountain in Gstaad and provides sufficiently challenging runs to keep even jet-setting *High Life* columnist Taki happy. Though the marked runs here are good, there is also plenty of off-piste and in powder this can be superb.

Frankly, Gstaad is not the place to come if you want a lot of good skiing in one continuous area: the skiing here is disjointed and of uneven quality. But if you are happy to do a bit of driving and to buy all sorts of different lift passes, then there are some interesting resorts within a radius of about 30 miles. Besides Les Diablerets, two of the better-known resorts within day-tripping distance are Villars and Leysin, both long-established and relatively old-fashioned places.

Lunches

The best place for lunch in Gstaad is said to be the **Eagle Club,** but unless you are fortunate and rich enough to be a member – or at least be a friend of a member – then you have no chance of being admitted.

The Eagle Club's eyrie is up at the top of

Wasserngrat and just below it is the socially unacceptable man's lunch place, the **Wasserngrat Restaurant.** This is a wooden building typical of the mountain restaurants in this area. It has a small terrace and waiter service. The regional speciality around here is *Rösti Oberländerart,* which is bacon, ham and onions topped with a gratinée of cheese and a fried egg. If you are driving to or from Les Diablerets, the **Hotel Baren** at Gsteig is a wonderful old building where it is worth stopping for lunch or even just a drink.

Ski schools

There are two official Swiss ski schools in Gstaad. One of them provides lessons in classes while the other one deals solely in private lessons. The Private Ski School produces a big poster with photographs of all its instructors so you can make your choice on looks if you like. Private lessons are not cheap, so you should expect a very high standard of teaching and spoken English. The feeling is that both of these are provided.

Ski shops

As you would expect, these are good but pricey.

KITZBUHEL

Situated at the western extremity of the Tyrol, Kitzbühel is most easily reached via Munich airport or by train to one of the town's two stations.

Kitzbühel was a fashionable resort for the British until about 15 years ago, but nowadays serious skiers find it unsatisfactory because it is relatively low and has a fairly short season. It is difficult to be certain of good snow conditions at Christmas time and the season is normally over by the middle of March.

Surrounded by hills rather than mountains, Kitzbühel does feel a low place, but its excellent rail and road links with Vienna, Salzburg, Munich and elsewhere, mean that it is still popular and, indeed, fashionable with both the Austrians and the Germans. In fact, if you get out of the train at Kitzbühel's Hannenkahm station it is only a short walk to the bottom of the cable car.

The town itself is very pretty with mediaeval walls and pastel-painted houses. It has a good selection of attractive shops, including several selling Persian carpets, florists and lots of expensive cafés and *konditorei* (cake shops).

Accommodation

Although there are a lot of chalets in Kitzbühel, the resort is not featured in the programmes of British chalet operators as the season really isn't long enough to make it worth their while. There are, however, lots of hotel beds in Kitzbühel and many of the middle-market British tour operators can negotiate very good rates on these hotel beds. Half-board holidays here represent quite good value and the principal tour operators are people like Inghams, Thomsons, Global and Neilsons.

The **Weisses Rossl Hotel****** is one of the oldest and nicest in the town and has been receiving the British for many years, as the ancient AA plaque outside the door testifies. The **Goldener Greif** is another long-established hotel (parts of the walls date back to 1271) with a loyal clientele. The **Zur Tenne** is a popular choice with members of the international jet set who still frequent Kitzbühel. There are many other reasonably priced three- and four-star hotels, as well as countless bed and breakfast establishments about whom the Tourist Office can supply details.

Après-ski

Café society still thrives in Kitzbühel and the main après-ski rendezvous is **Praxmair's,** a large café-konditorei with wonderful furnishings that are seriously let down by the rather grotty Formica tables. There is a remarkable display of old Austrian musical instruments all over the walls and the ceiling. The café serves excellent hot chocolate with masses of whipped cream on top, as well as sublime florentines and it stays open for drinks and snacks until 2am, with Fritz the pianist playing in the latter part of the evening. Sometimes Toni Praxmair himself stages Tyrolean evenings here. Just opposite is **Café Langer,** another good café which unfortunately closes at 6pm.

For simple drinking there are two pubs called **The Londoner,** both part of a chain owned by Rick Durrel. His other pubs are in Kirchberg, St Johann and Kurzen.

The larger of the two Londoners in Kitzbühel is the better. It is a vast place covered in lurid tartan wallpaper and is popular with Australian and American ski bums, workers and tourists. Alternative drinking places are **Seppi's Pub,** which is always very full of British, and **Winnie's Bar,** which is a good place to find the locals and fills up after 1am.

The **Unterberger** is the best restaurant in Kitzbühel and although it costs about AS600 per head it is often fully booked and in high season you are wise to reserve a table a few days ahead. The **Alt Kitzbühel** and the **Neuwirt** both serve good traditional Tyrolean food at reasonable prices. The Neuwirt is the rougher of the two and is popular with the locals.

For very cheap meals, try the **Zinnkrug,** which does very good spare ribs, or the **Spa Restaurant,** which is part of the supermarket and stays open until 8.30pm serving very good cheap menus of the day. In the main street, **Wienerwald** is doing for the Wienerschnitzel what McDonald's did for the hamburger.

After dinner, the **Tenne Bar** in the Zur Tenne Hotel is a large and expensive nightspot which often has a live band or a floor show. Beneath the Weisses Rossl Hotel is **Take Five,** a sophisticated nightclub where they scrutinise you through a spy-hole in the front door before allowing you in. There is also a smart casino here, although its standards vary according to the season – you need a jacket to get in in high season but in low season they're happy to take anyone. The chicest disco at present is the **Drop-In.**

For cheaper nightlife, you can hear Horst, the electronic zither expert, in the **Greifkeller,** or you can go to the **Goldener Gams,** a young disco with a lively atmosphere where there's often good live music. If none of these places appeals, you can always go the cinema, which specialises in films with titles like *Catrice die Nymphomanin.*

Après-ski in Kitzbühel is at its best at the time of the World Cup Downhill on the Hahnenkamm, which usually takes place in January.

The skiing

There are two main problems with the skiing in Kitzbühel: the areas are not interconnected and queues are frequently bad. The worst queuing is for the Hahnenkamm cable car, where great piles of cigarette ends by the fences testify to the long waits for a cable car that takes only 48 people at the most. As an alternative, there is the Streifalm chairlift but this does not take you up as high as the Hahnenkamm. There is some very good skiing on the Hahnenkamm section but here again the lift system is really inadequate – there aren't many top resorts that still have single chairlifts. The Hahnenkamm run is every bit as good as David Vine makes it sound, but you must do it before the end of February to enjoy it at its best.

On the other side of town is the Kitzbühlerhorn lift system. The skiing here is really best for beginners and intermediates and as the slopes are south-facing the snow is liable to be gone by early March.

The other main lift system in the Kitzbühel area is at Pass Thurn, which is quite a long way from the town – at least a 15-minute drive and sometimes as long as 30 minutes when the roads are busy. It starts from a vast car park by the side of the road with one double chairlift, which makes Glenshee seem favourably equipped. Queues can be bad here in high season. The Pass Thurn/Mittel area has some good broad intermediate pistes above the tree line, and because they don't get too much sun you will usually find the best snow in the whole of the Kitzbühel region here towards the end of the season.

There is a route called the Ski Safari that allows you to ski from Kitzbühel to Pass Thurn or vice versa by following a series of runs marked with placards of silly elephants. This safari can take a whole day. Intermediates will probably find it a challenge, but it will be

rather tedious for experts. If you are going to ski the Kitzbühel area properly you need your own car, otherwise you will be forever taking taxis or at the mercy of the rather infrequent local buses.

Lunches

At the top of the Hahnenkamm cable car there's a large restaurant with two sun terraces, one for diners and the other for deckchair loungers. (You seem to get many more non-skiers up the mountain in Kitzbühel than in other resorts. Some of them seem to have come out on their first holiday and decided halfway through that they really don't like skiing.)

The self-service restaurant here offers every conceivable type of wurst, schnitzel and zuppe at fairly reasonable prices. You will find an amazing variety of English regional accents around here. Most of them are the sort of package holidaymakers who like to be packaged: 'We've got a free night tonight. I don't know what to do, Trixie,' and so on. Indeed, the atmosphere is one of holidaymakers rather than skiers.

The **Schützhutte Restaurant** on the Steinberkogel has a good view and a nice sun terrace but has a limited choice of food – essentially just frankfurters and *germknödels.* The **Hochbrünn Restaurant** at Streiteck is away from any lift junction and so not too busy. It's a beautiful sun-trap and specialises in *Tiroler Gröstl mit Speigelei.* The restaurant down at Ehrenbachgraben, on the other hand, is a modern self-service place that has about as much character as the refectory of a contemporary university hall of residence. The menu is also unexciting.

The **Berghaus Tirol** is a much more attractive modern restaurant situated on the ridge between Ehrenbachöhe and the Hannenkahmm. It has a limited menu but very pleasant service and a good balcony and sun terrace. Over on the Kitzbühlerhorn side, the **Vordergrub Restaurant** is slightly off the beaten track. You can ski to it in good snow conditions but otherwise you need to drive there. It has a wonderful tranquil garden, which is a beautiful place to sit in fine spring weather.

Along at Pass Thurn, the smart **Holzer Hotel** is just down the road from the car park and is a good place for an indulgent lunch if you decide you can't be bothered to queue for the chairlift. At the top of the chairlift, however, there are three mountain restaurants close to each other. The nicest of these is the one below the top of the chairlift to the left as you go up. They are all self-service places, but this one has friendly staff and a relatively quiet, secluded balcony.

Ski schools

Kitzbühel has a typical traditional Austrian ski school with a high proportion of English-speaking instructors. The disadvantage of the school is that classes tend to be on the larger side, sometimes with as many as 15 or even more.

Ski shops

Most of the ski shops here are fairly competitive in the service they offer and their prices. Probably the best place to hire equipment is Sport Ober, where an Englishman called Peter runs the hire department. Euroski and Kitzsport, which has several shops, have good equipment but do not offer a particularly personal service.

KLOSTERS
Links with Davos

Klosters is in the eastern corner of Switzerland, not far from the Austrian border and just a few miles north of the very much larger resort of Davos, with which its skiing connects. It is a large, pretty village that has been popular with the British for many years, and there is a generation of British skiers (now mostly in their forties and fifties) who return frequently. With the exception of the much-publicised visits of Prince Charles in the late 1970s, it has not been particularly popular with younger skiers. (However, a return visit by the Prince and Princess of Wales, not to mention Princess Fergie, in the winter of 1986 may make it more fashionable.) It is rather an old-fashioned, staid resort, with a very sedate nightlife, and it is significant that this is where the Ski Club of Great Britain chooses to bring its geriatrics' parties.

Klosters itself is divided up into Klosters Platz and Klosters Dorf, though the two areas now almost sprawl into one. Platz is the larger and more convenient of the two areas with quite a number of shops, including an enormous Co-op supermarket – nobody knows how to do jumbo supermarkets better than the Swiss. Platz is also best placed for the Gotschnagrat lift system where the best skiing is found.

Klosters is most easily reached by Zurich airport, which is a couple of hours' drive away. It has its own railway station – on the best trains you have to change only once (at Landquart) to get here from Munich. On Saturdays and Sundays during the skiing season, there is now a through service from Zurich Airport to Landquart. This takes just over two-and-a-half hours.

Accommodation

The chalet operators have experimented with Kosters in recent years, but demand has never been high because the resort is not young enough for the kind of people who prefer chalet holidays. However, Bladon Lines will still provide you with a staffed chalet to order in Klosters.

For most people who go to Klosters the price of Swiss hotels will not be a significant deterrent. Many Brits who could actually afford somewhere more luxurious choose to stay at the **Wynegg Hotel,** which has that slight feel of austerity, and the vaguely bossy management that the old-fashioned Brits seem to love. It was here that Prince Charles used to stay in his bachelor days and Ruth Guler, the proprietor (she was a member of the Swiss ski team in days gone by), was one of only three people from Switzerland to be invited to his Royal Wedding. Some regular residents have described the Wynegg as the 'Albany Chambers of Klosters'.

The most famous hotel in Klosters, the Suvretta, in its heyday one of the great Swiss hotels, has finally closed down. The building has been gutted, but the facade has been preserved. A modern complex of shopping centre and apartments is now being constructed. The **Hotel Alpina****** opposite the railway station is now owned by an American group, First Western Hotels. It has plenty of financial backing and is consequently well-maintained.

The **Aaba Aparthotel******* has just been built in Klosters. This was proudly advertised as Switzerland's first vegetarian five-star hotel. Not surprisingly, the management had trouble filling it up and lately its policy has been altered. Meat-eaters are now accepted and catered for.

There are several good clean Swiss bed and

breakfast hotels in Klosters, including the **Madrals** and the **Minerva.**

Après-ski

Immediately after skiing, **A'Portas Tea Room** is very popular for its excellent ice creams and hot chocolate. Early evening drinking tends to be done in the hotel bars, particularly the **Cellar Bar** of the Chez Grischuna.

As far as dinner is concerned, the compulsory culinary experience in Klosters is the *fondue chinoise* at the **Wynegg.** The two other best restaurants are both slightly out of town. The **Alte Post** is at Aeuja and serves local food, including an excellent rack of lamb. The **Walserhof** restaurant also has a very high standard.

After dinner, **Leo's Snack Bar** (below the Kaiser Hotel) is just about the only late-night drinking spot for young people in Klosters. It is not a pretty place – Formica and aluminium mostly – but there is a good atmosphere when it's full. And at least it's fairly cheap.

As far as discos are concerned, the **Casa Antica** in Platz is fashionable and expensive, while **Rufinis** at Dorf is rather less trendy.

The skiing

The skiing in Klosters divides into two main areas on either side of the valley: the Gotschnagrat and the Madrisa. The Madrisa telecabine starts from Dorf and gives access to half a dozen or so draglifts serving easy and intermediate pistes. The run back down to Klosters Dorf at the very bottom, however, is rather more challenging. There is a bus service between Dorf and Platz.

The Gotschnagrat is the ski area for really serious skiers and is reached by a two-stage cable car from Klosters Platz. Unfortunately, queues for this cable-car can be really bad in high season. There were plans to build a six-man telecabine up from Surneus just along the valley to the Gotschnagrat, which would have alleviated the cable-car queues. However, unusually, these plans were vetoed by the locals themselves.

From the Gotschnagrat you can take a further cable car up to the Weissfluhjoch. This enables you to connect with the Parsenn/Jakobshorn lift system that starts at Davos. Alternatively, you can ski to the right of the Gotschnagrat and descend towards Surneus and Surneusbad in the valley below. The beauty of the area to the right of the Gotschnagrat is that although there are no more lifts, there is a huge variety of different runs down into the valley. Steep parts through the trees give ample opportunity for that favourite SCGB pastime, birdsnesting, or longer gentler paths will take you as far up the valley as Kublis.

The most difficult run on the Gotschnagrat is the Wang – a steep, dangerous piste that is hardly ever open. Even the best skiers only manage to 'get down'.

For the adventurous expert skier, the most

challenging skiing in the area is over in Davos, so it is worth investing in a REGA pass, which allows you to use all the lifts over there as well as the rail service connecting the two resorts.

Lunches

The best lunching places in Klosters are the **Schwendi** houses dotted about in the woods on the way down from Gotschangrat towards the Surneus valley. These Schwendis share the special atmosphere of all the mountain restaurants that are not actually at the top or bottom of a ski lift. The food and service is first-class – dishes of the day cost around SF12 and the bread is likely to be home-made. Most Schwendis do very good *Rösti*.

There is a more conventional mountain restaurant at the top of the Gotschnagrat cable car with a self-service and a service section. In fact, the prices in the unpretentious service section are not much higher than in the self-service. Next to this restaurant is a rapid ski service booth for waxing, sharpening and quick repairs. This is a service that many other resorts would do well to offer.

For a really bizarre lunch, it is worth skiing down to Surneusbad, where there is an amazing health hydro full of fat Germans hoping to buy themselves fitness. It's somehow very funny to wander in here in your ski clothes and watch the aforesaid Germans wallowing about in the magic pool with its built-in jacuzzi jets. Fortunately, the restaurant has an expensive menu with the potential to do your body quite a bit of damage, though as a concession to fitness freaks there is a section on it called Fitness Corner.

Ski schools

Because British visitors do not come here in large numbers, it is hard to find an English-speaking class in Klosters. On the whole, you are better off taking private lessons with an instructor who speaks good English.

Ski shops

This is not a cheap place to rent or buy equipment but it will be of a high standard.

LA PLAGNE

Situated above Aime, about three hours' drive from Geneva, La Plagne is the centre of six residential complexes, all with similar names. In fact, you have to stay in La Plagne for several weeks to work out the identities and geographical positions of all the satellite complexes: Belle Plagne is different from Plagne Bellecôte, which in turn is different from Plagne Villages, which is by no means the same thing as La Plagne. In view of this identity problem, it is ironic that La Plagne chooses to advertise itself on the basis that it has the world's largest single resort lift system.

Certainly La Plagne has a good lift system (some even argue that it is superior to the pistes it serves) but it is an exaggeration to claim that all the complexes are one resort, particularly as transport between them is not always easy.

The controlling company here is SAP, which is believed to be responsible for the resort's silly logo of a bobble hat wearing sunglasses.

Accommodation

This is essentially a place for self-catering enthusiasts, especially those with families. Most of the buildings here are apartment blocks, although there are a few chalets and one or two hotels.

La Plagne itself is the original development and is about 25 years old, so many of the flats here are now tacky. On the other hand, this is geographically the most convenient complex. The smartest and newest area with some of the best-equipped apartments is Belle Plagne. It is convenient for the pistes, but connections with La Plagne itself are bad – you have to go via Bellecôte. The buildings here are in the chalet style, making it the most aesthetically pleasing of the complexes. Nightlife is limited, but the telecabine connection to Bellecôte runs until about 1am.

Plagne Bellecôte owes much to British northern industrial architecture – it's full of pseudo-mill chimneys in need of detonation. Nor is the interior any more appealing: you walk along dreary corridors that seem subterranean, even if they aren't. There is as much atmosphere here as there is in the tunnels underneath the tarmac at Geneva airport – but at least at Geneva they have moving walkways. There are a reasonable number of shops here, most of them facing on to the corridors. There are some decent flats, though, and they are cheaper than those in Belle Plagne. Above La Plagne is Plagne Villages – another modern satellite built in chalet style, none of the buildings being more than about six floors high. It is convenient for the slopes, but lacking in any exciting nightlife. Plagne 1800 is the newest of the satellites, but inconveniently situated. For instance, it is difficult for beginners to get to ski school from here as they have to negotiate a narrow bumpy path.

The vast lump of futuristic-looking apartments perched on the side of the mountain is Aime la Plagne. It looks, as many people have observed, like a ship on the rocks. Not only is this satellite ugly, it's inconvenient. Avoid it at all costs.

Après-ski

The après-ski life would never be a reason for coming to La Plagne, but there are a decent number of bars and restaurants, if one takes all the complexes into account.

The most popular bar with the British has traditionally been the **Pescalune,** well patronised by all the chalet girls. This is a popular place for British companies to hold office hours and welcome drinks parties. It is also a restaurant and specialises in fondue evenings.

In the main La Plagne subterranean shopping centre, the **Chomego Bar** is popular in both the early and the late evening. It does draught Guinness as well as a large range of bottled beers, including McEwan's for the Jimmies. It is depressing, however, to look out of this bar not towards a snowy street but towards a gloomy heated corridor.

The **Refuge Savoyard,** also in La Plagne itself, offers some of the best-value food in the area. It is patronised by workers as well as visitors – always a good sign – and you can eat very well for around FF50.

Unlike many purpose-built resorts, La Plagne has one restaurant where both the cooking and the service are of an incredibly high standard. This is the **Matafan** up at Belle Plagne. The food here is traditional French, although the sauces are not too heavy. Veal escalope aux bolets is one of the specialities. There is also a wonderful selection of sorbets and ice-creams – passion fruit sorbet with champagne is a typical concoction.

Just opposite the Matafan is **Au Vieux Tyrol,** another slightly cheaper French restaurant. If you are making an excursion to Belle Plagne by car to visit these restaurants, be careful not to leave your cars in one of the many tow-away zones. The sign *'Mise en Fourrière Immédiate'* is no idle threat and you may have to go all the way to the pound at Aime 2000 to retrieve your car.

In Plagne Villages is **Au Bon Coin,** a typical Savoyard restaurant with a disco next door. **Le Bistrot** is also in this satellite but there have been one or two reports of food poisoning from there recently. Below Aime la Plagne is a pleasant old restaurant, **Au Bon Vieux Temps,** seating only about 30 people. You poubelle down there and then have to walk back up, but the food is worth the effort.

In Bellecôte, the centre of après-ski activity is the **Piano Bar.** Formally owned by Tom Mongellaz (now at the Bar Jacques in Val d'Isère), this large bar has a good atmosphere and is usually full of Bellecôte ski instructors. At the end of the evening, the most popular disco is **Video 5** in La Plagne, although the **Jet 73** in Bellecôte also has a following. In Aime 2000 there is **Gordons,** while the weirdest place in the whole resort is **Challenger** in La Plagne itself.

The skiing

The great pride of La Plagne's skiing is the Bellecôte Glacier, which is also open for summer skiing. Unfortunately, getting up to the top of the glacier from La Plagne itself can take two hours, allowing for minimal queuing – queues can be bad in peak holiday periods. The runs down from the glacier are not worth the trouble of getting to the top: there are some decent red and black runs but they are so heavily littered with reckless, intermediate wally skiers traversing the pistes that it is very hard for a cautious expert skier to pick his way down the fall line. Apart from these problems, the fact is that the skiing offered by the more accessible glacier in nearby Les Arcs is much more challenging.

Most of the rest of the on-piste skiing at La Plagne is better suited to intermediates than experts. This is an ideal place for an intermediate skier to build up the confidence that will turn him into an expert, especially as there are lots of opportunities for gentle off-piste skiing just beside the marked runs.

For the expert skier, it is likely to be the variety of off-piste tours that appeal most about La Plagne. You need a guide for most of them, but with a bit of poling and the occasional use of buses, you can make day trips to Les Arcs and Courchevel, taking in some of the older villages that are part of the lift system – Peisey Nancroix, Champagny and La Praz, for example.

Lunches

La Plagne is famous as the home of what has become the most celebrated mountain restaurant in the Alps to British skiers – **Le Kitchen.** Min Bell and Liz Andrews set up the Kitchen five seasons ago after they had both worked several seasons as tour operators' representatives. The food is simple: one *plat du jour* as well as soups, salads, cheeses and distinctly English pâtisseries like chocolate brownies and crunchy flapjacks. Min is now running the restaurant on her own in its new premises at Plagne 1800.

Most of the other good mountain restaurants in the La Plagne area are in the old villages further down the valley: there's **Le Sauget** and **La Ferme** in Montchavin and **La Tormente** in Montalbert, where there is a wonderfully sunny verandah.

For serious lunchers, the most hallowed destination in this area is **Le Bouquetin** (otherwise known as Chez Thérèse) at Champagny, where you get a five or six course (estimates vary) lunch and unlimited wine at a very favourable price. The only problem with Le Bouquetin used to be getting back from it, but there is now a new telecabine which solves this problem.

Ski schools

With so many satellite villages, it is inevitable that there should be several ESF ski schools, each with different directors and teaching hours. The Bellecôte ski school is the most enterprising and is particularly recommended for children and families as they are genuinely concerned if you have any problems.

Ski shops

Allais and Portillo are the two ski shops here: the former tends to have better equipment, but there is not much to choose between them as they are virtually controlled by SAP, the management company of La Plagne.

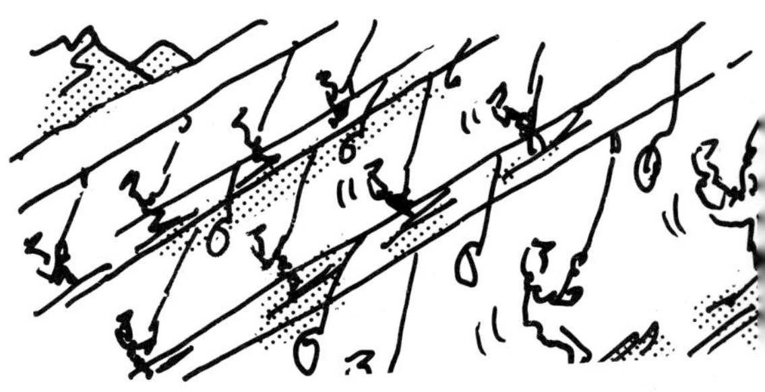

LECH

Also see St Anton

Lech is a traditional Austrian ski resort with an amazingly sophisticated international clientele. It is no coincidence that the suave Tourist Director, mentioning his fondness for the British, should cite two lords as close friends. Nor is it surprising that this same man should receive invitations to stalk and shoot grouse on the Scottish estates of his aristocratic acquaintances. Lech operates very much on this jet-setting social level.

Paparazzi photographers constitute more of a danger on the pistes of Lech than the unmarked rocks: they are everywhere. Abba come here, as do Queen Beatrix and ex-Queen Juliana. Nikki Lauda has a chalet here and King Hussein and the Prince and Princess of Wales have been known to stay in neighbouring Zürs. One star the paparazzi missed, however, was Anthony Andrews, who turned up in the same pew as a troupe of devout chalet girls at communion service on Christmas Eve. As in all the most fashionable European resorts, there is quite a high proportion of American visitors.

Although Lech has a pretty situation and its buildings are traditional in style, the overall scale of the place is quite large. This is not a pokey little mountain village with narrow streets – it is a small town intelligently planned around the demands of the 20th century. This means, though, that there are several large hotels and nothing much in the way of small, intimate bars. This is equally true of the satellite village of Oberlech, which is reached by road or by a cable car (included in the lift pass) which runs until 1am. Here again, social life centres around the bars of large hotels.

The closest airport to Lech is Zurich, although Munich is not much further away. (Innsbruck is actually the nearest airport but there aren't many flights there.) Lech is also easily reached by train via Langen or St Anton. Cars are allowed to move and park fairly freely in the resort. There is also a sleigh service, but if the driver happened to go overboard on the schnapps he may well not turn up – the excuse will always be that the horses were exhausted.

Accommodation

As the eating out is expensive and not particularly varied at the bottom end of the scale, chalet holidays are a good way of coming to Lech – both Supertravel and John Morgan have good chalet accommodation, but beware of being stuck in the John Morgan chalet at Zug.

Otherwise, hotels are the main type of accommodation, most of them being four-star or three-star and accordingly expensive. There are not many cheap hotels in Lech. The **Tannbergerhof****** is generally accepted as being the smartest hotel in Lech, but the **Arlberg Hotel** is also well thought of. The **Gasthof Post** has a striking pink facade with trompe l'oeil murals. It has modern comforts (fridges) concealed in old-fashioned wooden chests. In fact, most of the hotels in this resort can be relied upon to provide a very acceptable standard of service and comfort.

Après-ski

Here again the Tannbergerhof is a crucial place: it has a smart nouvelle cuisine restaurant and a popular disco which is also open for tea-dancing in ski boots. (The tea-dancing has become so popular of late that the management now charge AS35 for this pleasure which used to be free.) In fine spring weather, the bar outside the Tannbergerhof will be packed at round 5pm.

The **Rote Wand** at Zug also has a great reputation for its nouvelle cuisine, although it offers more traditional fondues and so on as well. The tomato and gin soup here is always a great hit with visiting British punters. Halfway towards St Anton is the famous **Hospiz** at St Christoph, where a superb dinner will cost about AS1000 per head if you can get a table. (The Prince and Princess of Wales have eaten here.)

In Lech itself, the **Haus Ambrosius** is a big, good-value restaurant and **Pizza Charly** offers snail pizzas, among other toppings. The **Milktrinkstube** is a lot more than simply a milk bar, serving basic dishes at very reasonable prices. Up in Oberlech, the **Goldnerberg** is a traditional Austrian restaurant where the British are particularly welcome. The **Sonnenbung Crêperie** up here has the best snails in the region, as well as the inevitable crêpes.

For a change from the hotel discos and the pricey **Scotch Club,** a visit to the **Hubertusklause** is recommended. This is one of the oddest après-ski spots in the Alps and never fails to amaze and even enchant visiting punters. The entertainment comes from Hans, the legendary electronic zither player, who spends his summers doing the same thing in a bar in Argentina. He has a slightly limited repertoire of waltzes, drinking songs and neutralised pop tunes which fill the dancefloor every night.

Holidaying middle-aged Germans seem to love it here, so you feel very young on the dancefloor if you are only in your twenties. Curiously enough, this is probably the closest Lech comes to an authentic Tyrolean nightspot.

The key nightspot in Oberlech is the slightly rowdy **Reblaus** in the Hotel Bergkristall. The **Kellerstube** of the Pension Ilga is also worth trying and serves good Glühwein.

The skiing

The most striking thing about the skiing in Lech is how well maintained the pistes are. Many European resorts have now stopped using Ratracs at night because they have to pay the drivers such high wages, but here piste-bashing goes on round the clock. As the lower slopes are fairly low, the resort has sensibly bought half a dozen or so snow-making machines which help to prolong the season. The pistes are also extraordinarily well marked with large spherical markers at each side.

Most of the skiing in Lech is on the south-facing slopes above Oberlech, and is for intermediate-to-good skiers. The Mohnenfluh cable car takes you up to the highest point in the system, from where there is a difficult descent to Zug, which can be delightful or dreadful, according to the snow conditions. It gets a lot of sun so it can be incredibly slushy and hard work later in the season, but in fresh powder it is the best run in the resort.

Approaching the end of this run, it is crucial to control your speed as you have to negotiate a sharp corner to avoid going straight into the river. And the danger doesn't end there: on

the chairlift back up again you have to be sure to close the safety bar immediately you get in or you risk being tipped out into the river.

The other main skiing accessible from Lech is Zürs, but getting there used to be a problem. You had to take the Rufikopf cable car, for which there were long queues (up to an hour at weekends) or else take one of the infrequent buses round to Zürs. However, there is now an additional, brand-new cable car up the Rupikopf so queues should be much rarer.

When the queues aren't too bad, the Rufikopf lift is the start of what has become known as 'The Circuit'. This involves going up to the top of the Rufikopf, skiing down to Zürs (which is a nice enough place but plagued by a recurrent smell of sewage), up to the Madloch, down to Zug and then up to Palmenalp and thence into the Kriegerhorn system and on back down to Lech.

It is important to be well-behaved on the impeccably-ordered Lech lift system. *'Die Pistenrowdys'* have their lift passes taken away, as exemplary newspaper cuttings posted at the bottom of certain lifts remind you. Swedish tour operators were banned from Lech some time ago and Swedes now try to dodge the ban by booking with British operators, so you may find some hurdy-gurdy talk in your chalet party.

Sensibly, there is only one lift pass for the whole of the Arlberg area, but the irritating lift men seem to want you to produce it every time you go up. The lift company is generally very bossy and has installed all sorts of gadgets like a continuous tape-recorded announcement in several languages stating the obvious. 'This is a double chairlift for two persons only' is a typical announcement. The lift men make you queue as though you are about to board Noah's Ark.

Beware going to Lech if you *really* want to go to St Anton – they do not connect very well. It is a mistake to go to one in order to ski the other.

Lunches

The crucial meeting place in the Lech ski area is the Red Umbrella outside the **Petersboden Sport Hotel** at Oberlech. This is an enormous hydraulic umbrella about 25 feet in diameter with a circular bar, run by Hasser, underneath it. The umbrella is raised late in the afternoon or if the weather is bad. There are stools right round the circumference of the bar and you can sit and consume local specialities such as *Glühwein, Jägertee* (tea with rum) and *Vodka Feigen* (vodka with figs in it). On a cold day you can warm up your gloves on the *germknödel* cooker. *Germknödels* are extraordinarily stodgy steamed dumplings filled with jam, and sprinkled with ground poppy seeds.

The Red Umbrella is perfectly placed not just for lunch but for meeting people in the mornings and for the final pit-stop of the afternoon. If the weather is very bad, then the inside restaurant of the Petersboden Sport Hotel is a good place for a long lunch. There is a log fire and the owner is very keen on the Brits. (He has been known to throw people out into the blizzard as soon as they have finished their meal so as to make room for his favourite chalet girls.)

Directly opposite the Red Umbrella is the **Burg Hotel,** which has a rather grotty self-service restaurant. For most skiers, the greatest attraction of the Burg Hotel is its loos, which are the most luxurious in the Alps, with lavish carpet and piped music. Other than the Oberlech complex, however, this is not an area over-endowed with mountain restaurants.

Ski schools

There are two ski schools here, one based in Lech and the other at Oberlech. They are both traditional Austrian schools with good reputations. English is fairly well spoken and there are one or two non-Austrian instructors who speak it as their first language.

Ski shops

The great trading dynasty in Lech is the Strolz family: they deal in everything and have several shops. They sell a lot of very up-market ski equipment and clothing Head suits are de rigueur on the pistes here. Those in search of Piste Cred in Lech and St Anton know that it is essential to have their own pair of Strolz boots, custom-fitted at the brand new Strolz boot shop. Strolz also do more basic boots for rental.

LES ARCS

One of the most successful of the new French resorts is Les Arcs. It is situated directly above Bourg St Maurice (about three and a half hours from Geneva) from where it takes only five minutes by cable car or half an hour by road to reach the resort. Les Arcs manages to remain popular with the most chic of French skiers, while still attracting low-budget self-catering skiers from all over Europe.

Opened in 1972, some years later than most comparable resorts, Les Arcs has avoided a lot of the mistakes of its predecessors. The architecture is innovative but unobtrusive, the buildings are clad with wood, in low, flat units built into the hillside at a variety of intriguing angles. The shops and restaurants open on to the snow, but are protected from the worst of the elements.

From a skiing point of view, Les Arcs has consistently been in the vanguard of the sport's development. It is the home of *ski évolutif,* which is taught with as much enthusiasm now as when it was invented. It is also the home of a Flying Kilometre speed-skiing course, where British competitors have enjoyed considerable success in recent years. You will also find plenty of users of monoskis, wintersticks and any other ski gimmick in Les Arcs.

The resort comprises three settlements: Arc 1800, Arc 1600, and Arc 2000 which is mostly given over to the Club Mediterranée.

Accommodation

Les Arcs is a guaranteed Chalet-Girl-Free Resort – it consists entirely of apartments and hotels. But there are plenty of tour operators' reps about, many of them working for Neilsons, which is one of the biggest operators here with 400 to 500 clients a week in high season. The company advertises its presence with enormous placards nailed gratuitously to the walls of innocent little wooden huts all over the piste.

The main part of the resort is Arc 1800 and most of the hotels and facilities are located here. As most of the apartment buildings are about the same age, there is little to choose between them. The British operators generally concentrate their operations in 1800, but Ski Val has its Club Winston in a converted two-star hotel in the satellite complex of Arc 1600. The standard of accommodation is very reasonable, but a holiday there involves all sorts of organised activities and fancy-dress dinners. As Miss Jean Brodie once said: 'For those who like that sort of thing, that is the sort of thing which they like.'

The smartest place to stay in Arc 1800 is the **Hotel du Golf***.** It has good bedrooms, a marvellous central lounge with open fire, and a gastronomic restaurant, the Green, which has a considerable reputation for its nouvelle cuisine. The hotel arranges special gastronomic weeks during the season, when leading chefs from Lyons and Paris come up to cook at the hotel.

The only argument against staying in the Golf is that it is virtually impossible to find your bedroom. There are no staircases: the whole hotel is built lengthways with a series of ramps (sloping horizontally as well as vertically) leading to the different floors. There seems to be no logic about the way the rooms are numbered and the lifts at reception go to a Floor 5 that bears no relation to the Floor 5 served by the lift at the other end of the building. The porters will give you a map but it is of no practical help. It should be easier to find your room in the new **Hotel Club Latitudes***** which has just been constructed at 1800. It offers half-board, inclusive of a ski package which features all-day instruction.

There are all manner of special events designed to induce people to come to Les Arcs in low season weeks. As well as the Gourmet Weeks, there is a Disc Jockey Week, a Monoski Week and a Wine-Tasting Week.

Après-ski

The main British bar in 1800 is the **Gabotte,** to which people ski back at five o'clock for pre-prandial drinks, and to which they return after dinner. A darker, more intimate bar for early-evening drinking is the **Santaline,** which turns into a restaurant for the second half of the evening.

For dinner, the **Laurus** does good traditional French food, as does the **Ti-Punch** next door. The **Gangantus** is the best pizza/pasta restaurant in the resort and you have to book to be sure of a table. The **My-Lihn** is a very

proper Cantonese restaurant run by French-Cambodians. The food is authentic and you eat with chopsticks or starve. For a really excellent dinner, there is always the **Green** restaurant in the Hotel du Golf (see above).

After dinner, **Zagrim's** is a fashionable nightclub for the younger set, particularly the French. The older and richer will probably prefer the **Fairway** club in the Golf. Here you find a lot of rich, sophisticated French still sweating in their furs and wearing dark glasses at midnight. Down in Arc 1600, there is always a good atmosphere at the **Abreuvoir Bar,** where jazz goes on very late, as it does at the **Arcelle,** a good, largely French disco. The **Cabuche** is a jolly bar here where many of the ski instructors meet. (Since the Navette bus linking Arcs 1600 and 1800 stops at 8pm, you can't really enjoy the nightlife in one complex if you are staying in the other, unless you have a car.)

The skiing

The lift system in Les Arcs is well designed and there is little queuing except on the lifts outside the resort at peak times. (Although a speedy new four-man chair has improved this bottleneck.) With the exception of one cable car, all the lifts are chairs or pomas, which means that uphill travel is often cold and unpleasant, particularly early in the season.

The greatest development at Les Arcs in recent years has been the Aiguille Rouge cable car. This now gives access to some truly challenging skiing. The top part of the run down is really narrow, steep, icy and generally dangerous. This section gives way to some broader, steep areas, some pisted, others not. The Face d'Aiguille Rouge and the Piste des Lanches by the Dou de l'Homme chairlift are both difficult runs that are anything but flattering.

The Ski Total concept (meaning that both on and off-piste areas are patrolled) makes Les Arcs an ideal place to start learning off-piste and powder skiing. There are a lot of trees on the lower slopes, all ideally placed for skiing between – not so close together that it is dangerous, or so far apart to be boring.

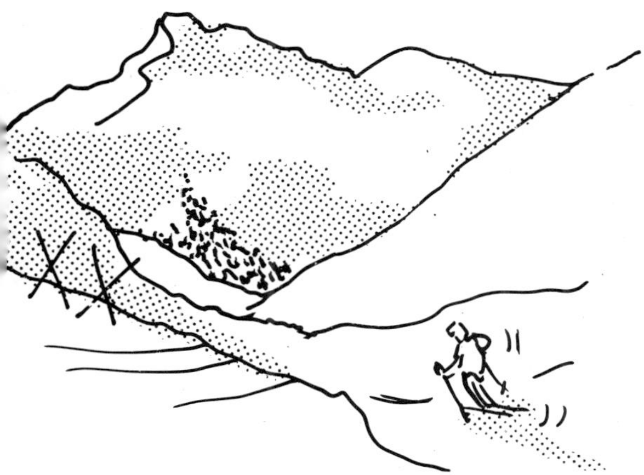

Lunches

Unfortunately, the main mountain restaurants in the Les Arcs area are owned by SMA, the management company, and tend to be nondescript. **L'Aiguille Grive** at 1800, however, is conveniently situated and is a popular place for skiers of different standards to meet their friends at lunchtime.

The nicest restaurant in the main ski area is **Tanière,** a chalet building with a sun terrace above 1600. It does an excellent *vin blanc chaud.* **La Cachette** in 1600 itself does a good lunch at around FF100 for unlimited wine and food. This is a good place to come when the weather is bad. Another fine independent restaurant is **Bois de Lune,** which is in an old village near the bottom of the valley. It is a difficult place to find; you really need a guide as you have to go a long way along tracks through the trees. There is a marvellously informal atmosphere about Bois de Lune: you feel very much as though you are eating in a private house. Slippers are provided for you to change into and masses of cushions for you to lounge on. After lunch, the patron will take you down to Bourg St Maurice in his ancient minibus and decant you into the cable car back up to Les Arcs.

Ski schools

It is generally agreed that *ski évolutif* is the best way for older adults to learn to ski, and the resort's special *évolutif* package, which includes ski hire, tuition and lift passes for two weeks, represents good value. There is one main ESF ski school in Les Arcs with several sections – the *évolutif* experts have a reputation for being the best instructors. There is also a section of the ski school teaching Ski New Way. This involves monoskiing and things called *ski extrème, ski espace* and 'apocalypse skiing', as well as the Powder Circus which specialises in off-piste skiing.

Ski shops

There are three ski shops in Les Arcs. They are all owned by SMA and all treat customers equally badly. The ski technicians don't bother speaking to anyone and charge a lot for their hire services.

LES DEUX-ALPES

Les Deux-Alpes is a large purpose-built resort in the Grenoble area, just about equidistant from Lyons and Geneva airports. It is a predominantly French resort that is in the process of being discovered by the British.

Architecturally, Les Deux-Alpes is a farrago of just about all styles known in the Alps. There are some harsh, square concrete blocks as well as other more recent chalet-style buildings which seem to have been erected to atone for earlier atrocities. But with 20,000 guests beds, it is always a lively place, and once you get inside the rather unattractive-looking restaurants and bars, the atmosphere is usually quite fun.

Unlike many purpose-built resorts, Les Deux-Alpes is not in the grip of one controlling mafia, so free enterprise flourishes. This means that there are lots of well-run shops and restaurants, and although prices are not cheap, they tend to be competitive.

Accommodation

A few years ago, there were no British operators in Les Deux-Alpes, but nowadays they are queuing up for accommodation. Companies like Supertravel, Activity Travel and Ski MacG now operate here, all of them with chalet accommodation as well as hotels and self-catering. There are a number of extremely nice family-run hotels. The Mayor, Monsieur Fourre, proprietor of the **L'Adret Hotel****, is a great character, a considerate hotelier and famous for the wine he makes. The food at his hotel is also of a high standard.

Chalet Mounier** has a standard of cooking worthy of a four-star hotel. Monsieur Mounier himself (one of the coolest characters in town) works in the kitchen, while his glamorous wife supervises the dining room. This is one of the oldest hotels in Les Deux-Alpes, dating from before the Second World War. Originally, it opened only in the summer. **La Berangère***** is a stylish hotel which is a member of the hallowed Relais et Château category. This place also serves superlative food and deserves to be a four-star establishment; however, the owners seem to prefer three-star clientele. It is probably the most pleasant hotel in the resort, and has the advantage of being right on the piste with a draglift only yards away.

As parts of Les Deux-Alpes are now more than 25 years old, some of the apartment blocks are getting a little scruffy. It is very important, therefore, to enquire about the age of the building and its condition when booking your holiday. Most agencies from whom tour operators get their apartments have a star system of rating similar to hotels. In the more modern apartments, the standard is high and the value reasonable.

Après-ski

For tea, **Gégé Pilloud** is an excellent pâtisserie, although as there are only four tables it is always crowded and you may have to wait a while before you can sit down. They do a superb *tarte tatin* as well as *pavé au noix* (a chocolate and nut speciality of the Grenoble region) and a large selection of mousses including *mousse de thé.*

There is a whole symphony of piano bars in Les Deux-Alpes. They are mostly reasonably cheap before dinner but with prices rising sharply to around FF30 a drink after 9pm. **Le Pressoir,** run by Serge, is the most lively, with music (often live) that's not so loud that it drowns conversation. The drinks are fairly cheap here and you can often negotiate special prices if you're in a large group. The **Baron**

Piano Bar is run by Jean-Claude and Rémy who usually employ an American or British pianist. There is a good selection of skiing and hang-gliding vidoes here. **L'Arlequin Piano Bar** is fairly expensive, although it has a live group early in the evening and a pianist later on. **L'Ile au Rhum** is a video bar with good music.

There is an enormous choice and variety of restaurants in Les Deux-Alpes. The **Café Suisse** is very good for fondues and raclettes, and there's a pianist here, too. Another popular place for raclettes is **La Patate** which represents a particularly good deal for heavy drinkers as the all-in price of FF80 includes as much wine as you can drink. **La Cheminée** is another popular place for groups enjoying a night out. The **Crêperie des Sagnes** is the best place for crêpes and galettes (savoury crêpes), **Chez Lee** is a reasonably priced Chinese restaurant, but the cheapest place for a meal in this town is probably **L'Oasis,** where you can have a dinner, including wine, for around FF100, or slightly less if your tour operator has negotiated a special reduction.

La Bougie, formally one of the best restaurants in the resort, has changed hands recently and the cooking has become erratic. **Les Camélias** offers good nouvelle cuisine food for prices of around FF250 per head. The food at **La Petite Maison** is not exceptional but this really tiny place, run by Georges and Marie, has a wonderful ambience.

After dinner, the best disco in town is the **Casa,** situated right at the entrance to the resort. (There's a free jeep taxi service to take you there.) The Casa has a big dancefloor area with seating all round it and the management are very keen on any kind of special events, displays, competitions, etc.

The French seem to have no inhibitions when it comes to organising Miss Nude, Mr Nude or Miss Grosse Poitrine competitions. There are photographs in the entrance hall to the Casa which prove events to be every bit as gruesome as they sound. The management have also framed a peculiarly unlikely commendation from, believe it or not, the *Daily Telegraph*. Admission, which includes the first drink, varies according to the day of the week and the season but is around FF70. There is a piano bar here as well, which is much quieter than the disco.

L'Avalanche is a new disco which caters for a slightly younger crowd and is popular with the locals, although it has now introduced a special night for the English. **Le Hippy** is the nightclub for those on a low budget. The piano bars are all very popular late at night when the French obsession for cocktail drinking is indulged to the full.

The skiing

There is skiing on both sides of the valley in which Les Deux-Alpes is situated, but by far the bigger of the two areas is that on the eastern side. Several different lift passes are available covering areas of increasing size – for instance, the cheapest pass allows you to use only the lifts on the lower slopes. If you are a good intermediate skier or above, it is worth getting the full (red) pass which allows you to use all the lifts and also gives you free access to the (outdoor!) swimming pool. As you cannot change your lift pass or pay a supplement, it is important to decide at the beginning of your holiday exactly what you want.

The skiing on the western side is fairly easy, but it's a very pleasant area for beginners and intermediates.

On the eastern side, the skiing goes right up to the Glacier du Mont de Lans at 3568m, where there is a good deal of summer skiing. This skiing area is unusual in that most of the steeper, more difficult runs are on the slopes immediately above the village, while the easier, intermediate runs are generally higher up.

The skiing on the glacier is not particularly difficult but the snow is always in very good condition and it's certainly the place to come if you want an ego boost. Lower down, the lifts up to Tête de la Toura and Tête Moute both give access to some difficult, interesting skiing.

The greatest innovation here in recent years has been the installation of the Jandri Express, an amazing 20-man telecabine which takes you from Les Deux-Alpes itself right up to the glacier in only 25 minutes – in the old days, this journey used to take hours. There are sometimes queues for this lift but it's worth waiting for.

Les Deux-Alpes is a good resort for families with young children as there are large numbers of short draglifts near the hotels and apartment blocks. As it is within easy day-tripping distance of Grenoble and elsewhere, queuing can be bad at weekends and is always dreadful during French school holiday periods.

If you tire of the skiing at Les Deux-Alpes, you can take advantage of the new helicopter service for a day's skiing at neighbouring Alpe d'Huez, another large French purpose-built resort, scarcely known in Britain. There are several good long black runs here. (You can also drive over to Alpe d'Huez – it takes about an hour.)

Lunches

For a resort with so many good restaurants in town, the mountain restaurants are surprisingly unimpressive. The few places that exist are self-service with food of indifferent quality.

At a test meal, **La Patache** at Lac du Plan was offering only boiled beef and carrots with noodles or dehydrated plates of salad. There were notices everywhere declaring that chips were not served on their own, but they were not serving chips, anyway. The French seem to overcome the gastronomic failings of this restaurant by purchasing endless family-size packets of chocolate digestive biscuits and guzzling them rapidly.

La Patache also has that most annoying French mountain feature – the FF1 charge for

the loo. Although this is certainly better than no loo at all, it is still a mean and irritating practice. Traditionally, a fierce woman from the village is employed to guard the two loo doors and extort money from the clients, using menaces when necessary. The woman employed is usually an expert knitter and combines the function of loo guard with that of cigarette machine. The ridiculous thing is that most restaurants only make enough from this enterprise to cover the attendant's wages.

At the next station up, there is a restaurant called **Le Panoramic** where the food is reasonable and the British are particularly well liked. The loos here are free, despite the discouraging signs to the contrary. Further up the mountain still, you come to the **Fast Food Glacier** – probably the highest pseudo-McDonald's in the world. Its speed is the only thing to commend it. A few yards away is the preferable **Glacier Self-Service** restaurant which has unremarkable food but a good sun terrace. **La Pastorale** at the top of the Venosc telecabine is a log cabin serving Périgord specialities, including goose.

Apart from guzzling their biscuits, the French tend to return to the village at lunchtime where they have more than 40 bars and restaurants to choose from. Here, many of the restaurants have south-facing sun terraces and good *plats du jour,* and being at the foot of the pistes and close to the lifts, there are no problems in getting back up the mountain afterwards. **Le Bimbo** is one of the nicest of these restaurants and has a lovely sunny terrace.

If you take an off-piste trip to neighbouring La Grave (you will need a guide for this), make sure you stop for lunch at **Le Refuge** on the way down. This is an authentic mountain refuge in a fantastic setting.

Ski schools

The ski school here is very popular and you have to be sure to book first thing on Sunday morning for lessons starting on Monday. Now that there are more British skiers in the resort, there are special English-speaking classes. There are plenty of instructors who speak English well although the best English-speaking instructor is Giles Galvinet, who has even written a French/English glossary of skiing terms which the other instructors make use of.

Ski shops

There are plenty of good shops here but if you are British and want to hire equipment, probably the best place to go is Dode Sports. The tiny La Datcha is another good shop.

MERIBEL

Part of Les Trois Vallées area – also see Courchevel and Val Thorens

Méribel (often pronounced 'Maybelle' or 'Mirabelle' by Sloane Rangers and chalet girls) is right in the middle of the Trois Vallées with Courchevel on one side and Val Thorens on the other, and is reached via either Geneva or Lyons airports. It is a pretty resort of mostly chalet-style buildings set in sections up a sunny, wooded mountainside. It was founded in the late 1930s by a Scot, Peter Lindsay, with the objective of bringing to the French Savoie some of the charm of an Austrian Tyrolean village.

Méribel has always been popular with the British, who find the architecture much more appealing than that of the more austere French purpose-built resorts. It is particularly popular with families, who tend to drive out here during school holidays, when the roads of the resort are clogged with British-registered Volvo estates, but the authorities deny that there are plans to make the resort left-hand drive.

The main and original part of Méribel is Méribel-les-Allues. On the hill above Les Allues (and sprawling into it) are, in ascending order, Altitude 1600, Plateau de Morel and the Altiport. But some three miles up the valley is the smaller and much more modern Méribel-Mottaret. This complex dates from the 1970s and has a couple of good hotels, but it is really an unexceptional purpose-built resort lacking the character of Méribel proper. However, it is better placed if you want to take full advantage of the Trois Vallées ski area.

Accommodation

Chalets are by far the most popular form of accommodation in Méribel. Both Supertravel and Bladon Lines have a good selection, while Snowtime, which operates only in this resort, has more beds than anyone.

Snowtime's operation is centred on the Saulire, which is run more as a hotel than a chalet, with dinner being available from 7.30 to 9.00 rather than at 8.00 precisely, as is the case in most chalets. Supertravel have two jumbo chalets: Le Dahu, on the edge of the piste, and Le Tremplin at the bottom of the resort.

Most of the chalets here are situated pretty close to the piste, so you can more or less ski to and from your front door. At night, however, communications are more difficult. The principal centre for shopping and night-life, such as it is, is down at the very bottom of the resort. If you want to take full advantage of these facilities, make sure your accommodation is fairly near this main complex.

As there are no bus services after 8 pm, if you are staying up the hill at Altitude 1600 or even right up at Plateau de Morel, you must either have your own car or be prepared for a long walk up the winding road or up the side of the piste, or want to stay in and make your own entertainment. There are a small number of bars and shops up the hill, but they are not very exciting. So make sure you know exactly the whereabouts of your accommodation when you book it.

The **Hotel Grand Coeur***** is probably the best in Méribel with an excellent standard of food, but it is fairly small and you have to make reservations well in advance. The **Hotel de la Chaudanne**** is also good value.

If you are staying in a hotel in Méribel, always choose half-board rather than bed and breakfast, as there are not really enough restaurants to make a week's eating out interesting.

Up at Méribel-Mottaret, the **Hotel Taren-**

taise*** is modern with a good atmosphere and a beautiful situation right on the edge of the piste. The food is also exceptional. **Le Mont Vallon****** is a brand-new hotel run by the suave former owner of the Tarentaise, Georges Lalou. This is a luxurious establishment, also on the edge of the piste, which has its own indoor swimming pool. The food is even better than that at the Tarentaise but, of course, it's more expensive too.

There is quite a bit of self-catering available in Méribel, mostly in the form of apartments in chalet-style blocks. Bladon Lines has a particularly large selection. There is still a lot of building in progress in Méribel-les-Allues, particularly of chalet-style apartment blocks, so new accommodation is becoming available all the time.

Après-ski

When it comes to nightlife in Méribel, the brochure writers, not normally noted for their coyness, start hedging ('après-ski life tends to centre around parties in chalets', 'in the evening, activities tend to revolve around the chalets', and 'nightlife in Méribel is informal'). What they really mean is that there is not much to do in Méribel after dark. In fact, the lack of nightlife is Méribel's biggest disadvantage as a resort. A fun chalet girl and a case or two of wine is a definite advantage.

Nevertheless, the nocturnal entertainment situation in Méribel is improving and the resort as a whole deserves praise for making an effort in this direction in recent years. All the signs are that this improvement will continue.

A great deal of drinking goes on in the **Club Mark Warner Pub,** which has lately been greatly enlarged and redecorated. However, the place still suffers from off-hand and inefficient service. There are various bar snacks but the ridiculously complicated American-style system for ordering them is hopeless. Avoid the rather nasty toasted cheese and tomato

sandwiches, which are served on stale baguettes with a slice of tinned pineapple concealed beneath the cheese.

The **Refuge** and the **Roc** are two other possible drinking places but neither of them is particularly lively. The **Capricorne Bar** is probably the most amusing bar in the resort, which is not saying much. There is hope that the new Supertravel bar in **Le Tremplin** may recreate the kind of fun atmosphere that was found in its lamented Jump Bar in Courchevel. It will also serve food.

Snowtime now has the **French Connection Piano Bar** on the ground floor of its Hotel Saulire up at Altitude 1600. This is an important rendezvous point for people staying in this part of the resort and is as popular before dinner as it is after. It has recently been expanded and features include a giant video screen and, occasionally, live jazz bands.

The best restaurant in Méribel is probably **Chez Kiki,** but **Chez Gérard** is also very good – they both do traditional French cuisine. The restaurant attached to the **Saint Pères** nightclub also has a high standard. For cheaper meals, there is the **Santa Maria** pizzeria in town and a crêperie up on the Plateau de Morel.

In the basement of the Club Mark Warner Pub is a new restaurant, **Scott's.** This is a French restaurant, run by a German with English staff. The name refers to Scott of the Antarctic and this theme is pursued sporadi-

cally in the décor. However, the greater part of the furnishings seem to have been purchased from a defunct Aberdeen Angus Steak House. The food is robust French fare and portions are very generous. Service can be slow. Prices are reasonable and the wine list is impressive – good clarets at good prices. The manager is Jurgen, an alpine legend, formerly of the Matterhornblick in Zermatt and latterly of the Club Mark Warner Résidence Le Clos in Val d'Isère.

Méribel's oldest nightclub is the **Saint Pères,** which is some way below the village on the road towards Moûtiers. The same owner is now providing himself with some competition in the form of **Les Nuits Blanches** in the main shopping area. This place is younger and trendier and has a good mix of French and English clients. There are special 'Company Nights' when you get reductions for being with certain British tour operators. During February, they sometimes have jazz bands here playing from 4pm to 8pm, which makes this a good place to come on a snowy afternoon.

The trendiest new nightclub in Méribel-Mottaret is the **Magic Mountain** which opened in 1986. This place has a kind of semi-circular opulence about it, with masses of mirrors and lights, as well as a good sound system. It is a chic, glib French disco with a clientele to match. However, it is also popular with the Brits in Mottaret and does a number of 'Company Nights'. It also has more cabaret acts than other nightclubs in this area. The only other disco in Mottaret is the rather dull **Le Catina.**

If you have a car or are prepared to spend a bit of money on taxis, there are a couple of other restaurants outside Méribel which can be recommended. Rowdy groups in search of a fun, cheap night out will enjoy **Le Plantin** on the road to Courchevel. On the road from Les Allues to Mottaret is the excellent **La Petite Rosière,** a refined, relaxed restaurant with a menu that ranges from elaborate dishes to very straightforward fondues. However, although the menu here is enormous, many of the dishes are off at any one time, so it is often best to start your ordering by asking what the staff particularly recommend that evening.

The skiing

Méribel advertises itself as being at the heart of the Trois Vallées and, certainly, this is strategically the best place to be based if you intend to ski as much as possible of this vast area. From here you have easy access to the skiing of Courchevel 1850 and its satellites on one side and of Les Menuires and Val Thorens on the other side.

The slopes on the western side of Méribel get the sun in the mornings and are probably the best place to start your day's skiing. Both

Mont de la Challe and La Tougnette offer interesting skiing, especially the Bartavelles run. Alternatively, you can go over the ridge into the next valley towards Les Menuires, where there are demanding runs around La Masse. (Incidentally, many aesthete-skiers staying in pretty Méribel-les-Allues have been known to suffer acute culture shocks on coming over this side of the mountain and seeing Les Menuires for the first time. Be warned: this is one of the least successful of the purpose-built resorts.) From Les Menuires, you can go up to Val Thorens and take the massive cable car that gives access to the superb skiing on the Cime de Caron.

The eastern side of the valley gets good sun in the afternoons and here the skiing is generally better suited to intermediates, unless you plan to go on over to Courchevel. The skiing around the Méribel Altiport at the top of the village is easy and well suited to beginners.

There are also good opportunities for off-piste powder in the Méribel Valley, given the right snow conditions. Later in the season, there is also excellent spring-snow skiing to be had, particularly down to the newly opened-up areas of St Marcel and St Martin-de-Belleville.

You can buy lift passes either for the Méribel

Valley or for the whole of the Trois Vallées area. As in Courchevel, you can pay a supplement to upgrade your Méribel pass. One problem with the Méribel-les-Allues ski area is that the lifts are owned by a private company, Méribel Alpina, which is a law unto itself and which does not cooperate particularly closely with the neighbouring lift companies in the Trois Vallées. Basically, this means that the company opens and closes its lifts for the season on prearranged dates, regardless of snow conditions. Thus Méribel can have plenty of snow in early April, but all its lifts will be closed, while in Courchevel everything will be functioning. However, there is some hope that Méribel Alpina will be forced to come into line in the next few years.

Lunches

The most elegant place to have lunch in the whole of the Méribel area is the **Hotel Tarentaise** at Mottaret. In fine weather, lunch is served outside on a large sun terrace. There is always an amazing cold buffet, as well as a very good selection of desserts. The hotel is managed by an Australian, John Godisson, who looks after the interests of British guests assiduously. It is not a cheap place for lunch, but it's far better than anywhere else you will find in Mottaret.

There is a reasonable self-service restaurant, **Les Pierres Plats,** at the top of the Saulire side, but you are really better advised to come down to **La Chouca,** which is just below the middle of the Les Allues to Saulire six-man telecabine. This is a small modern restaurant with a sun terrace. It has been very imaginatively designed with a large semi-circular wooden stool bar. The service is good and the restaurant specialises in a variety of exotic salads. Further down, the **Belvedere Hotel,** which can also be reached from Les Allues by dustbin lift, is a popular place for a high-quality lunch. It has a large sun terrace and you know it must be a good sun trap because there are solar energy panels just above the terrace. The Belvedere is slightly off the beaten piste and so makes a nice change from the usual mountain restaurants.

For a cheap lunch, the British flock to the **Dahu Spud,** which is part of Supertravel's jumbo chalet Le Dahu just on the edge of the piste above Les Allues. As you would expect, this serves baked potatoes with various fillings and has become popular with the French, as well as the British. For this reason, you often have to book in advance, although remember that it's closed on transfer days (Saturdays), of course. Just above the Dahu is the **Adray Telebar.** This has a lovely interior with masses of plants and flowers, including a Swiss cheese plant that is entwined all over the ceiling and roof beams. Like all the restaurants here, it has a big sunny terrace.

Ski schools

The ESF ski school in Méribel has a very go-ahead young director, Gérard Guervin, who has now started an international section. It is run by David Lindsay, whose father founded the resort, and this will be its second season. It runs for all except the three weeks around Mardi Gras. This section is geared specifically towards British holiday skiers, but it is very popular and you are well advised to book in advance – ask your tour operator about this. David Lindsay himself is one of the great characters of Méribel and he is shadowed everywhere by his black labrador, Romy.

Ski shops

There are plenty of ski shops to choose from in both parts of Méribel, some more dynamic than others. In Les Allues, Manduit Sports, La Varappe or one of the many shops owned by the Front family offer the best service to the British, while up in Mottaret the biggest and most efficient is Mottaret Sports.

MURREN
(Links with Wengen)

Mürren is not so much a ski resort as a very traditional Alpine village where there happens to be some very good skiing. It is not just the local Swiss who are conservative and traditional – British visitors (many of whom have been coming for years – generations even) are just as protective of the status quo in their village. Many of these Brits are stalwarts of the exclusive Kandahar Club: Peter Lunn, son of the father of skiing, Sir Arnold, is an important official in the club and usually spends a couple of months in Mürren in the winter.

Like Wengen, Mürren is traffic-free and is reached from Geneva or Zurich by a two-stage mountain railway from Lauterbrunnen, or by cable car from Stechelberg, where you can leave your car in a free outdoor car park. However, it is much smaller than Wengen and life is generally much quieter – Supertravel is the only British tour operator to have penetrated this conservative society, so most of the skiers come independently and are consciously opting for a relatively peaceful village.

The few shops in Mürren look as though they exist to serve the locals rather than to rip off the tourists.

Accommodation

Many of the wealthy regular British visitors to Mürren have their own flats or chalets to which they return for the same periods every year. (One SCGB representative tells how he worked here for three weeks one year, returned for the same three weeks five years later and found the British skiers were precisely those he had met during his first visit.)

Apart from the two Supertravel chalets, most of the accommodation in Mürren is in hotels. Most of them have regular clients who return for the same periods every year, so it is essential to book well ahead if you want good rooms at peak holiday time.

The best hotel in the village is the **Eiger*****, which has 100 beds and is just opposite the mountain railway station. This is a typically professional family-run hotel with efficient but friendly service. The **Jungfrau Hotel***** is a smaller, very reasonable alternative to the Eiger and is ideally placed for the slopes. The **Mürren Hotel*****, formerly the Palace and owned by the Lunns, is still custodian of the Kandahar cups, but it is not a particularly good hotel nowadays.

Après-ski

Not surprisingly, this tends to revolve around hotels.

Mürren is the sort of place where you feel you have to take tea after skiing – the **Hotel Bellevue** opposite the nursery slopes is a favourite haunt for the British, as is the **Stagerstubli.** There is some very relaxed tea-dancing at the **Jungfrau Hotel.**

As far as eating out is concerned, the choice is really limited to the various hotel restaurants, unless you want to go to the **Stagerstubli** for a fondue or raclette. Both the Eiger and the Jungfrau have good food and extensive menus – they both excel in Swiss specialities. The **Inferno Pizzeria** is part of the Mürren Hotel, but it is not especially cheap and has less atmosphere than the average branch of Pizza Express.

The only real disco in Mürren is the **Bliemli Challer** in the **Hotel Blumental.** It is popular with young people but you have to be prepared for a few oompah numbers thrown in with the pop records. Otherwise, both the Eiger and the Jungfrau have more conservative live bands.

The skiing

The remarkable thing about the skiing in Mürren is that although there is not that much of it, there are some very challenging runs. Unassuming little T-bars give access to fairly difficult black pistes. There are four separate but connecting ski areas – Winteregg, Almendhübel, Schiltgrat and Schilthorn – and it is the last two which offer the most demanding skiing.

At the top of the Schilthorn is the famous revolving mountain restaurant where sequences for the James Bond film *On Her Majesty's Secret Service* were filmed. Some people recommend having breakfast up here

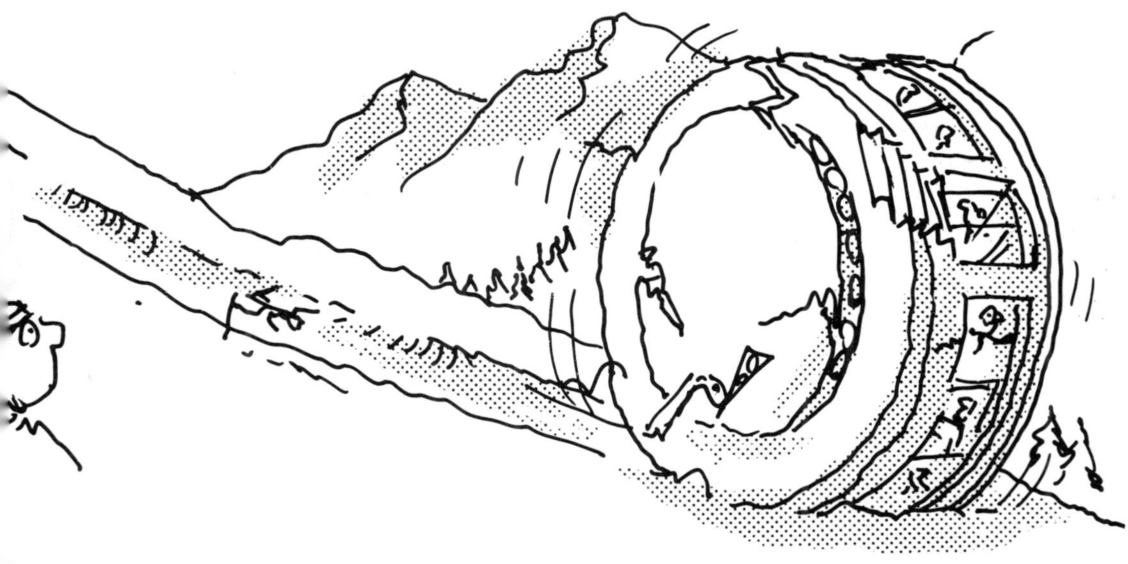

at about 9.15 and then tackling the run down, but this is a black run and perhaps not ideal as the first run of the day. The top of the Schilthorn run is very difficult, with large icy moguls covering a steep narrow path. After this section, the run widens out for a few hundred yards before it becomes a long schuss along a path. The skiing that the Schilthorn cable car opens up is not exceptional: the cable car was built more for summer than winter use.

The Gimmeln T-bar and the one next to it give access to difficult, short black runs known as the Kandahar and the Black Line. The festivities for the annual Inferno race organised by the Kandahar and the Mürren Ski Club now last about a week during the second half of January. The problem with the race itself is that even with two people starting every 30 seconds from 9am to 4pm, only about 1500 people can participate, whereas 4000 want start numbers. The race starts from the top of the Schilthorn and goes all the way down to Lauterbrunnen, if snow conditions permit.

Lunches

Up at the Schilthorn, the **Piz Gloria** revolving restaurant offers some amazing Alpine panoramas and the slow service ensures that you have plenty of time to enjoy them. The restaurant takes just under an hour to turn 360 degrees, but don't put your gloves down on the windowsill as this is stationary. The menu is neither exciting nor cheap, but it is not bad value when you consider you are 10,000 feet above sea level – and rotating as well.

A large immobile self-service restaurant occupies the floor below the Piz Gloria. There is something slightly pathetic about the way the management cling to the reflected glory of having been featured in a 20-year-old James Bond film – all the table mats, for instance, proclaim this dubious association.

The other key lunching places in the Mürren area are all unpretentious little wooden chalets. The restaurant at the bottom of the **Gimmeln** lift is renowned for having the best (most alcoholic) *Kaseschnitte mit Ei* on the mountain. It also has a juke box with speakers outside on the terrace that play fairly up-to-date British records. After lunch try one of the popular, but lethal, *Café Fertig Melange.*

The **Sonnenberg** in the Blumental Valley is a good self-service lunch place with a large sunny terrace. On the way home, the best place for a pit-stop is the nearby **Sunnenalp,** where they serve another of Mürren's alcoholic concoctions, *Alpenrosetee,* a bizarre but addictive blend of framboise, white wine, schnapps and anything else that happens to be around.

Ski schools

The ski school here is, as you would expect, a traditional Swiss one with very high standards and all the instructors speak good English.

Ski shops

The better of the two shops in the resort is Eddy Abegglen. It is now run by young Edy *(sic)* who speaks excellent English and offers good discounts to English customers. The other shop, Stager, is better for ski clothes.

ST ANTON

Also see Lech

Although more British skiers go on holiday to Austria than to any other country, serious skiers tend to feel that France and Switzerland offer skiing of a higher quality, so Austria does not figure prominently in the programmes of tour operators catering for the more experienced skier. St Anton is, of course, the great exception to this prejudice. It is certainly one of the top five resorts in Europe and has a sense of tradition that cannot be matched by any of the purpose-built French stations.

The British connection with St Anton dates back to the beginning of this century and the formation of the famous Arlberg Ski Club. Lord Roberts of Kandahar and Sir Arnold Lunn were some of St Anton's earliest skiing patrons. British skiers are still warmly received by the locals, many of whom speak a reasonable amount of English.

To reach St Anton by air, the best route is via Zurich airport, which is about three hours' drive away. However, by far the most romantic way to travel to St Anton is by train direct to St Anton am Arlberg Bahnhof, right in the middle of town. You can take the Arlberg Express or, more romantically and expensively, the Venice Simplon Orient Express which has a weekly through service during the winter. This means you can leave London Victoria on Saturday morning and be in St Anton 24 hours later. It is a marvellous experience to come through the Arlberg on this beautiful old train with two engines at the front and two at the rear.

The centre of the town has now been made a pedestrian precinct, which makes it much easier to get around but does not make it any prettier. Architecturally, the town is a bit of a mish-mash. Old wooden chalets lie next to concrete hotels, but skyscrapers have been avoided and the overall effect is cosy enough.

Accommodation

St Anton has been a popular resort for chalet parties ever since they began, but since the beginning of this decade the Austrian police have been enforcing all kinds of employment laws rather more stringently. This means that chalet girls must refer to themselves as 'hostesses' and must be very careful not to reveal to the police the true nature of their job.

The most awkward of the Austrian laws is the one that requires at least one Austrian citizen to be working in a large chalet in order for it to be legal. Try as they might, the British companies simply cannot get Austrian girls to work in their chalets, despite offering them much more than the meagre wages paid to the British girls.

There are numerous instances of chalets being forced to employ the local idiot or kleptomaniac in order to stay within the Austrian law. One company found the ideal solution, employing a Canadian girl who is Austrian by marriage.

Assuming your chalet girls are not deported across the border to Germany in the middle of your holiday, chalets still remain a very good way of holidaying in St Anton. They have been particularly popular in recent years, and companies like Supertravel, Bladon Lines and John Morgan have all increased their capacity here lately.

Hotels are also very popular in St Anton, which is not big on self-catering accommodation. The **Sport Hotel***** is right in the middle of town, while the **Hotel Berghaus Maria***** is just outside, but they both have indoor swimming pools, saunas and a generally high standard of accommodation. The **Schwarzer Adler** dates back to 1570 and is another fine old luxury hotel. The finest interior décor is perhaps to be found in the **Alte Post** which has beautifully furnished rooms (Austria's answer to Laura Ashley) with hand-painted furniture. For a cheaper hotel, the **Valluga*** is very good value, although you must be prepared for the irritation of paying every time you want a bath.

When booking accommodation in St Anton, it is as well to remember that this is a large, rambling resort and that if you want to benefit from the best of the skiing and après-ski, then you need to be located near to the centre. Nasserein, for example, is pleasant enough, and fairly convenient from a skiing point of view, but it can be quite a long walk back after a night on the town.

Après-ski

St Anton is very much a skier's resort: the nightlife tends to revolve around a few amusing and inexpensive bars rather than expensive, chic nightclubs. For a drink before dinner, the tiny **Pub 37** is always popular with ski instructors as well as punters, although it can get very sweaty at peak times. The **Platzl**

Après is a relaxed, rustic kind of bar with a log fire, and it never gets too packed. It has good taped music and, although it's not cheap, it does offer a welcome respite from the more frenetic drinking places. The **Valluga Bar** just behind the church is a ritzy cellar bar with black and gold Arab-style décor. It is run by Joan and has live music every night and serves good cheap food.

In Nasserein, at the eastern end of St Anton, there is an incredibly grotty bar called **Tom Dooley's.** It is like a transport cafe with Formica tables and austere décor. Nevertheless, British punters love it, although the proprietor has been known to throw them out when there is no room for the locals. The **Toby Bar** is also in Nasserein – this is a jolly place with occasional live music.

As in most Austrian resorts, if you want to eat well at dinnertime, you will probably have to go to a hotel. The **St Antonerhof** is the best place for dinner and for just around AS500 a head you will get as much as you can eat and drink. The food here is basically Tyrolean but there is an enormous choice on the menu. The **Hotel Schwarzer Adler** also has a good dining room, as does the **Alt St Anton Hotel** up at the Nasserein end of town. The restaurant of the **Berghaus Maria** serves an excellent Austrian version of nouvelle cuisine. In terms of atmosphere, one of the most unusual restaurants is housed in the **Ski Museum** and specialises in fish.

For a seriously good meal, the **Hospiz** at St Christoph is worth the journey and the vast amount of Austrian schillings you will have to pay, but remember to book several days ahead to be sure of a table.

If you have the transport or are prepared to pay for taxis, there are two other good restaurants in neighbouring villages.

The **Brunnenhof** in St Jakob serves good local food in informal surroundings. You are likely to find yourself sitting at a large communal table rather than an individual one. Out of St Anton in the other direction is **Ferwal,** a wonderful old inn in the middle of a forest. The road through the forest is long and you can come by sleigh or four-wheel-drive vehicle when there's a lot of snow. A dinner here is a real adventure and the menu includes robust Austrian venison dishes.

Back in town, for a cheap dinner you can go to the **Pizzeria Pomodoro** or to the **Bahnhof** restaurant, which is a very popular rendezvous point for ski bums and friends. Also good for a fairly cheap dinner is St Anton's most famous après-ski complex, the **Krazy**

Kanguruh (most people simply call it the KK). It is some way out of town and up a steep hill, but this does not stop it being the most popular nightspot for the British. It has a restaurant, as well as a bar and disco. (This is also popular at lunchtime, but it closes for an hour or so at 6pm.)

After dinner, the **Post Bar** is a popular place for dancing to American and British pop music. The **Stanton** is one of the newer and larger nightclub/disco complexes with a couple of bars and giant video screens. The **Piccadilly** has loud European music and is often packed to overflowing. This place has a reputation as a pick-up joint but, with an estimated male to female ratio of six to one in St Anton, there are many more people trying to pick up than those waiting to be picked up. The **Klause,** attached to the Schwarzer Adler hotel, plays very good music but is unfortunately often full of drunken 15-year-old Swedes. (The Austrians hate the Swedes even more than the French do. They say the Swedes steal a lot and forge lift passes.) **Pinnocchio's** is always very crowded but, given the combination of tinkly German music and bad English music, it is impossible to dance.

The skiing

There are three main areas in St Anton: Gampen-Kapall, Galzig-Valluga and Rendl, which goes up the opposite side of the valley to the other two areas. All these systems are easily accessible from the middle of the village. From Nasserein, simply take a connecting T-bar to get up into the Gampen-Kapall and the Galzig-Valluga systems, or take a (rather crowded) free bus round to the bottom station of the Rendlbahn.

There is some very good skiing on the Kapall section, as well as some good runs down from the Schindler Spitzer. There are masses of opportunities all over St Anton for good off-piste skiing. Although the Valluga area does offer the very best skiing, it also offers the very worst queues. The Valluga cable car is in three sections, and in high season, if you want to get right to the top to ski down to Zürs, you really have to take the first cable car of the morning to avoid spending hours queuing. (Keen skiers should note that things start very early in this resort – first lifts up at 8am, so it is sometimes necessary to restrict après-ski activities in deference to these early starts.)

The run down from the Valluga itself is off-piste and, in fact, only skiers with guides or people without skis are allowed on to the third section of the Valluga cable car. When you have got to the top, you still have half an hour's steep and treacherous climb to do before you start the long descent to Zürs.

There are always queues for the second section of the Valluga cable car, but the system of giving you the number of your cable car means that by allowing seven minutes for each car before yours, you can get in a bit of skiing, and come back at the right time. If you miss your car, you go back to the end of the queue.

An alternative to this cable car is the new Schindlergratbahn triple chair. It gives access to much the same skiing and queues are not nearly so long. It is important to remember that many of the best, steepest slopes in St Anton are south-facing and get quite a bit of sun. This means that they are not good late in the season, but also that they are often very icy in the mornings and should be treated with respect.

The Steissbachtal is the valley that runs between the Valluga and the Kapall and forms the run down from the Schindler Spitzer or the Mattenjoch. It is called Happy Valley or Ego Valley because it is remarkably flat and offers easy, flattering skiing. The run down from Tanzhoden into the Steissbachtal is known as Backsider, being steep and ridden with moguls. It is a favourite with the large numbers of St Anton ski bums, but does nothing for the ego of a lesser skier.

The skiing on the Rendl side is generally easier but offers some very good powder skiing through the trees when conditions are right.

There are great opportunities for heliskiing here, but it is very expensive.

Lunches

The best lunch place in the whole area is the **Rodelhutte** in Nasserein and to the right of the Gampen lift. It is a rustic wooden place with a marvellous sun terrace, staffed by jolly men in leather aprons and, occasionally there is an accordionist playing outside. The speciality here is *Tiroler Grostl,* which is a mixture of potatoes, bacon and other meats together with lots of herbs, served in individual little copper frying pans. (You can eat here in the evenings and toboggan down.)

At the top of the second stage of the Valluga cable car, there's a good-value self-service restaurant where the staff are particularly friendly. This is infinitely better than the **Galzig** restaurant at the top of the first stage of the cable car, where the food is indifferent and expensive.

From February onwards there are a number of ice-bars in this area, including one at Gampen and one at Ulmerhütte on the way up from Raus. There is also an ice-bar at the top of the Rendlbahn in what is known as Rendl Beach because it is such a good area for sun bathing.

If you are skiing outside the St Anton area, the **Hotel Post** at Stuben, the legendary **Hospiz** at St Christoph and the **Zürserhof** all do very good, if rather expensive, lunches.

Ski schools

The Arlberg ski school is one of the oldest and best known in the world and now has more than 300 full-time and part-time instructors. The standard of tuition is still good, although there are those who now accuse the school of resting on its laurels. Classes have been known to take as many as 15 and even private lessons are not always satisfactory. The best thing is to seek local advice and choose an instructor by personal recommendation. The instructors at St Christoph are said to be particularly good.

In years gone by it was possible to have lessons from one of the 300 or so ski bums who winter in St Anton, but the regulations have been tightened up so much lately that no ski bum who values his skiing will risk being seen giving lessons.

Ski shops

Pangratz Sports, run by the charming Tony Pangratz, is a popular choice with the Brits for ski rental, as is Fauner Sports at the other end of town. Fauner lets you leave your skis at the shop overnight instead of having to lug them back to your chalet or hotel. For fashionable clothes, there is plenty of choice in the boutiques and ski shops along the busy main street.

ST MORITZ

The first thing that strikes you about St Moritz is not its style but its silliness. There is something intrinsically ridiculous about all these enormous plush buildings perched on this tiny mountainside. Badrutt's Palace Hotel is the silliest building of all and would not look out of place in Disneyland. The next thing you notice is the vulgarity and ugliness of the buildings: the town itself is not pretty at all, although its situation is beautiful. The views across the frozen lake are some of the most spectacular in the Alps.

St Moritz and its much-vaunted 'Champagne Air' remain as popular as ever with the international jet-set, and the standard of hotels and shops (and their prices) reflects this. A skiing holiday in St Moritz will never be cheap, despite the efforts of the Tourist Office, which produces brochures with titles like 'How to live at astonishingly reasonable prices in St Moritz'. It's really only worthwhile coming to St Moritz if you are prepared to spend a bit of money and enjoy the place as it should be enjoyed.

This is an ideal resort for wealthy non-skiers, as you do not find the obsession with skiing that you find in most ski resorts. There are plenty of other attractions: the Cresta run, horse-racing on the frozen lake, shopping and socialising.

Situated in the far south-western corner of Switzerland, St Moritz is best reached via Zurich airport. But the resort has its own railway station served by the wonderful Rhätische Bahn rack railway system, which connects with the main Swiss railway system at Chur. (If you really want to travel to St Moritz in style, you should take the Venice Simplon Orient Express, which leaves London Victoria every Saturday morning in winter and calls at Chur nearly 24 hours later.)

Certainly the most glamorous of all the trains serving St Moritz itself is the famous Glacier Express – billed as the slowest express train in the world – which winds its way through fantastic mountain scenery, including 291 bridges and 91 tunnels, to Zermatt. This unforgettable journey takes about seven and a half hours and the train conveys an excellent restaurant car. Excursions to Italy are also quite easy from St Moritz.

Accommodation

You can go to St Moritz and stay with Club Med, but that would really diminish the experience. Unless you have been invited to stay in a friend's chalet, the only way to visit St Moritz is to stay in one of its grand hotels. There are four top-quality hotels, each with its own atmosphere and type of clientele. **Badrutt's Palace******* is the biggest and most famous, with the greatest social cachet. The **Carlton Hotel*******, originally built for the last Russian Czar, is relatively small, offering particularly personal service. The **Kulm Hotel****** is rather flash but is great fun: it tends to appeal most to young people and wealthy pop stars. The vast and elaborate **Suvretta House****** is slightly out of town and is much used by families with children. It has its own ski lift and ice rink, among other facilities. More modest but pleasant hotels include the very central **Steffani****** and the attractively situated **Soldanella*****.

Après-ski

For afternoon tea, the obvious choice is **Hanselman's,** a wonderfully smart old café where the ground floor is considerably more fashionable than the first floor.

For early-evening drinking, all the top hotel bars are worth visiting, particularly the appositely named **Sunny Bar** in the Kulm. The **Chesa Veglia,** the oldest building in St Moritz, has a good cocktail bar and also a restaurant. In fact, upstairs in this famous building, there is an enterprising **Pizzeria** which is probably the best value for eating out in town. A pizza and half a litre of beer can cost as little as SF15, although there is an expensive wine list for the benefit of the rich, chic clientele. You are served by waiters in white jackets and white ties – particularly smart for a pizzeria. There is sometimes live oompah music also. They have even been known to hold beer festivals here: hardly the sort of thing you associate with St Moritz.

The **Cresta Bar** is an intimate little place at the front of the Steffani Hotel, which is a nice spot for early or late-evening drinking. Run by Marion, this bar is a favourite with key Cresta figures during January and February. From time to time, they sign their names and best times on the ceiling – unfortunately it gets repainted regularly. The Cresta run result lists for the season are pinned up here and make fascinating reading. They contain an extraordinary cross-section of European aristocracy: Prinz, The Hon, Archduke, Lord, etc.

As you would expect, the top hotels here take great pride in their dining rooms, and

dinner in any of them is unlikely to disappoint. Particularly worth a visit is the **Grill** at the Suvrettta House.

Later in the evening, there are plenty of parties going on and, ideally, you should secure an invitation to one of these. The **Prüveda** at the Carlton Hotel is the place for bowling parties, while fancy-dress parties are popular at Gunter Sachs' **Dracula Club.** Failing that, the most famous disco in town is the **Kings' Club.** It is, however, also the most expensive and you have to get past the papparazzi and discerning bouncers at the door.

The skiing

Curiously, lift passes in the St Moritz area are relatively cheap. It is possible to get a pass just for the Corviglia area immediately above St Moritz, but if you are a serious skier you will want a pass for the whole Engadine region. Although there is good skiing to be had in the Engadine, the problem is that it consists of several separate areas that are not interconnected. The only way you can make the best of this area from St Moritz is by having a car and being prepared to drive a few miles.

The best skiing in the Corviglia area, which also links up with Suvretta, is down from the Piz Nair summit. Unfortunately, the cable car up to the top of Piz Nair takes only 40 people so there can be bad queues here in high season. The run down, though not difficult, is long and interesting and as you go round the back of Piz Nair you feel you are getting away from the crowds. With the aid of one short T-bar, this run brings you out at Marguns. Most of the rest of the skiing around Corviglia is of an intermediate standard.

Because many people go to St Moritz as much for the nightlife as for skiing, they tend to get up late in the mornings so queues often build up at unusual times – 11.30am, for example. So get up the mountain relatively early to avoid the worst of the queues. The best skiing area in the Engadine is at Corvatsch. These north-facing slopes rise out of St Moritz Bad, an inferior suburb of St Moritz Dorf, a couple of miles away on the floor of the valley. There are decent red and black runs up here and the area goes up to the Corvatsch Glacier, where there is summer skiing.

Even further away from St Moritz is the resort of Pontresina (which incidentally has a good toboggan run) and the skiing areas of Diavolezza and Plagalb. Good as all these areas are – and Plagalb offers some very taxing black runs – they are not easily accessible if you are staying in the main part of St Moritz.

Lunches

At the top of Corviglia is **La Marmite,** probably the greatest mountain restaurant in the Alps. The food here is really outstanding and so are the prices, but they are not all that outrageous when you consider you are eating first-class nouvelle cuisine-ish food and getting superb service at the top of a mountain.

Truffles are the speciality here: they do a salad of black truffles, foie gras and Bel Paese with a dressing of egg yolk, olive oil and Savora mustard, as well as carpaccio with white truffles. The restaurant also makes its own gravad lax and offers an enormous selection of caviars. You can, of course, get steaks and other more mundane main courses, then move on to the delicious desserts, which are all displayed on an enormous buffet table.

La Marmite is presided over by Hartley Mathis, the head chef, whom the *New York Times* has dubbed the King of Alpine Cooking. The 2pm sitting is the most popular with serious eaters and you have to book several days ahead in high season. Princess Caroline of Monaco is a frequent visitor. When staying in St Moritz, she tends to lunch here several times a week but, on one occasion, was kept waiting an hour for a table – she hadn't booked.

The atmosphere is generally unpretentious and only a small glass partition divides La Marmite from a much cheaper self-service restaurant. Although you cannot eat outside, there is a sun terrace where really dedicated sun-worshippers lie covered from chin to toe in drab brown blankets looking like rows of wounded soldiers waiting for attention.

A little way above La Marmite is another restaurant where you can eat outside. Sensibly, it has windbreakers at either side of the sun terrace. There is also an ice-bar here later in the season, where trade in champagne-by-the-glass is brisk. This is a key meeting place for the young poseurs of St Moritz. Up at **Piz Nair** there is a small self-service restaurant.

Ski schools

Classes here are fairly small and most of the instructors speak good English. Naturally, the ski school has great experience in providing very tolerant private instructors who will pander to your every whim.

Ski shops

Nothing is cheap here but you can be assured that any equipment you hire will be of the highest quality.

SELVA

Although it is now in Italy, Selva is situated in a part of the South Tyrol that until the First World War belonged to Austria. This is why German is the local language and why it has the alternative German name of Wolkenstein. Appropriately, Selva is equally accessible from the German airport, Munich, and an Italian one, Milan. (But whichever you choose, it's a long transfer.)

Now that ski holidays in Italy are no longer ridiculously cheap, Selva is the only resort in the Dolomites served by the more up-market British tour operators. In the heart of the Val Gardena area of the Dolomites, Selva is famous to *Ski Sunday* viewers for having the World Cup downhill course, where Konrad Bartelski achieved his best ever result.

Selva is not especially pretty. It is rather a rambling place with old and new chalet-style buildings scattered on either side of the main street. Most services are run with Austrian efficiency but Italian charm.

Accommodation

The authorities do not seem to have clamped down so tightly on chalet operators in Selva as they have in other parts of Italy. Both John Morgan Travel and Club Mark Warner have luxurious chalets here, while Small World has its chalet Sonnenheim for 28 people. This is not really a luxurious chalet but it does have a good atmosphere. Bladon Lines, on the other hand, has the chalet hotel Solaia, which has an indoor swimming pool and is well situated for the skiing.

Apart from chalets, most of the accommodation in Selva is in hotels. The **Oswald** is probably the best of these, but the **Laurin,** which is run by a man called Marco who looks just like John Cleese, is also pleasant and efficient. It has a cheerful lounge bar where there is an open fire and often someone playing the piano after dinner. The **Hotel des Alpes** also has a jolly Tyrolean atmosphere. There are also plenty of modest two-star hotels and quite a few self-catering apartments.

Après-ski

The most popular drinking place in Selva after skiing is the **Luislkeller Bar,** a subterranean place where there is live music on Tuesdays and Thursdays. It is owned by a ski instructor, Luisl, and is well patronised by instructors, most of whom sit round the *stammtisch,* which is reserved for people from the village. The Luislkeller is equally lively late at night.

The **Speckeller** is another key drinking place. It is run by Franco, an enormous man in baggy lederhosen. When closing time approaches Franco puts on a large hat with feathers and goes round chucking people out: when he puts his hat on, it's time to leave.

For dinner, the best food is to be found in hotels, especially the **Laurin.** But there are lots of other good, unpretentious restaurants around town. The **Ciampinio Pizzeria** is fun – the waiters are easily smitten by English girls and have a habit of bringing them heart-shaped pizzas. It also serves schnitzels and other dishes. **Campa Freina** is a little restaurant at the bottom of Ciampinio. It serves lots of schnitzels and does big platters designed to be shared between two or three people. It also serves the most enormous helpings of *Apfelstrudel*.

After dinner there is a surprisingly wide choice of nightlife for a relatively small resort. The **Stella** is a large, cavernous disco with up-to-date music, whereas the **Savoy** is equally big but has a live band and is usually packed with Italians. The bands here change every fortnight and the quality varies enormously.

The **L'Medel** is a big disco just out of town run by an English DJ. It is quite a long walk but if you can get together a large group of people they will ferry you there and back by taxi. The usual policy with discos round here is that you pay on entry and that includes your first drink.

The weirdest après-ski event of the week in Selva is the tea-dance at the **Scoiattolo** (or Squirrel), where the owner and the director of the ski school both play the saxophone. Other instructors play the accordion and there is a great deal of yodelling and oompah dancing in ski boots.

The skiing

The most striking thing about skiing in the Dolomites is how different it feels from skiing anywhere else in Europe. The pink mountains are not like any others. The whole region is covered by the Superski Dolomite ski pass, which is very good value compared with the pass for the Val Gardena area. Any reasonably good skier should invest in it. Although it will be impossible for you to ski in all the areas covered by the lift pass, you may well wish to do the Sella Ronda, a circuit of those resorts within easy reach of Selva itself. The Sella Ronda takes about a day and can involve quite a lot of queuing. Intermediates may find that completing this circuit gives them a great sense of achievement, but experts may find it boring.

Because all the lifts in the Superski Dolomite area are owned by different companies, you have to bleep your lift pass through an electronic control system before every ascent. This is mildly irritating, but what is more annoying is that the lifts do not connect well – you often have to take your skis off and walk from the bottom of one run to the start of the next lift.

It is important to know the operating times of the lifts and make sure you get back to Selva using them, rather than relying on road transport. The buses across the Val Gardena pass can often be cancelled at short notice. And because there is a serious risk of avalanche, even when the road is clear you will often have to bribe taxi drivers to bring you back over it.

The most difficult and challenging skiing in the whole of the Dolomites is to be found at Arabba. It takes about an hour and a half to ski there from Selva but it is well worth the trouble for good skiers. Nearer Selva itself, however, is the Val de Mezdi. This is a difficult, narrow off-piste run for which you need a guide, and you have to walk uphill for half an hour before skiing down. You get to the top via the Passa Pordo cable car. There is a fantastic view, but the top of the run is the worst bit, as there is hardly any room to turn.

The run down from Sassa Lungo is incredibly steep and difficult. It is known as Death Valley and every season claims a few lives, or so resort gossip has it. For good skiing without the risk of death, the men's downhill course, otherwise known as Saslong, is a wonderfully steep run with a very broad piste. It has hardly any moguls and is always well maintained.

Lunches

The **Panorama** mountain restaurant at the bottom of the Danterceppies draglift is a fantastic rickety wooden construction built in a wonderful sun-trap. It specialises in fried ham and eggs. The **Roland Hutte** between Ciampinio and Plan de Garlba is run by Roland and his wife (both ex-ski instructors) and their vast St Bernard dog. They make the most ambrosial *Apfelstrudel* here and serve endless glasses of *prunier,* the most popular post-prandial drink in the area.

The **Badger Hut** by Ciampinio (so named because of the stuffed badger wearing sunglasses that lives by the fireplace – its real name is the Clerc Hutte) is famous for its *Jägertee.* This is an incredible concoction of rum, schnapps, brandy and more or less anything else you care to name: because of the fumes you have to let it cool down before you can drink it. Occasionally, *Jägertee* drinking competitions are held here. No one is on record as having consumed more than three in any one session. A less alcoholic-tasting, though, still fairly potent, alternative is *vov caldo con latte,* which they make very well here.

Halfway down the Col Raiser lift is the **Gamsblut Hutte,** where they serve an excellent brew called *Gamsblut* which is believed to be sloe wine and gin. On the Lagazuoi run down from the Passa Falzarego cable car, there is a marvellous restaurant called **Scotini,** where in good weather they barbecue whole pigs outside.

Ski schools

The ski school here is one of the best in Italy and about half the instructors have been in the national team at one time or another – in fact, many of them are now national trainers. The instructors also own most of the shops, bars and restaurants and many of them are related to each other. One instructor once asked a chalet girl how many first cousins she had. 'Ten,' she replied proudly. 'That's nothing,' said the ski instructor, 'I've got 70 first cousins and they all live in Selva – 20 of them are ski instructors.' The instructors tend to be either very young (19-25) or fairly old (late 30s to 60). For some mysterious reason, a lot of the young instructors go down to Venice or Florence in the summer to study architecture.

Not a lot of English is spoken in Selva, but those instructors who speak the language tend to speak it quite well. Despite the language barrier, the British are by far the most popular visitors to Selva – the locals much prefer them to the Germans.

Ski shops

All the ski shops are pretty good here: Arnold's shop, alias Sport Fulminino, is the most friendly towards the British.

TIGNES
Links with Val d'Isère

Tignes is really three separate, and not particularly well connected, complexes (Le Lac, Lavachet and Val Claret) near the end of the Isère valley, above Bourg St Maurice. It is about three-and-a-half-hours' drive from Geneva.

This is an ugly, purpose-built resort that has sprung up in a variety of architectural styles over the past 30 or so years. Some of the more appealing buildings are the giant chalet-style ones that have recently been built at Val Claret. But Tignes wisely makes no claims to architectural distinction. This resort's raison d'être is the vast ski area which it shares with Val d'Isère. It is generally thought that while Val d'Isère as a village has more character, Tignes offers easier access to the best of the skiing.

For years there were regular disputes between these two resorts and their respective lift companies, but they have finally hit on the idea of calling the Val d'Isère/Tignes area *L'Espace Killy* which seems to be a meaningless term agreeable to both sides. (There is only one type of lift pass and it covers both areas.)

Lac de Tignes is the principal Tignes village and is quite spectacularly ugly. However, it is very convenient for the skiing, with lifts radiating up on both sides of the valley. The Tourist Office, the Mairie and all the main facilities are based here. There is also rather a good market one day a week in the main square.

Below Lac de Tignes is Lavachet. This is popular with British holidaymakers as well as many of the resort's workers – liftmen, pisteurs, shop assistants and so on. There is not much in the way of shops or restaurants down here – there is no bank or chemist – nor is it well situated for the ski lifts. However, there is a telecabine that connects with Lac de Tignes and this runs until midnight during the main part of the season, although it inconveniently closes at about 8.00pm in very low season. During the day you can also take the triple-chair out of Lavachet which takes you

close to the bottom of the Tovière telecabine station.

Beyond Lac de Tignes is Val Claret, a bigger and newer satellite than Lavachet with much better facilities. Val Claret is almost entirely apartment blocks, but at least there is a semblance of architectural uniformity here. There are plenty of restaurants and bars in Val Claret as well as several shops, some of them distinctly up-market. Val Claret also offers brilliant access to the Grand Motte lift system, as well as the lifts up to Tovière and up the other side to the Col du Palet. There is a free bus service linking Val Claret with Lac de Tignes during the day. Taking everything into account, Val Claret is probably the best place to stay in the whole Tignes area. But it should be mentioned that the place becomes infested with Germans at peak holiday times. (A lot of German money went into the building of Tignes.)

Accommodation

There is a good selection of hotel, chalet and self-catering accommodation in Tignes. The resort is served by a large number of British tour operators, the biggest of them being Ski Val, whose operation is based where it has several buildings including its large chalet-hotel **Club Tovière** at Lavachet. Other operators have a good selection of smallish, modern chalets.

Hotels in Tignes are mostly two-star but on the whole they are good value. The **Neige et Soleil**** is right in the middle of Lac de Tignes, ideally situated for the skiing and the nightlife, while **Lo Terrachu**** is also good but is rather inconveniently situated between Val Claret and Lac de Tignes. The **Ski d'Or****** in Val Claret has earned a Michelin star for its good food, although the standards in the kitchen do vary considerably.

The standard of apartments in all three parts of Tignes is very mixed and doesn't necessarily relate to the age of the buildings. Chalet Club in Val Claret is a new development but the studios designed for four people are extremely small. Their counterparts at Home Club in Lavachet are much more spacious, though make sure you request the new part of the building when booking. One block, Inter Résidences in Val Claret, is worth noting since there is a swimming pool for clients' exclusive use. The apartments here are well-maintained – perhaps because they are run by the Swiss.

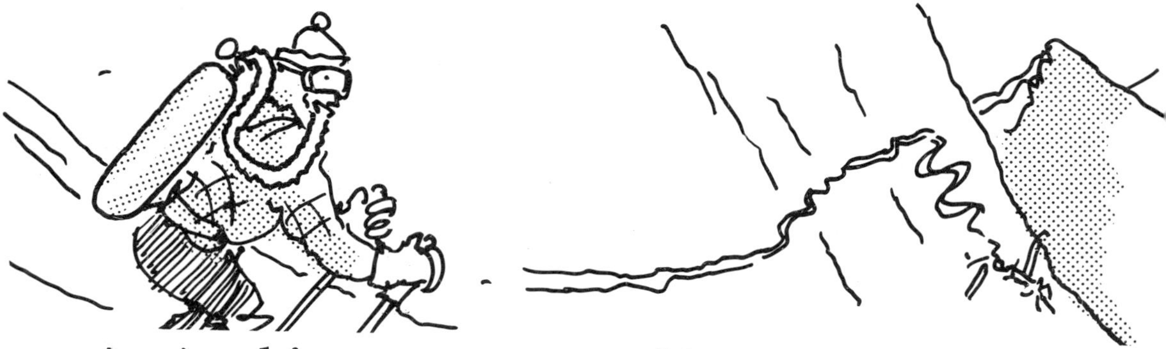

Après-ski

There is not a great deal of après-ski in Lavachet, but **Harri's Bar** in the Club Tovière (named after Ski Val's car-dealing proprietor Mike Harris) is a popular drinking place with the British. Ski Val have also just acquired a bar restaurant which is likely to be called **Oliver's.** Skiworld has a small cheap bar called **La Poêle d'Or.**

L'Armoric is a good place for fondues and raclettes and is very popular for a punters' night out. The owners, Jean-Claude and Anne-Marie, are particularly charming. For cheaper meals, the **Pignatta Pizzeria** also does grills, etc.

Up at Lac de Tignes **Le Refuge,** right at the centre, has an amusing rustic bar as well as a very good restaurant which serves particularly good mussel soup and a large variety of salads, among other things. (Be warned that the Madame here is not best renowned for her love of the English.) The **American Bar** is not a very inspiring place but for some reason is packed with Brits. Some tour operators have their office hours here.

La Chantignole is a pleasant place with old-fashioned décor specialising in seafood. **Le Clin d'Oeil** is an intimate restaurant, seating about 20, with the kitchen actually in the dining room. It is run by an eccentric, Claude, who spends his time hang-gliding and jumping off Mont Blanc with a parachute. **Le Tocade** is a pizzeria with an additional à la carte menu. It is a good place to eat out in a large group. **Clouso's** is a bar-restaurant owned by an English couple, Thea and Phil, but the chef is French and produces good-value, straightforward French dishes.

The best disco in Lac de Tignes is probably **Le Palaf** in the Palafour building underneath the Tourist Office. They have a particularly good selection of ski videos here also, but you must expect to pay chic French nightclub prices. **Club 73** is a fairly tacky place that seems to change hands every season, though for the very poor it is useful because it does not make an entry charge. **La Boum** is cheap, small and the staff are very friendly.

Up at Val Claret, the **Why-Not Bar** is a modern, dimly-lit piano bar with a very laid-back, sophisticated atmosphere. It is popular both before and after dinner, when there is live music. **La Corniche** tends to get a bit full of Swedes but it's not a bad bar all the same.

The **Myako** Japanese restaurant in Val Claret makes a refreshing change from run-of-the-mill Alpine cuisine. It is run by a Japanese man with a German wife who looks increasingly Japanese. For less surprising French food, the **Boeuf Miche** can be recommended. **Le Poutrerie** is a terrific place for après-ski drinks and also serves good raclettes and fondues. (Again, it can become overrun by Swedes.) **Le Caveau** is a rather up-market and expensive restaurant beneath the Poutrerie – both are run by a mountain guide called Jean-Claude Glasser. **Le Pub** is an execrable imitation of a British pub and has no atmosphere whatsoever.

Les Chandelles is quite a decent disco – it's certainly better from the point of view of music and service than the **Playboy,** which is the other principal nightclub in Val Claret. If you want to stay up really late, the place to go is the **Weinstube**, a jolly Germanic place that often stays open until about 5am.

The skiing

The Grand Motte glacier probably offers the most demanding skiing in Tignes, with its good long run from top to bottom. Queues for the double telecabine and the final cable car can be bad at peak periods, although the building of two new chairlifts most of the way up the Motte have helped to alleviate this problem. (Irritatingly, the first chairlift has three-man chairs, but the second has only two-man chairs.)

Because of their altitude, the runs from the Motte to Val Claret tend to stay in good condition until late in the season. (In a good year, you can still ski all the way down to Val Claret in the middle of May.) When open, the Wall on the right-hand side of the lifts is strictly for experts. To the right of the Grand Motte, the cold chairlift up Col des Ves leads on to some interesting skiing and, when off-piste conditions are suitable, you can traverse and ski down the Face of the Grand Balme. This is another popular lift for late-season skiing.

The Aiguille Percée chairlift takes you up to this striking summit, where there is an eye of the needle-like hole through the rock. There is a fairly easy run down to Lac de Tignes from here, but it is more important as the starting-point for the long run down to the old village of Tignes les Brevières, way below at 1550m. One red run here takes you to the Vallon de la Sache and well away from the crowds. Another run down here is named Cocaine, for reasons skiers must deduce for themselves. But there is also an easier and longer blue run.

There are lifts from both Lac de Tignes and Val Claret up to Tovière, the summit where the Tignes and Val d'Isère ski areas connect. A luxurious new ten-man telecabine – in which you stand rather than sit – has just been installed on the route up from Lac de Tignes.

The runs back down to Val Claret are considerably easier than those back to Lac de Tignes. The latter part of the run from Tovière to Lac de Tignes is a steep mogul-ridden wall, a challenge for the best skiers. In fact, in the winter of 1986, this was the slope used for the spectacular first-ever World Freestyle Championships.

Lunches

The best lunch in the Tignes area is probably in the upstairs restaurant at **Tovière,** which has an extraordinarily high standard of cooking and service for a mountain restaurant. There is also a good self-service section here. The terrace outside has spectacular views but it is often too cold or windy to sit there.

There are several lively pizzerias in Val Claret itself where you can eat at lunchtime – often outside in good weather. At the bottom of the Grand Motte lifts is the **Bar de la Grand Motte,** a bar/restaurant that is universally known to the Brits as Pouftah's Bar, for reasons that soon become apparent – females are seldom sighted working here. The atmosphere is jolly and in good weather the south-facing sun terrace is an incredible sun-trap, even on a windy day. The food is adequate rather than excellent, but the bar is always well-stocked.

The **Panoramique** is an enormous, new, self-service restaurant at the top of the Grand Motte telecabines that was opened in 1983/84 and was built to replace the one which had been accidentally blown up by avalanche explosives the year before. For a modern self-service restaurant, this has a surprisingly good atmosphere and most of the fittings are in carved wood. The food is not cheap but there is a good selection. Just about the only safe drinks here are Coke and Perrier – otherwise you may find yourself getting packet soup or powdered Glühwein. There are plenty of tills so queuing is kept to a minimum.

There are a couple of good restaurants on the slopes to the right of Tignes, but for a really ethnic Alpine lunch it is worth skiing right down to **Les Brevières.** This is a pretty, undeveloped Savoie village with a couple of unpretentious lunch places just by the church.

There is now a comfortable new six-man telecabine that takes you most of the way back towards Tignes.

For a really extravagant lunch, **Le Refuge,** right in the middle of Lac de Tignes, is an ideal place, particularly in the spring, when there are a large number of tables outside. The *noisettes d'agneau à l'estragon* are particularly recommended.

Ski schools

For several years now, the ESF ski school here has been one of the best in France, especially from the point of view of British clients. It has a young director who is keen on the British and even arranges special classes for them on Sundays. He also works closely with British tour operator reps so any complaints can be sorted out quickly.

The facilities for children learning to ski, however, are not particularly good here. There are no special classes and there is not a great deal in the way of nursery slopes. Also, Tignes is very high up and cold, so not an ideal place for beginners.

Ski shops

Ski Fast is the most friendly and efficient ski shop in Lac de Tignes – there's a helpful English guy called Jeremy. In Lavachet, Micks Sport is a good shop, while in Val Claret, the British patronise Pierre Favre, where the staff are usually exceptionally friendly and helpful.

VAL D'ISERE
Links with Tignes

In architectural terms, Val d'Isère is a rather messy ski resort, situated at the far end of the Isère valley. By road, it is reached via Moûtiers and Bourg St Maurice, but the nearest airports are Lyons and Geneva, both of which are at least three hours' drive away. At peak holiday periods, it can take many hours longer than that as the traffic bound for Val d'Isère, Tignes and the Trois Vallées has a habit of thrombosing some way before Moûtiers.

No-one could describe Val d'Isère as a pretty Alpine village, but it is not a modern, purpose-built resort. (In fact, the travel brochure cliché is that it was once the hunting village of the Dukes of Savoie.) The hotchpotch of buildings signifies that the resort has grown organically and for that reason, it has considerable character, if not in terms of the buildings themselves, then certainly in terms of the hotels, bars, restaurants and shops that occupy them.

Val d'Isère is situated on the floor of the valley so the views from the resort itself are not particularly dramatic and it is not recommended for people who suffer from claustrophobia. But being on the floor of the valley has its advantages – Val d'Isère is fairly flat and compact, so walking from one place to another is not much trouble. During the day, the free Train Rouge bus service is one of the most efficient ski bus services in the Alps and it runs very frequently between the bottom stations of La Daille, Solaise and Le Fornet. At night, there are half-hourly bus services between Val d'Isère and the satellite apartment complex of La Daille.

In recent years, alas, the invasion of British tour operators who have rented several hotels to run as chalets has led to an invasion of British skiers. The resort is now saturated with the British and is thus less desirable as a holiday destination.

Accommodation

You can choose whatever kind of holiday you like in Val d'Isère: there are plenty of chalets, apartments and hotels.

The two biggest British operators here are Bladon Lines and Ski Val. The Bladon Lines operation is run by the formidably efficient John Yates-Smith, who heads a team of around 50 staff. It has two jumbo chalets, the Eau-Vive, recently upgraded, and Les Crêtes Blanches. They also have a large number of smaller chalets. The Ski Val operation centres on its two big chalets, the Solaise in the middle of town and the Rond Point, just at the bottom of the Solaise lifts. The décor in the Solaise makes you feel that the building may once have been run as a brothel, but the Rond Point is much more tasteful. There are grandiose plans for a large new complex to be built on the site of the Rond Point by Pierre Schnebln, the man behind the development of Tignes.

Ski West has the famous Fjord chalet just at the entrance to the village, while Supertravel has the rather old-fashioned Grand Nord, the more modern Les Bruyères and a very attractive small new chalet, Costerg, right up at Le Fornet. Club Mark Warner has the chalet hotel Moris in the centre and Les Clarines on the way into the town.

Undoubtedly the smartest and most convenient apartment block in Val d'Isère is Les Andes, which is right on the main street. The apartments in Les Hameaux on the road to Le Fornet are all quite modern and of a good standard, as are those at L'Albaron, though they are both slightly out of the way. Les Hauts de Val d'Isère and the Résidence d'Isère are all blocks of apartments behind the Tourist Office complex, which is reasonably convenient although you have to walk up a steep drive to get to them. These are not really recommended as, unless they have a careful private owner, the apartments are getting rather tacky now and many of them have school dormitory-like tin bunks. Ski West has a lot of self-catering accommodation and its faithful representative, Debbie Kitchen, is one of the most helpful in the Alps.

Mountain Lodges, run by Val d'Isère veterans David MacCallum and Patricia Killy, has some very, very luxurious and imaginatively converted chalets for rent. These come with a host of extras and excellent service and are priced accordingly.

There is a large new development of self-catering apartments at the satellite station of La Daille on the way into Val d'Isère. This has been put up by the ubiquitous Pierre et Vacances company. However, La Daille is not recommended as a place to stay since nightlife there is limited and the place has very little character.

The most sophisticated hotel in Val d'Isère is **Sofitel****** above the Tourist Office, but most of the best value hotels are in the three-star category. These include the **Gelinotte*****, an informal place that has always been popular with the British, reached by a fairly steep path; the **Bellier*****, near the centre of town, which is quieter and more formal (and Monsieur Bellier's food has a great reputation); and the **Savoyarde***** which has attracted the British for some time, but is becoming increasingly expensive now. (Check your reservation here twice, since over-bookings are not unknown.) The **Squaw Valley***** hotel has a slightly transatlantic atmosphere in keeping with its name but the bar is lively and the food good.

For a simple bed and breakfast hotel, **Le Kern**** in the main street is hard to beat, while **Les Lorès****, formerly a John Morgan chalet, is a pleasant hotel run by the temperamental but normally charming Madame Taillfer. The dining room here has a marvellous atmosphere with a large sunken fireplace in the middle.

Après-ski

The most popular tea-time rendezvous in Val d'Isère is **Les Petites Anglaises,** started in 1981 by Amanda Shakespeare and Belinda Boston. It has changed hands twice since then and is now run by Paula. It serves an enormous selection of teas, as well as milkshakes and lots of home-made English cakes such as banana bread and flapjacks. It also does good trade for breakfast in bad weather and is as popular with the French as with the British.

The epicentre of Val d'Isère nightlife for visiting Britons is the seminal **Dick's T-Bar.** Opened in 1979/80 by the enterprising Dick Yates-Smith, and constantly improved ever since, this bar/disco complex caters for the après-ski requirements of the holidaying British in a way that no other place in the Alps succeeds in doing. The décor in the bar is thoroughly modern, although there are too many plastic plants and not enough windows. The new adjoining cocktail bar has an expensive feel to it, although the décor seems straight out of *Dynasty.*

In the early evening, there are skiing videos as well as a constantly changing slide show. Many reps have their office hours here and almost all British visitors to Val d'Isère come in here for at least one pre-prandial drink. Just before eight o'clock, the chalet dinner witching hour, the bar suddenly empties and enjoys a quiet period which lasts until the disco begins at 10 o'clock.

The old Cocktail Bar has now become the Members' Bar and is arguably the most exclusive drinking place in the resort. Dick confers membership upon local and regular visitors to the resort, so the gossip here is always up-to-the-minute. For those who can prove themselves credit-worthy, there is also an account facility in this bar.

The entrance charge of FF50 for the disco includes your first drink. The records and videos are usually cued and introduced by the diminutive Dick himself from his gadget-filled booth known as Mission control. Although he sometimes lags behind the British charts, he has good taste in music and is sympathetic to requests. (The newest gadget is likely to be a very expensive laser for use inside the disco and also for writing messages outside on passing clouds.)

Some people argue that Dick's T-Bar is far too British, but apart from the fact that it has a significant minority of French clients, the inescapable truth is that the British on holiday enjoy mixing with other British on holiday. In any case, the success of this establishment speaks for itself. For many years, Dick protested that he wasn't making any money, but now he openly admits to doing rather well and has been transformed from a fidgeting, midget DJ to a suave, nightclub patron. He is well supported by his large staff, including manager Tim and star bar staff like Lucy and Mango.

A new British-run bar, **Playbach,** opened in the 1985/86 season. It is owned by Nick Montlake (formerly with Snow Fun) and John Allan from Tignes. It is a basement piano-bar/disco that attracts a younger crowd than Dick's and is more popular with people working in the resort. The disco is not so sophisticated, but then nor are the prices. Watch out for a clever scheme whereby you are charged an entrance fee that gives you your second (not your first) drink free. This enterprise has now expanded and opened a restaurant called **Feedbach.**

Other popular places for early-evening drinking in Val d'Isère include the amusing **Alsace Taverne,** which also serves rather stodgy Alsatian dinners, and the comfortable **Saloon Bar** of the Brussels Hotel. **Bananas** is popular for cocktails and also has a restaurant doing burgers and so forth.

Val d'Isère's immense selection of restaurants includes some very good ones. One of the best is the idiosyncratic but stylish **Au Bout de la Rue,** run by the engaging moustachioed José and Isabelle, his *serveuse.* The menus are written out in school exercise books with the day's special additions on the blackboard. It specialises in some very inventive fish recipes but also does good duck and rabbit. The **Grand Ourse** provides haute cuisine in the traditional French style, but starve yourself before going here as you can find yourself faced with gargantuan portions. **El Cortijo,** beneath the Les Andes apartment building, also has a great reputation for its fish, but this is not such a cheap place as it can at first appear. Another good place for fish is the **White Ocean** in the Squaw Valley hotel, a modern restaurant serving nouvelle-ish food.

For braserade, **L'Arolay** restaurant right up at Le Fornet is well worth visiting, if you have transport. Also out of town is **Le Châtelard** which does fondues to order as well as more sophisticated dishes and has a good selection of Alsace wines. Nearer to the centre of town, **La Mourra** does braserade and good fondues. For cheap pizzas and pasta, **La Perdrix Blanche** is a very large, efficient restaurant that is always good value; the bar here is always popular with locals. **Chez Nano** is a smaller pizzeria with a less frenetic atmosphere. If you're feeling really down on your

luck, you can always get a carry-out from **Valburger** beneath the Bladon Lines Eau-Vive building.

Bar Jacques, now owned and run by veteran ski champion Tom Mongellaz and his wife Annie, is another key bar/restaurant. It is a long narrow building and the small bar area is frequently packed. (It's a great achievement to install yourself on one of the six bar stools.) In the rather cramped restaurant section, the food is expertly cooked and charmingly served by Jean-Baptiste, the *serveur. Magret de canard* and tournedos are just some of the specialities here.

Bar Jacques advertises itself as being *Ouvert le nuit* and sometimes does not shut until five or six in the morning. After dinner, genial Tom will allow you to sit at the table and drink. He is happy to serve snacks well into the early hours. The auld alliance still means something in the Savoie and this bar is particularly popular with the many Scots who frequent Val d'Isère. Tom has been presented with an award from an outfit calling itself The Scottish Après-Ski Display Team. (The coat of arms is a pair of crossed skis and a pint of heavy.)

Besides Dick's T-Bar, there are also discos at **Club 21, Mephisto** and the **Sagittaire,** but none of them has such good music and they are usually more expensive.

The skiing

There are three main starting points for the lifts in Val d'Isère. These are the Solaise/Bellevarde complex, which is close to the middle of town, Le Fornet, at the far end of the valley, and La Daille in the opposite direction.

The cable car at Le Fornet takes you halfway up the mountain and a connecting six-man bubble takes you up to the Glacier de Pissaillas, which is also open for summer skiing. The slopes up here are really very easy but the snow stays in good condition late into the season. For good skiers, however, there are some marvellously challenging off-piste opportunities, especially in powder or spring snow. The Col Pers is a particularly dramatic long off-piste run, but you must take a guide as the terrain is quite dangerous. On the lower part of Le Fornet, there is some good, steep tree skiing beneath the cable car and this, too, is excellent in powder.

From the Solaise/Bellevarde bottom station, cable cars (and alternative chairlifts) rise up on both sides of the valley. To the left, they go up to Solaise, where there is skiing to suit all standards. The runs from the Madeleine and Cugnai chairlifts are fairly easy, while the Marmottons and the Arcelle are more difficult, as are the off-piste runs over the back from the top of the Cugnai chair. (These can be very good in spring snow, although, you risk sliding a long way if you fall.) You can connect with the Le Fornet area by means of an up-and-over chairlift, which also operates in the opposite direction. The most difficult piste skiing on Solaise is below the top station of the cable car on a slope simply but accurately known as 'The Bumps' – a vast mogulfield.

The Bellevarde cable car and chairlifts rise up, above the steep Face de Bellevarde, on the right-hand side of the bottom station. From here, you can either come straight back down the black run on the Face, or tackle off-piste runs such as the Tour de Charvet and the terrifying Face de Charvet. Alternatively, you can ski on the easier slopes by the Grand Pré or over towards the La Daille area and even on from there to Tignes.

From La Daille up to the top of Bellevarde, there is now a brand-new (mostly underground) express funicular, called the Funival, similar to the Sunnega Express in Zermatt, which does the journey in four minutes. If you prefer a more leisurely trip, there is still a two-stage telecabine which runs up to the top of Bellevarde and the start of the World Cup Downhill course, which runs all the way back down to La Daille. This run has now been equipped with 40 snow canons to ensure good cover at the beginning and end of the season.

Alternatively, a triple-chairlift takes you as far as the middle station of the telecabine, from where you can connect with the double triple-chairlifts up to Tovière and the Tignes ski area. All around here there are long, broad pistes well-suited to experts and very good intermediates. On the lower part of the slopes, there are plenty of trees so this is a useful area in bad visibility. There is also an intriguing off-piste run from the middle station of La Daille down to the bottom. This is called the Piste Perdu and is just as isolated as it sounds, but make sure you go with someone who knows how to *trouver* it.

Lunches

At the top of the **Le Fornet** cable car, there is a self-service restaurant with an even better service one upstairs, but really the best place to eat at this end of town is **L'Arolay** in the old village of Le Fornet. It is an ideal place for a long lunch on a bad day.

On the Solaise side, there is a big new self-service restaurant at the top of the cable car. This is not a particularly exciting place to eat, although the food is quite reasonable. The new, enlarged **La Datcha** restaurant, in a sun-trap beside the Cugnai chairlifts, is not as good as it used to be, but it is in a useful position and there are both service and self-service sections, the latter often being packed. Prices here tend to be rather steep.

The restaurant at the top of **Bellevarde** should be avoided at all costs – you are much better advised to ski down to the **Folie Douce** at the middle station of La Daille. (This is now run by Luc, who used to run Val d'Isère's superb nouvelle cuisine restaurant, La Petite Folie, which is no more.) The Folie Douce is a self-service restaurant but the food is very fine and Luc's girlfriend and mother help to provide excellent service.

The upstairs service restaurant up at **Tovière** is as popular with skiers from Val d'Isère as it is with those from Tignes. It is managed very efficiently by an amazingly thin, chic woman laden down with expensive jewellery. The place is run like a proper restaurant with an extensive, interesting menu. The cooking is of a good standard – the meat is always of the highest quality and the selection of coupes for dessert is good. There is a decent self-service restaurant here as well. The sun terrace offers

beautiful views, but it is often very windy up here. (Tovière is one of the few mountain restaurants in this vast area equipped with lavatories, so long queues form. It is a scandal that restaurant proprietors are not obliged to provide loos. All Swiss mountain restaurants have them.)

Close to the bottom of La Daille is **La Crech'Ouna,** run by another powerful Madame who is fine, providing you remember to brush all the excess snow off your ski boots before you walk into her restaurant. They do an excellent steak tartare here which you mix yourself.

Ski schools

There is an ESF school here, but it is not much used by the British. For beginners and intermediates, the English-speaking Snow Fun ski school is recommended by nearly all the operators since it caters so well for the British market. (Although there are classes for beginners, it is worth stressing that Val d'Isère is far from being the ideal place to learn to ski.) For more experienced skiers who want a bit of off-piste guiding as well as teaching, the Top Ski school is strongly recommended. The instructors are all experienced and well-qualified and they carry radios, as well as giving you avalanche bleepers if you are skiing off-piste.

Ski shops

As well as its ski school, Snow Fun also runs some of the best ski shops in Val d'Isère, hiring equipment to the clients of most British operators. (The company runs a special Wally of the Week competition to see which operator can produce the largest number of stupid punters. Points are awarded to people who try to put their skis on back to front or who put their boots on the wrong feet, and so on.) Snow Fun specialises in Dynastar and Dynamic skis and Salomon boots, while Top Ski has a shop dealing mainly in Kästle skis and Lange boots.

Killy is the most chic label to have on your ski suit in Val d'Isère and there is a large Killy shop selling every conceivable piece of ski clothing – all marked with the Killy name. Next door, Pitte Sport is almost as fashionable and deals in the other major skiwear manufacturers.

VAL THORENS

At 2300m above sea-level, Val Thorens is the highest ski resort in Europe. This means it is well above the tree-line and often very cold. On the other hand, it also means that the resort is surrounded by fairly steep mountainsides and snow is pretty well guaranteed.

Val Thorens is the southernmost of the Trois Vallées resorts and is reached from Geneva via a tortuous 20-mile-long road from Moûtiers through the Belleville valley. It is a very long way by road from the other major Trois Vallées resorts – Courchevel and Méribel – so it is very important to get back over to Val Thorens before the lifts close.

This station was opened in 1973, so it is one of the most modern of the purpose-built resorts. It is not a pretty place, but few buildings could look pretty in this bleak setting. Some of the more recently built blocks are very attractive in themselves and have well-designed interiors.

Unless you are a very keen skier, you will probably hate Val Thorens. It is very much a skiers' resort and everything else is secondary to the sport. But if you are a deeply committed skier, you will appreciate being able to walk out of the door on to the piste and having immediate access to very difficult skiing. You don't have to get up the mountain before you reach the good runs – you are already up the mountain.

Accommodation

Val Thorens is still a developing resort and there is still a lot of building in progress, so the accommodation scene changes year by year.

This is primarily an apartment resort, although there are several hotels. The most impressive apartment block here is one of the newest, Les Temples du Soleil. This is a really imaginatively designed complex which incorporates restaurants, a bar and a supermarket as well as the flats. Unlike most blocks of apartments in ski resorts, you get the feeling that the builders have spared no expense to make the place look good. The communal parts of this building all have a wonderful feeling of light and space, while most of the apartments themselves have sunny balconies. Unfortunately, the building does not appear to have been managed so well since being taken over by the vast Pierre et Vacances group.

The Résidence de Val Thorens is another large, recently built block. Generally speaking, the east end of Val Thorens is the slummier end and several apartments in the Les Névés and Les Glaciers buildings have been wrecked in the past by the Swedes, whose numbers in Val Thorens are now limited by the authorities.

Le Val Thorens**** is a newish, smart hotel owned and run by resort guru Branko Perkov. The **Fitzroy******, new for the 86-87 season is right next door. Among the smaller, more modest hotels, **Le Sherpa**** is a friendly little family-run French place, whose only drawback is the rather tasteless décor.

At the other end of the scale is the **Chalet du Thorens,** in the middle of the piste, a mile from the resort. This is the 'world's highest chalet party' and features dormitory-style accommodation. Like a boarding school in that you are not allowed out into town at night.

Après-ski

Although by no means exceptional, the après-ski life here is probably superior to that of neighbouring Méribel. If you haven't managed to get enough exercise during a day's skiing, you can always go to the **Club Pierre Barthes** sports centre which includes a swimming pool, sauna and jacuzzi as well as tennis courts, squash courts and a gym.

For early evening drinking, the bar in Les Temples du Soleil is a good place to relax and gets a lot of sun in the spring evenings. **Le Gloulou** is a popular bar where some reps hold their office hours. It is run by a woman called Marie-Jo, whose manner is too sugary-sweet for some. There is a restaurant here but it's not very good and rather over-priced. **Les Saints Pères** is a pleasant little bar that also does good snacks such as crêpes. **La Pause** is another popular spot for reps' office hours, but the service is notoriously slow.

There is quite good selection of reasonably priced restaurants for dinner. **Hot Beans** is an American restaurant in a cellar which serves lots of burgers and similar fast-food delicacies. **Goa Beach** is a bar and restaurant that often does special 'theme' evenings – for example, Italian or Mexican. This is always a popular place with ski instructors. **Le Bistrot** is famed for its couscous evenings and good-value set menus. The **Nectar Inn** is a milk bar/restaurant serving good-value French food.

There are two pizzerias in Val Thorens – the **Pizzeria du Loup** and the **Pizzeria** in Les Temples du Soleil. The latter is run by Albert, who used to have a renowned pizzeria in Canada and is very disappointed that he doesn't have facilities for *au feu de bois* here. Nevertheless, he turns out pretty good pizzas.

For a more up-market meal, the **Gaboulet** is probably the best place. Although busy, this place has an intimate atmosphere and serves good traditonal French food. Similar fare can also be found at the **Chalet des Glaciers.** Unfortunately, the popularity of this place with the Swedes is reflected in the fact that it is the only place in the Alps to have several copies of its menu written in Swedish.

There are two discos here, the newer and bigger is the **Agoora** which is decorated in Egyptian style and can be good fun. The **Pop 3000** is smaller and cosier and charges similar prices – FF70 for entry and first drink. From time to time, there is live music down at Les Temples du Soleil in the **Eldorado Hall.**

The skiing

The most exciting run here is down from the Cime de Caron (3200m) which is reached by what is one of the world's largest cable cars. This carries 150 people and has a built-in stereo system but a limited choice of tapes – it has been Pink Floyd or Wagner for about five seasons now.

The runs down from Cime de Caron are not especially long. But they are straight, steep and ridden with moguls, and demand the greatest concentration even from experienced skiers. The delightful thing about these runs is that, being so high, the snow is almost always in perfect condition. After a good snowfall, this area can be paradise for powder skiers. There is also some very good skiing up Mont de la Chambre and Aiguille du Peclet.

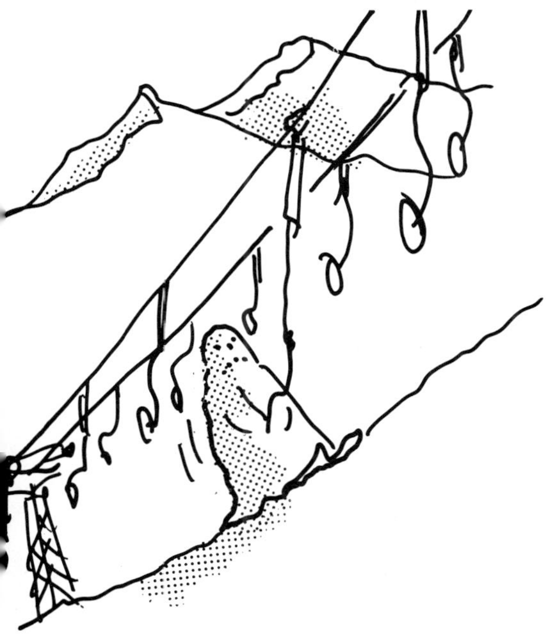

It is very easy to ski down to Les Menuires and enjoy the skiing there, although you are well advised to avoid the resort itself, which is one of the dreariest in Europe. There is some good skiing up La Masse and, of course, you can always go over into the Méribel valley and even on to Courchevel, though you need to make an early start if you intend to go this far.

Lunches

Many people who come on self-catering holidays to Val Thorens choose to return to their apartments for lunch. This is relatively easy to do and most of the balconies face more or less south. The **Chalet du Caron** is very social and an ideal place to stop if you have come from Courchevel and are doing the Three Valleys.

There is a tiny refreshment hut at the top of the Cime de Caron, but it is so cold up there that it is against all natural instincts to hang about a minute longer than necessary. **Camille's Restaurant** at the top of the Glacier du Chavière in the summer skiing area, is a really ethnic mountain hut. Platters of bread, cheese, Savoie meats and so on are served, as well as beer and carafes of wine.

If you choose to come back to Val Thorens for lunch and want to eat out, the **Galoubet** is a large trendy restaurant with a good sun terrace. The waiters in their white dungarees are slightly disconcerting, however.

The ESF ski school is of the usual good standard here but there is a shortage of English-speaking instructors. However, as the number of English visitors to Val Thorens is growing rapidly, things should improve. The school offers a course it calls 'Ski Tonic' in which you can sample a day of nearly all types of skiing – mono-skiing, deep powder, slalom courses, *ski voile* (where a mini-parachute is attached to you) and any other variation of skiing you can think of.

Ski shops

Inside the Temples du Soleil complex, there is the Eskiador shop run by the Jean-Pierre. In the village itself, the Ski-3V shop is the best.

VERBIER

Along with Zermatt, St Anton, Courchevel and Val d'Isère, Verbier is one of Europe's top five ski resorts, the relative merits of which are constantly and inconclusively discussed by ski fanatics.

Verbier sits on a sunny hillside (not quite flat enough to be a plateau) on the south side of the Rhône valley, a few miles up from the station town of Martigny. One of its greatest advantages for British skiers is that it is only about two hours' drive from Geneva airport. For those rich enough to afford the air fare, a weekend's skiing in Verbier is a perfectly feasible proposition.

It is sometimes rather hard to believe, but Verbier is, in fact, a post-war, though not quite purpose-built, ski resort. It is a large village but, as almost all the buildings are in chalet style, it is also very pretty. It has superb views and a lot more sunshine than most top resorts.

Although most of the services you buy in Verbier are pretty good value, the fact remains that you are spending Swiss francs, of which you get lamentably few to the pound. The much-publicised minimal inflation rate in Switzerland is all very well, but it does not alter the exchange rate. If you are having a reasonably extravagant holiday, eating out in mountain restaurants as well as drinking and eating in the village itself, you will probably find yourself paying about a quarter as much again in Verbier as you would in, say, Val d'Isère. For a fortnight's holiday, this difference can easily turn out to be £100 or more.

Of course, if you stay in a catered chalet party and monitor your casual expenditure carefully, then a holiday here will not be very much more expensive than one in France.

Accommodation

As Verbier consists mainly of chalets, there are plenty available for rent and, consequently, the rental charges are low compared with many resorts. The knock-on effect of this is that British tour operators are able to offer chalet-party holidays in Verbier at remarkably reasonable prices.

Bladon Lines has an enormous, well-run operation in Verbier with about 20 chalets, most of them fairly small, although there are a couple with 20 or so beds.

Supertravel has a much smaller selection of chalets which includes its Jumbo Chalet Pleaide, while John Morgan's accommodation here includes very luxurious apartments in the Flaminia building which it runs as chalets.

There are a number of smaller chalet operators in Verbier, most of them specialising only in this resort – some of them having simply one eight-bedded chalet. Obviously, some of these smaller independent operators are better than others, so it is advisable to check them out before booking. There is no substitute for personal references in these circumstances. The scene changes every season and some of the better known names of the past, like Ski Jeannie no longer exist in Verbier. Ski Montagne is one of the more reliable newcomers.

There is plenty of good-quality, self-catering accommodation and Bladon Lines has a large selection of flats, as does Ski West. Most of the apartments in Verbier are in large chalet-style buildings. Some operators arrange for you to have self-catering accommodation with the services of a chalet girl to cook dinner if you wish.

There is a good choice of hotels in Verbier, all of them offering good Swiss service. The **Rhodania***** is one of the most luxurious and has the advantage for those keen on nightlife that the Farm Club is in the basement. The **Hotel de Verbier***** is situated in the main square and is run by Patrick and his English wife, Lynne. **Le Mazot***** is just behind the square and has an entertaining proprietor called Serge Tacchini. He is famous for making bets (usually bottles of wine) with his clients about when it will snow. He has a terrible tendency to lose these bets and, on one occasion last season, he lost so many and owed so much wine that he was forced to give a vast free Glühwein party for all his guests.

Après-ski

As Verbier is essentially a place for skiers rather than poseurs, the nightlife is lively without being particularly sophisticated. The **Mont Fort Pub** (also known as the Mark Warner pub because the rest of the building is run by Mark Warner as a large chalet) is situated just above the Medran lift station, where many of the runs back to the resort end up. Consequently, it is a popular rendezvous point at the end of the afternoon's skiing. Prices are cheap here and draught beer (including Guinness) is consumed in large quantities. Down in the village itself, the **Milk Bar** is a key tea-time haunt for many of the resort's estimated 250 chalet girls and quite a few of the resident army of ski bums. They drink fresh fruit frappés and hot chocolate and eat cakes and ice-cream. (The sunny outdoor terrace here is popular in spring.)

The favourite early-evening drinking place is **La Luge,** a rustic bar that is particularly popular not only with the statutory Sloane crowd, but also with the heavy-drinking Scottish contingent in Verbier. (Because Scots get plenty of skiing practice at home, they want to go to the very best resorts when on holiday. And there are a lot of very rich Jimmies who ski.) However, La Luge is not a large bar and it oftens becomes unpleasantly crowded. When this happens, the best idea is to escape a few yards down the hill to the very agreeable **Rodeo** bar, a laid-back place full of large, comfortable black-leather sofas. One of the specialities in this bar is Dôle Blanche, a delicious hard-to-find Swiss wine. There is also a selection of hot bar snacks, like *croque monsieur,* which are served until closing time.

Many bars in Verbier close at midnight (Francis, the proprietor of La Luge, and his staff clearing the bar at witching hour is one of the great sights of the resort), so those places which stay open until 1am tend to be very busy in the final hour. One such place is the **Nelson Pub,** a very pseudo-British pub run by men in suits who look like suburban bank managers.

The most popular hotel bar is that of the **Hotel de Verbier,** which is the definitive rendezvous point for the English-speaking in-crowd in Verbier. Many British reps have their office hours here and the place is a centre for gossip and trading in air tickets and airport transfers. There are delicious home-made crisps most evenings, although, occasionally an inferior substitute of popcorn is put out. For sophisticated cocktails and expensive drinks in a really luxurious atmosphere, the bar of the **Rosalp** hotel is recommended. There is very comfortable and discreet alcove seating here, as well as very elegant waitress service.

For a simple but excellent dinner, La Luge is almost unbeatable. The menu is unremarkable but the quality of the meat and the cooking is superb. All meals begin with a self-service salad buffet which is followed by a choice of meats, all charcoal-grilled in the middle of the restaurant. The finest cut is *coeur de filet,* but there is a slight tendency to under-cook, so it can be worth ordering your steak slightly better cooked than you normally would. Quibbles apart, these are some of the finest steaks served in any ski resort. For good value wine, drink the Patron's Réserve Dôle.

Up at **Le Carrefour,** you can get an excellent *fondue chinoise* (various meats cooked in bouillon rather than fat), after which you can poubelle back to the village. **Le Mazot** hotel is much more centrally situated and its menu includes a *fondue chinoise* that is arguably even better.

For a cheaper meal, the **Pizzeria Fer à Cheval,** next to Ski Service, is probably the most social place in town. The atmosphere and the pizzas are both worth savouring. The **Robinson,** just off the main square, has no atmosphere but does have an extensive menu of good-value dishes and is well patronised by locals.

For burgers and so forth, the basement of the **Mont Fort Pub** is the place to go. Although very slightly out of town, both the bar and restaurant in the Pub are well patronised in the evenings.

For dancing, the best place is undoubtedly the **Farm Club.** This lively, rustic-style disco run by brothers Giuseppe and Serafino has lately become famous in British newspaper gossip columns because it is much frequented by Paddy McNally, the former Miss Sarah Ferguson's former boyfriend. It is certainly the smartest nightclub in Verbier and prices itself accordingly. Entrance is technically about SF20 (including your first drink) but on a busy night the strict doormen will only grant admission to regulars and their friends, or those who look as though they are going to be big spenders. In fact, most regular visitors to the Farm Club do not buy individual drinks but rather bottles of spirits. If you ring in advance, you can reserve a table, but space around it will still be at a premium.

Cheaper but less stylish nightclubs include **Tara's** and **Marshalls,** both of which have a tendency to have rather tacky Miss This and Mr That competitions on stage, as well as the dancing. The cheapest place of all is the **Scotch Club,** a phenomenally sweaty dive which, nevertheless, plays decent music and is popular with impoverished chalet girls.

The skiing

For expert skiers, particularly those in search of powder skiing, Verbier offers almost unparalleled opportunities. The most difficult skiing is to be found on the Ruinettes/Attelas/Mont Gelé complex. Below Attelas, the runs are suitable for intermediates, but above here the runs are really for good skiers. There is an ageing single cable car (which actually came off its wire last winter) that takes you to the top of Mont Gelé, from where you can either ski down the face (very difficult) or walk a little way round the side of the mountain and ski down the back (not quite so difficult). From here, you eventually join up with the run from Col des Gentianes down to Tortin. The more usual route to Tortin is via the chairlift up from Lac des Vaux to Chassoure and then down the notorious Tortin run itself. This is a steep mogul-ridden run which takes you to the bottom station of the new Mont Fort cable car. This takes you up to Col des Gentianes, from where another cable car takes you to the top of Mont Fort. The run down is very steep indeed and inadequate skiers who attempt it are often admonished by a pisteur near the bottom of the steep section.

There are tremendous off-piste possibilities on the Tortin side of Mont Fort, but on the other side there is a good long piste run down La Chaux. If you have the stamina, you can go right on down to Le Châble, below Verbier, and have the satisfaction of knowing that you have skied one of the longest runs in Europe. However, the Verbier to Le Châble section of this run is only open when there is particularly good snow cover. Even then, care must be taken as the piste runs through orchards and vineyards which, though very pretty, contain many hidden hazards in the form of stone walls and water pipes.

Téléverbier, the lift company, are in the process of constructing a large (150 persons) cable car which will run from La Chaux up to Col des Gentianes. This will give much easier access to the Mont Fort/Tortin complex and will eliminate the dreadful queues that occur at the bottom of the Lac des Vaux to Chassoure chairlift. Whether it will create other queues elsewhere remains to be seen. There is also hope that the six-man telecabine which presently runs from Medran to Ruinettes will be extended to Attelas, parallel with the existing four-man telecabine. However, planning permission for ski lifts in Switzerland is becoming increasingly hard to obtain.

There are good, longish runs down from Attelas right down to the resort itself, via either Ruinettes or Carrefour, while the Fontanays chairlift is excellent for those who enjoy steep mogul-bashing. In bad weather, when few lifts are open, there is decent skiing in the wooded area below Ruinettes. Although the corridor beneath the telecabine is not technically a piste, it is reasonably wide and does offer excellent skiing if the snow is deep but the visibility is bad.

On the other side of Verbier is the Savoleyres ski area. This is not so easily reached from the centre of town as you have to take one of Verbier's charming, but from a skier's point of view, irritatingly old-fashioned buses. (You can't take your skis inside – they have to be wedged into a basket at the back.) The skiing over here is mostly of an intermediate standard with plenty of good, wide pistes. From the top of Savoleyres, you can ski down to La Tzoumaz – a small village where you can stop for lunch. There are also some good off-piste possibilities in this area but, because much of it is wooded you certainly need a guide.

The Verbier lift pass gives you access to the skiing of the Quatre Vallées, the collective name for Verbier and the many resorts to its east. These other resorts include Haute-Nendaz and Super-Nendaz where some British operators have accommodation, but as places to stay they are poor substitutes for Verbier itself.

It is possible to ski the Quatre Vallées area in one day if you start early, but it is fairly exhausting. It is the sort of tour best suited to good intermediate skiers, who will feel a great sense of achievement. Experts may find it rather boring, as the skiing is not as interesting as that around Mont Gelé and Mont Fort.

Another all-day expedition is the Super St Bernard. You drive or take an excursion bus to the mouth of the St Bernard Tunnel, from where there is a telecabine up to the top of the mountain. From here you can ski back down to the bottom of the telecabine, a long and fairly steep run. But the real reason for coming here is to go over the top of the mountain and ski down into Italy. It is a beautiful, long

descent (11km) which although, technically off-piste, is usually well-prepared by the preceding skiers. The skiing itself is not particularly demanding – there are quite a few traverses – but you have a wonderful sensation of being in the mountains away from all ski lifts and buildings. The reward for completing this long descent is an even longer Italian lunch at one of the restaurants in Etroubles from where you are driven back to Verbier by bus. (You need your passport for this expedition.)

The one drawback to Verbier is that its queues are almost as famous as its skiing. So it is a place best visited at low or middle season. Of course, it is usually possible to avoid the queues, but it often means skiing where there aren't queues, rather than where you would ideally like to ski. The worst bottlenecks are probably the lifts from Medran to Ruinettes, Ruinettes to Attelas, and the telecabine up Savoleyres. You can avoid the worst of the morning queues by getting up early or late.

There is a single supplement of SF10 per day payable if you use the Mont Fort cable cars, but if you are planning to go up Mont Fort more than twice in a week, then it is worth buying a lift pass that includes the Mont Fort section. (In high season, the queues for people wanting to buy the supplement are often longer than those for people who already have the Mont Fort lift pass.) If two parents buy full-price passes, then two children can have free passes – quite a useful reduction.

Lunches

The disadvantage with all the best mountain restaurants in Verbier is that they are relatively low down, with the consequence that you often have to queue again to get back to the best skiing areas. However, the best place to lunch and to be seen lunching in Verbier is upstairs at **Ruinettes,** a large but not particularly attractive restaurant building with a self-service department on the ground floor. The prices upstairs are not much higher than those downstairs but the atmosphere is much more fun. There is a large team of hard-working and entertaining young waiters and waitresses, the funniest being a Manuel lookalike called Vincent. There are plenty of expensive main courses, but most people will be satisfied with one of their many *croûtes au fromage* or a *croûte aux champignons.* There is also a fine range of desserts here, including a vast selection of fruit tarts and various ices which appear on the menu from time to time – the finest is a *soufflé glâcé au Grand Marnier.* There is a sunny, south-facing terrace here with terrific views over the Rhône valley. A lunch outside on a good day, with a bottle or two of the pétillant local Fendant, is as pleasant a one as you will find anywhere in the Alps.

Lower down, on the run down to Medran, is the tiny hamlet of Clambin, famous as the home of top ski photographer, Mark Shapiro, and the location of **Chez Dany.** This is a wonderful little hut in the middle of pinewoods just beside the piste. The food is simple and good, but the service can be frustratingly slow on a good (busy) day. There is an attractive terrace here also. **Le Carrefour** is a bigger place at the top of the nursery slopes and is very popular as the final pit-stop of the day as well as for lunch. There is no more fitting conclusion to a good day's skiing than sitting outside at Carrefour with a glass of beer sparkling in your hand, watching the sun sink slowly.

Over at Savoleyres, you have to go down very low and risk very long queues to get back up again. If you are prepared to do this, however, **La Marmotte** is a beautiful little wooden chalet run as a service restaurant on the way down to the bottom station. It has a small terrace outside. La Tzoumaz is a popular lunching spot and there are several restaurants down here. They all serve much the same sort of food and have terraces, so it is worth going a little way away from the end of the piste to find somewhere quieter and cheaper. **Fougère** is a relatively small restaurant with a tiny little terrace at the back, but it serves an excellent selection of *croûtes.*

Ski schools

The Swiss Ski School in Verbier is renowned for its Cours de Godille. These are intensive advanced classes which last a week, and which take place about four times a year, always in low season. The courses in early December are particularly popular. All of them tend to foster a great esprit de corps within the class, since you ski, eat and drink together every day for a week. Otherwise, the ESS ski school is not as good as it once was and there have been rather too many instances of dissatisfied British pupils in recent years. Relations between the ESS and British tour operators have become strained recently over the tiresome issue of the operators' ski guides. Classes take place in the mornings only, except for children. Children are quite well taught here, but it is not really an ideal resort for adult beginners.

Ski shops

Verbier has some of the best ski shops in the whole of the Alps, so it is a good place for serious and/or trendy skiers to buy their gear – providing they can afford the Swiss prices.

The most famous shop in Verbier is the recently-enlarged Ski Service, run by the legendary, laid-back figure of Dale Anderson. It stocks the classic Powderhorn clothing, as well as the incredibly sought-after, high-fashion Jet Set range. The equipment section also has good gear, including K2 skis and Lange boots. Recently Ski Service has become well-known for its sweatshirts, including the celebrated 'Not Normal' range. It also has a very efficient ski hire department staffed by English-speakers. (Jack, who used to work at Ski Service, now has his own wine business, Macbirch, just across the road.)

Just across the road from Ski Service is Mountain Air, another fine shop with good English-speaking staff. It does an extensive range of Event clothing. It has a sister shop of the same name in the Fulham Road which is currently London's best ski shop.

WENGEN
Links with Murren

It is generally accepted in skiing circles that David Vine does go over the top a bit, but in his traditional Lauberhorn preamble about Wengen it would be hard to accuse him of hyperbole. You would have to be very unromantic not to be moved by the funicular journey up to Wengen from Lauterbrunnen.

You pass through tunnels, through deep cuttings with snow up to the top of the carriage on either side, and then through pine trees keeling over under the weight of freshly fallen snow. Going to any modern purpose-built resort is not half so exciting as this.

And this is the only way to get to Wengen: private cars are not allowed into the resort and there is no road up there, anyway. Lauterbrunnen is the valley town for both Wengen and Mürren and is reached by road or rail via Interlaken. (Zurich and Geneva airports are almost equidistant but Berne is nearer than either.)

At Lauterbrunnen there is a vast multi-storey car park for private cars. This is Switzerland, so the car park is naturally linked to the station. Once you have taken a special ticket to remind you which floor your car is on, you put your luggage into a trolley with a special ski-rack attachment and trundle along to the station.

The last train up to Wengen is at 23.00 and not a second later. (Incidentally, it is worthwhile getting a pocket timetable for the Jungfrau Railway, since you are likely to be using its services quite a bit if you are spending time in Wengen.)

Wengen is car-free, but there are a few vehicles – a handful of Land Rover taxis and lots of funny little electric buggies that look as if they have strayed from an American golf course. Each hotel has its own electric buggy, and a whole fleet of them turns up at the station to meet a crowded train.

It is this station scene that shows Wengen at its most traditional: uniformed porters from smart, long-established hotels turning up to meet a smart, rich, long-established clientele from Britain, America and other European countries.

Wengen is still a resort where the British are treated with respect and reverence, as the nation that invented skiing. The very social Downhill Only Club makes its base here, though nowadays the active members of the club are principally the parents of the junior racers. Piers Benson-Browning, Chairman of the DHO, is a great Wengen character and spends most of the winter here. The fact that there is usually an Anglican chaplain in residence gives some idea of the social status of Wengen.

Accommodation

This is really a resort for hotel-dwellers: there are only a few chalets and hardly any apartments, but there are lots of hotels of all standards. The most expensive is the beautifully situated **Jungfrau,** just by the railway up at Wengernalp. (You must reserve months – even years – in advance here.) The **Victoria Lauberhorn****** and the **Regina** are both large, old hotels, while the **Sunstar****** is a relatively new place offering a high, standard of accommodation. The nicest small hotel is the **Alpenrose*****, which is run by Margaret and Paul von Allmen. Margaret is Scottish and employs quite a few staff from her homeland. The British have a special affection for the **Falken******, known to its regulars as Fawlty Towers.

Après-ski

The tone of après-ski life in Wengen is lively but traditional. Drinks parties are crucial functions and last season, the three most social ones were John Morgan (Monday), the SCGB and the DHO (Tuesday), and Supertravel (Thursday). Early evening activities include such genteel sports as curling and skating.

Before dinner, the **Pizzeria Bar** of the Victoria Lauberhorn is the key meeting-place for keen skiers and instructors, while the **Pickel Bar** of the Eiger is popular with all types of British and it keeps humming until about 2am. The **Gemstubli** is a cheap bar much used by locals, whereas the **London Pub** is a dreadful, kitsch place that attracts the worst sort of punters.

For dinner, the Pizzeria and the Gemstubli both offer fairly cheap, good-value meals. At the top of the market, any serious eating out must be done in hotel restaurants. The **Silberhorn** and the **Eiger** are both recommended: the Eiger is famous for its excellent *fondue chinoise*. The **Schonegg Hotel,** on the other hand, has a reputation for being both bad and expensive.

There is no entry charge for nightclubs in Wengen, but the drinks are expensive. **Tiffany's** in the basement of the Silberhorn is a good disco run by an English DJ called Jules, who has been there for several seasons by now. He willingly plays requests, but you have to beware of teenyboppers on the dancefloor. The **Carousel** at the Regina is geared towards an older age group and always has a live band playing somewhat dated music.

After the disco finishes, tobogganing home is a popular moonlight activity. Toboggans are the principal mode of transport in Wengen and only proper wooden toboggans are used – there is no interest in trendy French poubelling here. As they all look the same, the rules about the ownership of toboggans are irrelevant. If you tie up your toboggan outside a nightclub and come out to find someone has taken it, you just take someone else's. The system works quite well.

The skiing

There are nursery slopes in the village itself – this is a very pretty place to learn to ski – but to get to the main skiing area, you have to take the mountain railway up to Kleine Scheidegg.

There are some good short runs around Kleine Scheidegg and Wixi, including a black run down to Wixi from Eigergletscher. For a longer run, you can ski right down to Grindelwald Grund and connect with the Grindelwald lift system. (The Jungfrau Region lift pass covers Grindelwald and Mürren, so you are well placed for day excursions to both resorts.)

For some really dramatic skiing, there is the famous Lauberhorn World Cup Downhill course. In fact, Wengen is always at its most exciting in January when the race is held: the town is packed and the atmosphere is tremendous.

One of the great delights of skiing on the Kleine Scheidegg area is the four-mile run back to Wengen that you can enjoy every afternoon. This run is pretty and interesting but easy enough for most intermediates.

Non-skiers or inveterate sightseers should make the trip up into the Jungfrau mountain. Trains leave from Kleine Scheidegg and take you up through the mountain, stopping halfway for you to look out of the mountain through specially-built windows. At the top of the Jungfrau, there are all sorts of Disneyland-style tourist delights, including a palace carved out of ice and husky-dog rides. (This excursion is not included on the lift pass.)

Lunches

The **Wengernalp** is one of the best places to have lunch on a sunny day but, although the terrace has seating for 200, you need to book in advance to be sure of a table. There are dramatic views of the forbidding north face of the Eiger, as well as a remarkably comprehensive menu and the best carrot cake *(reublitorte)* in the Jungfrau region.

By the Lauberhorn T-bar near Kleine Scheidegg is the **Grindelwald Blick,** which is famous for having a perfectly framed view of the Eiger through the window of the ladies' loo. It also serves excellent hot chocolate. At the end of the day, **Mary's Café** at Inner Wengen and the **Café Oberland** are both strongly recommended as pit-stops for that final glass or two of Glühwein.

During the busy weekends (Wengen gets a lots of Swiss and German weekend visitors), all the mountain restaurants are packed, but you will usually find a seat if you bother to go up to the **Eigergletscher** restaurant.

Ski schools

Wengen Ski School is famous throughout Britain as the school where bearded, Channel Four guru, Ali Ross, used to teach. He doesn't work there any longer, but there are still signs of a strong British influence in the school – the instructors all have Event suits, for instance. English is spoken very well in the ski school, as it is all over Wengen. The older instructors are generally felt to be slightly less good than the younger ones, but the overall standard is very high. There is an alternative Kleine Scheidegg ski school but it has no real advantages.

The instructors you see clad in horrid maroon and green suits belong to Club Med (or Club Frog as it is known locally), which has taken over 400 beds in the Palace Hotel. But at least this resort is pretty well Swede-free.

Ski shops

The best ski shop in Wengen is Molitor. Herr Molitor is famous for having won the Lauberhorn five years in succession in the 1930s. He is a wonderful, friendly character and provides a very good service for the English companies operating in Wengen.

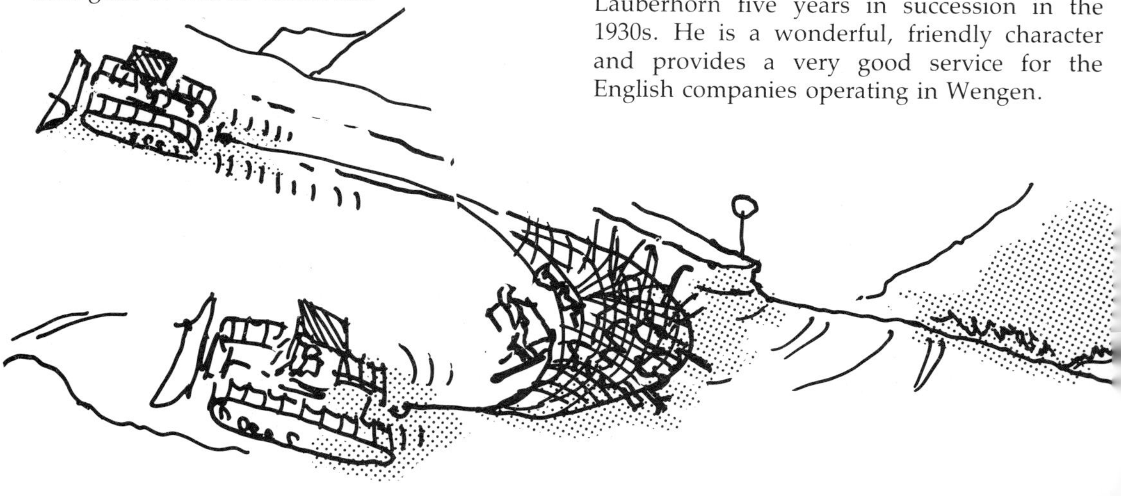

ZERMATT

If the 25 resorts featured in this book were to be listed in order of merit, there can be little doubt that Zermatt would be in the top three – possibly even in first place. In almost every category by which a ski resort can be judged, Zermatt scores highly. It goes up higher than any other resort in Europe; it is a carefree, pretty village with stunning views of the Matterhorn; it has three large skiing areas suitable for intermediates and experts alike; it has more and better mountain restaurants that any other resort in Europe; and it has lively, varied nightlife.

No matter where you have skied before, it is almost impossible to be disappointed by Zermatt. It has an incredibly romantic atmosphere which leaves almost no one unaffected. There are still a lot of rustic old Valaisian shepherds' huts here and all the newer chalets and hotels have been built in chalet style, so are fairly unobtrusive. The ever-changing views of the Matterhorn dominate the village and never cease to fascinate.

Zermatt is completely car-free: the only forms of transport are sleighs and almost silent electric buggies that have a worrying habit of creeping up behind you when you're not looking. Cars and coaches, in fact, have to stay down the valley at Täsch, from where you take a shuttle, rack railway to Zermatt. (Täsch can be chaotic at peak times on Saturdays, without a luggage trolley in sight. Normally, you can load the trolleys and then wheel them onto a special luggage van in the middle of the train.) The nearest airport is Geneva, which is some three-and-a-half-hours' drive away. (It is worth noting that traffic delays are much rarer between Geneva and resorts in the French Savoie.)

There are through-trains to Zermatt from Brig and Visp, both stations on the main Rhône railway line between Paris and Milan. There is also a direct link with St Moritz via the Glacier Express.

Accommodation

Being in Switzerland, Zermatt is by no means a cheap resort, so chalet holidays here make good sense. Good chalets are not easily available but both Bladon Lines, John Morgan and Supertravel have a reasonable selection. (Most of the chalets here tend to be old and very wooden with lots of creaking floorboards, but then that's part of the charm.) There is a limited amount of self-catering available but this does not seem to be a very popular option with the British.

Zermatt boasts a number of classic Swiss hotels. These include the **Mont Cervin******* and **Zermatterhof******, both of which have horse-drawn carriages to meet you at the station. The **Monte Rosa****** is nearly as good. It was one of the first hotels to be built in Zermatt. The **Schweizerhof****** and the **Alex****** offer a younger, livelier atmosphere. The **Sport Hotel***** is a small, friendly hotel, presided over by the charming Leo. Like so many people in Zermatt, he speaks excellent English. This hotel is always the venue for the weekly SCGB drinks party on Thursdays.

All the above hotels are pretty expensive but if you want something much cheaper, there are many bed and breakfast places, including the **Hotel Romantica**, where you can, if you wish, stay in one of the three 'mazot' huts in the garden. The bed and breakfast option, of course, gives you the opportunity to eat out every night.

Nowhere in Zermatt is convenient for all three ski areas, but if you know the resort well you can arrange to stay nearest the area you like best. Everyone in Zermatt has to do quite a bit of walking, or failing that take electric or horse-drawn taxis. (Be warned: you don't know what rudeness is, until you have seen a Zermatt taxi driver arguing.)

Après-ski

Unlike most resorts, après-ski in Zermatt begins up the mountain. There is a well-established tradition in Zermatt of stopping at a little hut on the run home for early-evening drinks, stay there until 7 or 8 o'clock, then ski down the last few hundred yards. On the Sunnega side, there's **Othmar's Hutte** and the **Olympia Stube**; on the Gornergrat, there's **Toni's**; and on the Kleine Matterhorn section, there's **Blatten** and **Zum See**.

In the village itself, the **Papperla Pub** is a good cheapish pre-dinner meeting place. It serves a wide range of beers from around the world, as well as bar food. It even has a couple of squash courts in the basement. **Elsie's Bar** has long been a key place for pre-prandials and snails, but it is small and rather crowded with fur-coat wearers, so it is advisable to reserve a table. The **S'Alt Hischi**, down what is known as Cat Piss Alley, is good for drinks and cheap meals. Hotel bars are also popular for drinks before dinner, particularly the ancient **Monte Rosa**. The tiny bar of the **Mazot** is another genial drinking place.

However, the Mazot is most famous as a restaurant – it is arguably the best in Zermatt – specialising in grilled lamb *au feu du bois*. It is not cheap but it is excellent. You need to book several days in advance.

The **Tenne** Hotel (now owned by the Alex Hotel) also does very good lamb and other kinds of grills. The **Stockhorn** is an up-market fondue restaurant that does a particularly food *fondue chinoise*. **Chez Gaby** is a small cosy upstairs-downstairs restaurant specialising in grilled meats.

As you would expect, the hotels also provide good food. The **Pollux** has a Restaurant Français that has a good reputation, and the **Arvenstube** deals in Swiss-German specialities and, towards the end of the season, has a lot of fresh asparagus. The **Whymperstube** and the Monte Rosa Hotel are also popular for dinner, as is the restaurant at the **Zermatterhof**. The **Bahnhof** restaurant may sound an unlikely suggestion for dinner, but, in fact, this is a wonderfully old-fashioned place with good food, attentive, flamboyant service and reasonable prices. This is also the best place to come for breakfast either if you are seeing somebody off on a train, or if you have been up all night – quite likely at Fasching, carnival time, in February.

For a really cheap meal, you cannot beat the **Brown Cow** (also known as the BC or the Green Sheep) in the Hotel Post. This is a glorified snack bar which does particularly good BLTs (bacon, lettuce and tomato toasted sandwiches). The sign in the men's loo 'Being a ski bum is sitting in the Brown Cow on a sunny day' says it all. Another ski bum haunt is the **North Wall Bar**, otherwise known as Vince's, which serves good, cheap pizzas. **Toni's Grotta** is likewise good for pizzas and Italian food generally, as is his mountain restaurant on Gornergrat.

At some point during the evenings, you are almost bound to end up in a part of the vast Hotel Post empire which has been built up over the past 30 years by American Karl Ivarsson. This includes **Le Village**, the most popular disco in Zermatt. Around Le Village dancefloor is a gallery housing the **Spaghetti Factory** Italian restaurant. If you book a table here, you can keep it for the whole night, which means you can go down to dance and then retire to your own table. This is quite an advantage as Le Village gets quite full.

The Pink Elephant, also known as the Piano Bar, is one of the more refined areas of the Hotel Post. The décor is art nouveau but no one can understand why the enormous plaster-of-Paris elephant is blue, not pink. There is often live jazz music or a pianist here and it's a comfortable place to drink cocktails or champagne and get away from the noise of the discos, particularly if someone else is paying.

The Post has two other restaurants, the **Zamoura** which is an expensive fish restaurant named after the owner's boat in the Mediterranean, and the **Broken Steak Bar** which does good-value, Mexican-style food.

The Zermatt in-crowd tends to gravitate towards the **Broken Bar** itself, in the basement of the Post, where they drink spirits at around SF12 a time and dance to good music on a smallish dancefloor. The principal feature of this disco is 'The Barrel', a cross-section of a large wooden barrel, on top of which great numbers of people attempt to dance at the same time, sometimes with disastrous results.

The **Hotel Alex** is also great fun after dinner. There is an enormous bar-disco complex with three separate dancefloors, although the same music is played everywhere. There are lots of comfortable seating areas and the music is never so loud that it kills conversation. (They play an amusing selection of good records here – not just boring music.) Mad George is the great character behind the bar – he has a ship's bell which he rings vigorously every so often for no particular reason. He also creates weird cocktails, including his Vitamin C Special, which is full of any alcohol he happens to have left over.

Usual après-ski entertainments here include ten-pin bowling beneath the **Hotel Bristol** and an indoor tennis court at the Hotel Alex. There are also plenty of hotel swimming pools, several of which are open to the public at a nominal charge.

The skiing

There are three main ski areas in Zermatt: Schwarzee/Trockener Steg/Kleine Matterhorn, Riffleberg/Gornergrat/Stockhorn and Sunnega/ Blauherd/Unterrothorn. The last two connect up with each other in both directions, but if you start on the first system you cannot get into the other two. (You can, however, ski across from Gornergrat to Furri on the Schwarzee system.)

The Schwarzee/Trockener Steg/Kleine Matterhorn system takes you up to the highest ski lift station in Europe, which is the top of the Kleine Matterhorn (3820m).

Although the lift systems here are fairly modern, queues still develop. A six-man telecabine or an oldish cable car take you up to Furri. From here, you can either go on up to Schwarzee or Furg by cable car or take the new 125-person cable car up to Trockener Steg. From Trockener Steg, you can then take a 100-person cable car up to the Kleine Matterhorn. This really is a spectacular ride, since the top station is actually built into the rock near the top of the mountain – and when you come out of the cable car, you have to walk a couple of hundred yards along a tunnel through the mountain before emerging at the back of the Kleine Matterhorn. This is no place to hang about even on a relatively warm day, so secure your boots, gloves and hat while you're still in the tunnel.

The descent from the Kleine Matterhorn starts with a long, broad and often windswept schuss: this is cold and not particularly exciting. In fact, the skiing opened up by this section of the Kleine Matterhorn cable car is by no means thrilling, but it does give good access to the runs over to Cervinia in Italy and it also improves the summer skiing possibilities. (Going over to Cervinia will cost you a not inconsiderable supplement of SF23. Good skiers should be warned that the runs are not very exciting, but it's a fun excursion for intermediates.)

There are a couple of T-bars stretching out from Trockener Steg, both of which serve fairly broad, easy slopes that are ideal for beginners, but it's a long way up for beginners to come and the runs below here are much more difficult. The runs down from Trockener Steg to Furg and Furri and the Aroleid from Schwarzee to Furri are all pretty demanding. Over beyond Schwarzee are good narrow black runs, like Mamatt and Tiefbach.

The main route up the Gornergrat is by mountain railway from the centre of town. This railway winds its way prettily, but rather laboriously up the mountain and the journey from bottom to top can take up to an hour. Many skiers treat this journey like a routine piece of commuting and bring their newspapers with them. (You can buy one-day-old copies of *The Times* at the newspaper stall just opposite the bottom station.) Below the top station of the mountain railway are several broad, open pistes well suited to intermediate skiers.

However, it you go up from Gornergrat to Stockhorn, something you can normally only do from the beginning of February onwards (any earlier it's too cold), you get to the Stockhorn and some of the most difficult skiing Zermatt has to offer. There are some wonderful powder runs on the north-facing slopes down to Triftji and Grunsee. The area is not often pisted by machines, so there is still good powder skiing to be had here several days after a snowfall. There are also one or two pretty taxing mogulfields. There is now a new cable car which cuts out the treacherous walk along the ridge from the top of Triftji (Rote Nase) to the Gornergrat cable car at Hohtalli.

From Grant and Findeln, you can get connecting lifts that you take up to Sunnega and Blauherd. Alternatively, you can get up to Sunnega from the village with great speed on the famous Sunnega Express, an underground funicular railway that carries more than 2000 people an hour. The runs on the south side of this area are generally fairly easy but the runs on the north side, the Chamois and the Marmotte down from the Unterrothorn and the National down from Blauherd to the bottom of the valley are all very demanding – even for good skiers.

Do not believe all you read in brochures about queues having been eliminated in Zermatt: they haven't. You find queues in different places at different times all over the resort, but they are seldom very serious and you just have to put up with them. The Sunnega area is probably the best one to ski if you are impatient to get up the mountain.

Because Zermatt is not a purpose-built resort, you will have to do a certain amount of walking in your ski boots carrying your skis. For those rich and enthusiastic enough to indulge in helicopter skiing, Zermatt offers some of the best possibilities in Europe – the most popular mountains for this are the Monte Rosa and the Aeschihorn. Details are available from Air Zermatt.

Lunches

For people who are as serious about their lunches as they are about their skiing, Zermatt is the ultimate resort. There are about 40 mountain restaurants in the area and this book cannot hope to cover them all in detail. For a full rundown, you must buy, beg, borrow or steal a copy of the *Zermatt Good Food Guide* pamphlet which was written by Julie Norman, who repped there for several years. Although now rather out of date, this is the definitive work on the subject and it is worth going to some trouble to get hold of it. (As Julie no longer spends the season in Zermatt, the guide is not really for sale any more.)

As a general rule, you should aim to eat in one of the little wooden huts scattered about the mountainsides, not in the large concrete restaurants that are built into the lift stations. At the Schwarzee end of town, **Simi's** is a little place below the Furri cable car station. It is owned by Simi Biner who is also head of the Ski School. It does excellent *Rösti* and has a small sun terrace. Its one disadvantage is that it faces towards the mountain, so has no real view. **Blatten** is below Simi's on the way down to the village and also has a sun terrace. The inside is built on two floors and to get upstairs you have to negotiate a very precarious, steep ladder. Getting up is easy enough, but people have been known to sustain injuries trying to get down after a heavy drinking session, so if you intend to have a long lunch, have it downstairs.

Between Simi's and Blatten is **Zum See**, a fun place which does superb *Apfelstrudel*. It does very good *fondue chinoise* dinners on Thursday evenings, followed by torchlight descents.

Further down the valley at Findeln is **Enzo's Hutte**, previously called Hans und Gerda's. This can be unequivocally recommended as the Best Mountain Restaurant in the Alps. It has a beautiful south-facing terrace here with fine views of the Matterhorn. There is a step ladder up to the flat roof, where there is an outdoor bar if fine weather. This is a fantastic sun-trap and is known as the Findeln Solarium. It is decorated with plastic palm trees stuck in the snow.

Enzo's is not easy to find: you have to leave your skis at the edge of a tiny wooden hamlet and walk down a small path to get here. Enzo himself is a wonderfully genial young patron and he employs very chic, hard-working, helpful staff, which is just as well as the place is packed on good days. Recommended dishes include the *Tortelloni* and various types of *Käseschnitte* and *Rösti*. Enzo also offers enigmatic dishes like Eskimo Spaghetti (priced on the menu as '?') and Jet Set Toast. There is a short but impressive wine list which includes Louis Roederer and several other types of champagne, some of which he serves by the glass and good Swiss wines, including Dôle Blanche. The most fatal drink here is a kind of coffee known as *Schumli Pflumli*. On a good day, it would be hard for the gastronomic skier to think of anywhere in the world he would rather have lunch than Enzo's Hutte.

A little way above here is another rustic restaurant, **Alpenheim** or Broni's, with beautifully carved wooden seats on the balcony, all carefully placed to get the maximum amount of sunshine. They have an outdoor *feu de bois* grill here which they use in fine weather.

Othmar's Hutte is yet another charming rustic place with a good-sized south-facing terrace. Its slight disadvantage is that once you have come down this far (it is just below the Standart run down from Sunnega), you have to go on all the way down to the bottom of the valley. But this is a very good late afternoon pit-stop, as it offers wonderful spicy *Apfelkuchen*.

Ski schools

There is one ski school here with about 170 instructors, a good proportion of them English-speaking. The standard of teaching is high, particularly at an advanced level. The ski school also provides guides for high mountain expeditions and heli-skiing.

Ski shops

There is a fixed tariff for ski hire, so prices do not vary from shop to shop and the standard of equipment is generally very high. The trendiest shop for fashion skiwear is Bayard Sport, which has a couple of branches. Head, Ellesse and Jet Set are the most fashionable labels in Zermatt.

SNOWSPEAK GLOSSARY

Airport Place where you seem to spend most of your skiing holiday.

Altitude (As in "It must be the") excuse used to explain crush on chalet girl.

Apremont Slightly pétillant white wine much drunk in French Savoie resorts.

Après-ski Blanket term used to cover all activities off the slopes.

BASI Mafia of British (i.e. Scottish) ski instructors often encountered in Alpine bars.

Beer Essential internal lubrication for relaxed skiing. Much used by BASI, see above. Readily available in all ski resorts.

Bird's Nesting Curious off-piste ritual practised exclusively by members of the SCGB.

Blood Wagon Reason for a crowd of gawping skiers in the middle of the piste. Actually a stretcher.

Bubble One of many British attempts to translate telecabine.

Bus Thing that drives away from the bottom lift station when driver sees you running towards it in your ski boots juggling your skis in your hands.

Cable-bindings What anybody who has been skiing for more than 10 years bores on about to more recent converts.

Cable-car Claustrophobia-inducing metal box containing up to 160 skiers swinging from a thin wire several hundred feet up in the air.

Chains Things that get twisted round the axle of your car. 'Man was born to ski but is everywhere putting on chains.'

Chalet Girl Real names: Caroline, Sophie, Lucinda, Henrietta. Known as Kettle, Bucket, Boot, Pudding.

Charter Flight Airborne equivalent of cattle truck.

Dead Ant Sloane Ranger game beloved of chalet girls in which they lie down on the piste and wave their skis and sticks in the air.

Delay See *Airport.*

Dôle Red Swiss wine that gives new meaning to the phrase 'Life on the Dole.'

Edge Excuse for falling. As in phrase 'I caught an edge.'

Egg Another British attempt to translate telecabine.

Fendant Pétillant Swiss white wine, the ruin of many a good skier.

Fohn Warm wind used as excuse for just about everything in the Alps, from murder to skiing badly.

Fondue Time-honoured Alpine ceremony in which locals rip-off visiting skiers by charging a lot of money for a bowl of congealed cheese.

Gamay Red wine of French Savoie.

Glühwein (Usually) clever way of selling undrinkable red wine by heating it up and putting a slice of orange in it. (Occasionally) delicious spicy mulled wine.

Goggles Headgear that mists up and makes it impossible to see the next bump.

Gondola Yet another British attempt to translate telecabine.

Hang-gliding Way of getting down a mountain if you are scared of skiing.

Heli-skiing Something rich skiers boast about incessantly.

Hip-flask Invaluable source of courage and consolation. Necessary at top and bottom of really terrifying runs.

Hired equipment Another useful scapegoat for bad skiers.

Ice-bar Outdoor refreshment post where you can get a drink without even having to take your skis off.

Jagertee Fatal Austrian drink whose relationship to tea is very tenuous.

Kick turn Useful type of turn you learned at ski school but now do not dare to attempt.

Kir Way of selling undrinkable white wine by flavouring it with cassis. See also *Glühwein.*

Langlauf Cross-country skiing, generally indulged in by geriatrics, freaks and masochists.

Lift pass That which you discover you have left at home when you get to the bottom of the lift in the morning.

Long lunches In bad weather these can become the highlight of the holiday.

Mogul Thing that you have difficulty turning on/around/above/below/beside.

Monoskier Show-off.

Motorway Type of easy broad piste about which the good skier is always disparaging but secretly enjoys.

Nightclub Place where lonely punters hope in vain to pick up a chalet girl. Most expensive place visited on the average ski holiday.

Nursery slopes Ego-boosting area where there are guaranteed to be lots of skiers much worse than oneself.

Off-piste Often much nastier conditions than on-piste, but off-piste skiers never admit this.

Parallel turns What most skiers think they do.

Piste Marked ski run where most skiers succeed in not bumping into each other most of the time.

Pizzeria Essential component of ski resort: rendezvous point for ski-bums.

Pole That which you keep forgetting to plant.

Poma Type of one-person drag lift which normally lifts you three feet in air as you get on.

Poubelling Method of sliding down snowy slope wearing a black plastic dustbin liner. V. popular with chalet girls.

Queues Opportunity to vent pent-up aggression and suppressed xenophobia.

Raclette Universal 'regional' speciality of melted cheese served with gherkins, pickled onions and potatoes. Induces incredible thirst which keeps you awake all night.

Ratrac Big red piste-bashing machine that nearly knocks you over.

Schuss The most fun, effortless part of skiing.

Ski Bob Snow tricycle that failed to catch on the 1960s and 1970s.

Ski bum Suntanned, laid-back Antipodean who skis well and has affairs with several chalet girls at once.

Snow Volatile white commodity of which there is always too much or not enough.

T-Bar Type of drag lift for two persons; each attempts to push the other off.

Transfer What always seems like 12 hours on an unventilated coach full of screaming babies in a traffic jam between airport and resort.

Uphill struggle Paradoxically, learning to ski is this.

Vodka Feigen Useful form of Dutch courage, often on sale in Austrian ice-bars. Because the figs taste horrid, you can pretend it is medicinal rather than pleasurable.

Wall Word used to describe vagely steep slope in boastful après-ski talk.

Wally Skier who traverses the piste in unpredictable, out-of-control manner, careering in front of you just as you are about to do a neat turn. Usually British.

White-out Complete loss of vision and co-ordination in which goggles are no use.

Williamine Pear eau-de-vie made and consumed in great quantities in the Valais region of Switzerland.

Xenophobia Practising this helps to pass the time in lift queues.

Yodel Alpine resident's method of scaring the tourists.

Zip Piece of equipment that always gets stuck open in sub-zero temperatures and gets stuck shut in blistering sunshine.

THERE TO WORK OR THERE TO PLAY?

HOW TO BE A CHALET GIRL

How to apply

You need to apply earlier and earlier every year – some of the big companies now start interviewing at the end of May – just a few weeks after the end of the last season.

Ideally, your application form should be returned by the middle of May, since if you are one of the first to be accepted, then you have a better chance of choosing your resort. (Those returning, more faithful than before, get first choice of resorts and chalets: the most popular resorts just now are Courchevel, Méribel, Verbier, Val d'Isère and St Anton.)

Later applications still stand a chance – some companies have vacancies at the end of September. Very late applications (late November/early December) also stand a very good chance since people always drop out at the last minute and replacements have to be found quickly. Sometimes it worth re-applying at this stage even if you have previously been rejected.

The leading tour operators seldom advertise for staff: you have to approach them and ask for an application form. Make sure you are applying for a job that you are putatively capable of doing: don't apply to be a rep if you don't speak the language fluently, don't apply to be a chalet girl if you can't cook.

In the first instance, it is worth applying to as many potential employers as possible – you may be offered more than one job, but that means you will probably be able to choose between resorts or possibly between working on your own or with others. (Wages, such as they are, do not vary much between companies.)

Some of the bigger companies put age limits on the jobs, but you can get round these if you know somebody in the company who can get you an interview. Alternatively, you can approach a smaller company where you will be more likely to get an interview regardless of age. These are the most common jobs and the usual age limits:

Cleaner or Scrubber (17–18+) These are employed in jumbo chalets or chalet-hotels. You do not need to be able to cook beyond being able to prepare breakfast. Most of your work will be cleaning bedrooms, bathrooms etc.

Chalet Girl (21+) You should have some kind of formal cooking qualification (Cordon Bleu or equivalent) and preferably some practical experience in a wine bar or restaurant. The age limit here really has nothing to do with cooking ability, it is just that more mature girls are better able to fend off the advances of lecherous punters without getting too worked up.

Cook/Chef (20+) These positions exist only in the larger chalets. You should have some experience and preferably a qualification in catering rather than 'private' cooking. You must be able to cook for 50 people.

Plongeur/MBO (18–20+) There are not many jobs for males in the chalet business, so these positions are much sought after. You can sometimes get one of these jobs between leaving school and starting at university, but generally the employers prefer people slightly older. Duties vary, but involve washing up, driving, clearing snow, serving in a bar, consoling lovesick chalet girls, etc. (MBO means either Maintenance and Buildings Officer or Muscle-Bound Oaf.)

Ski Guides (21+) These jobs are for either sex and the main requirement is that you are a good, responsible and patient skier. You do not need a teaching qualification as you are not allowed to teach, but a BASI certificate or the SCGB Rep's qualification help. Make sure your employer has adequate insurance so that you will not be personally liable in the event of a catastrophe. Remember, also, that this job does not leave you a lot of time for skiing on your own – often you will be skiing with people much less good than yourself.

Tour Operator's Representative (24–30) You must be fluent in the language of the resort in which you will be working, as well as literate, numerate and efficient. You are responsible for the welfare of all your company's clients and staff in the resort, so tact is an important attribute. Open to both sexes although most reps seem to be girls.

Most application forms just ask you to give details of nationality (Australians, New Zealanders and South Africans are weeded out immediately because of work permit problems), education, qualifications and previous experience. However, if you are applying to be a chalet girl you will have to complete an additional questionnaire with cookery questions. This will usually ask you for sample menus, as well as asking about budgets and quantities. It is worth getting a very good cook to help you with this form as it will decide whether or not you get an interview.

The interview

For most of these jobs, the interviews are fairly conventional, although some companies now use group interviews for some of the less important jobs. In this case, you will first be seen individually, but only for a couple of minutes; what is important is that your personality comes across well – but not too strongly – in the group discussion. Don't bluff if you can't carry it off: never say you know a ski area well if you don't, as you are likely to be cross-examined about it. If you say you speak a foreign language fluently, you will probably be expected to converse in it.

If you are being interviewed for a chalet girl job, then be prepared to answers questions about the menus you suggested. Make sure you know ten ways of cooking potatoes and interesting ways of re-using cold chicken. If asked for further menu suggestions, you must make sure they sound interesting: chicken casserole won't get you the job whereas chicken with orange and avocado just might. Remember that most operators have fairly tight budgets so make sure that you show a great sense of economy. The questions that really sort out the cooks from the bottle-washers are those about the quantity of meat required to feed x punters. The question about garnishes is a trick one: the answer is always chopped parsley as it is pretty well the only garnish available in Alpine supermarkets.

If you get the job – fine. If not, do not make a fuss or this will ruin your chances for next year or as a last-minute substitute. The greatest mistake is to allow your parents to ring up and complain about your rejection, especially if they claim they know one of the directors.

The briefings

In the middle of November most companies hold briefing sessions in London for all their staff. The length of these briefings varies between a couple of days and a week. You will learn about the company's general structure and policies as well as having lessons in basic accounting. You will also be issued with your company sweatshirt, puffa or parrot jacket.

Your pay will be confirmed at this stage, but remember that nobody is a chalet girl for the money. An average chalet girl wage is only £25 per week, but you do also get free board and lodging (though it's scarcely luxurious), free lift pass, free ski hire and, if you treat them properly, drinks bought by the punters. As a rule, you are more likely to be bought drinks and dinner by your punters if you are working in a small chalet than if you are part of a large team.

The job

Chalet girls usually arrive in a resort early in December, a week or so before the first lot of punters. Use this time to ingratiate yourself into the local community as much as possible. It always helps to speak, or attempt to speak the local language and you should always make a conscious effort to learn new words and phrases. The local tradesmen will be very important to you so start up some harmless (preferably) flirtation right away. If you always invite the butcher's delivery boy in for a coffee or a beer, then you will find that your meat has less fat on it than the stuff he's going to deliver to the unfriendly girls down the road.

Get to know the layout of your local supermarket, the quicker you get your shopping done the quicker you get on the piste. Do not make the mistake of imagining you are the first person to discover that supermarkets sell lots of luxury goods, which are nothing to do with your cooking but which can be charged to the same account. Just remember that if you get greedy you will probably get caught. (Most of the people who check your accounts have worked in the Alps themselves.)

Walking into bars – a string of your punters in tow with the obvious expectation of a free drink – does not go down well. It tends to aggravate bar owners. A more subtle, friendly approach will probably be much more successful in the long run. The bar owners look after the people who bring them custom, as do restaurateurs.

Get to know the other British people working in the resort as soon as possible: you never know when you may need to borrow spices or firewood. If the owners of your chalet live in your resort, always be especially nice to them, otherwise they can make your life hell. Establish good relations with the ski hire shop – this could mean you will be given a particularly good pair of skis. Flirt a little with the lift men and you should never have to queue for very long. The same technique will work with the doormen of the local discos. Above all, make sure you have good relations with the rep who is in charge of you – she must be able to trust you.

As far as the punters are concerned, you will find that most groups fit into one of three categories: 'desperate', 'pleasant', and 'really, really nice'. In an average season of 16 weeks, you should expect three with 'desperate' punters, ten with 'pleasant' punters and three with 'really, really nice' punters. When a new group arrives, the best policy is just to be jolly and polite until they indicate which category they are in and how much or little they wish to socialise with you. Try not to get too attached to any particular group of punters, as it can make you incredibly miserable when the new and comparatively dreary group arrives. Affairs with punters are very difficult to orchestrate because chalets have very few single rooms, not to mention notoriously thin walls. But there is nothing to stop you lining something up for your return to Britain. Affairs with punters are, at any rate, preferable to affairs with married ski instructors or Australian ski bums living in caravans, both of which are likely to result in dismissal. (If you are in Verbier, be especially careful as it is the herpes capital of the Alps.)

Your season is likely to get better and better as the months go by – not only does the weather get better, but you learn the shortcuts and get out skiing much earlier. This is one of the advantages of doing a second season – you know the ropes and you almost cease to think of the job as work.

Three main employers:

Ski Supertravel, 22 Hans Place, London SW1X 0EP (01-584 5060)

Bladon Lines, 56–70 Putney High Street, London SW15 1SF (01-785 2200)

John Morgan Travel, Meon House, Petersfield, Hampshire GU32 3JN (0730-68621)

Other employers:

Activity Travel, 19 Castle Street, Edinburgh EH2 3AH (031-225 9457)

Club Mark Warner, 20 Kensington Church Street, London W8 4EP (01-938 1851)

Ski-Val, 91 Wembley Park Drive, Wembley, Middlesex HA9 8HF (01-200 6080)

Ski West, Eternit House, Felsham Road, London SW15 1SF (01-785 9999)

Snowtime, 23 Denmark Street, London WC2H 8NA (01-836 3237)

HOW TO BE A PERFECT PUNTER

Most chalet operators' brochures contain a homily to the chalet girl, extolling the virtues of the breed. This always contains a subtle exhortation to the punter to be kind to the girls: "It's only natural if the way you treat her is reflected in the way she looks after you. Please, therefore, make their life fun and happy.'

So, to have the perfect holiday you have to be the Perfect Punter. Having booked his holiday with the minimum of fuss, the Perfect Punter obtains from the London office the phone number of the chalet and the names of the chalet girls. He then rings up about a week before he is due to arrive and introduces himself. He gives advance warning of any special requirements – vegeterian meals or a desire to change the night off, for example. He asks if there is anything the girls would like brought out from England and takes orders for famous Alpine non-obtainables like Marmite, Ribena, British Mars Bars (European ones are too chewy), bacon, gelatine and syrup. He will automatically bring out all the latest glossy magazines.

On arrival at the foreign airport, the Perfect Punter will please the rep by not complaining about the late arrival of the flight and not being drunk on his duty-free. Experienced reps can spot the dreadful punters during the first hour of the coach journey: they are often drunk, complaining about the driver being foreign and demanding to stop every few minutes. (Some downmarket punters have now obviated the need for these stops by making use of empty duty-free wine boxes.)

On the coach journey to the resort, the Perfect Punter will have impressed the rep by being one of the few people on the bus who knows what kind of lift pass he wants and having a photograph and the correct foreign currency to pay for it. He will give the rep a knowing sympathetic smile as she struggles to cope with the drunks and incompetents.

On arrival in the resort, the Perfect Punter will not complain because his chalet is not the first on the coach's route round the village. When he gets to his chalet he will take his bags up to his room and then come down to talk to the chalet girls – he will not disappear to spend two hours unpacking. He will immediately offer the girls a drink from his duty-free supplies and deposit the bottle for communal use. (In future evenings, he will always be sure to ferry the necessary gin and tonics into the kitchen.)

The Perfect Punter will not begin his holiday, as an amazing number do, by whingeing. He will not carry his brochure round with him picking holes in the description of the chalet and the resort. He will not preface any of his remarks with those phrases so dreaded by chalet girls and reps: 'It says in the brochure ...', 'Last year when we were in Courchevel ...' and 'Last year when we were with John Morgan ...' On the contrary, the Perfect Punter will have positive things to say about the resort and the chalet and will prove himself to be a lot better informed than the whingers. Although the Perfect Punter will tease chalet girls constantly, he will always sympathise with them and stick up for them if there are any problems with whingeing wally punters.

The Perfect Punter will be very happy to go skiing with the chalet girls, but it will certainly not insist that they ski with him. If he does ski with them, he will buy them lunch, or at least pay for the wine. In return for this, he will be granted that ultimate mark of chalet girl approval, an invitation to their picnic. (These are held at least once a week in spring, and when weather permits earlier in the year.) Most clever chalet girls manage to absorb the cost of these picnics into the budgets and each clique of girls has its favourite picnic spot. Getting the wine up to the spot is always a problem (nobody likes skiing with a heavy rucksack), but one groups of girls in Lech found a solution to this problem last year. They bribed a Ratrac driver to take a couple of cases of (boxed) wine up to their chosen spot and then buried this cache for use over the following few weeks.

In the evenings, the Perfect Punter will always offer to take the girls out drinking before dinner and probably afterwards as well. If he and his friends are rich, the Perfect Punter is very likely to pay a supplement to have better wine with dinner than is normally provided. 'It is only natural' that the chalet girls respond to this by going slightly over-budget and cooking more exciting meals.

On the chalet girls' night off, the Perfect Punter and his friends will have no hesitation in inviting the girls to eat with them as their guests. (It is not uncommon for thoughtless punters to ask the girls to come out and eat with them and then ask for their share of the bill at the end of the meal.) The Perfect Punter will choose somewhere other than the local fondue place for this meal out. He knows that by four weeks into the season most chalet girls and reps have developed an allergy to *fondue bourguignon* and the chip-shop smell that hangs on your clothes for days after you have eaten it.

Before he leaves, the Perfect Punter will always make some parting presentation to his chalet girls – a plant or a scarf, perhaps. He will take their addresses and arrange to see them in London. If he has got on really well with the girls, then he may even book to come back out later in the season. Most important, though, is writing a letter on his most official writing paper to the managing director of the tour operator praising the girls. He knows it means more to them than a more personal letter to the chalet which the bosses never hear about.

Meanwhile, the poor chalet girls are left wondering whether the next lot of punters will make their own beds or expect to have it done for them. (Of course, it's the chalet girls' job to make the beds, but the Perfect Punter knows that they hate this part of it more than anything ...)

LOCATION OF SKI RESORTS

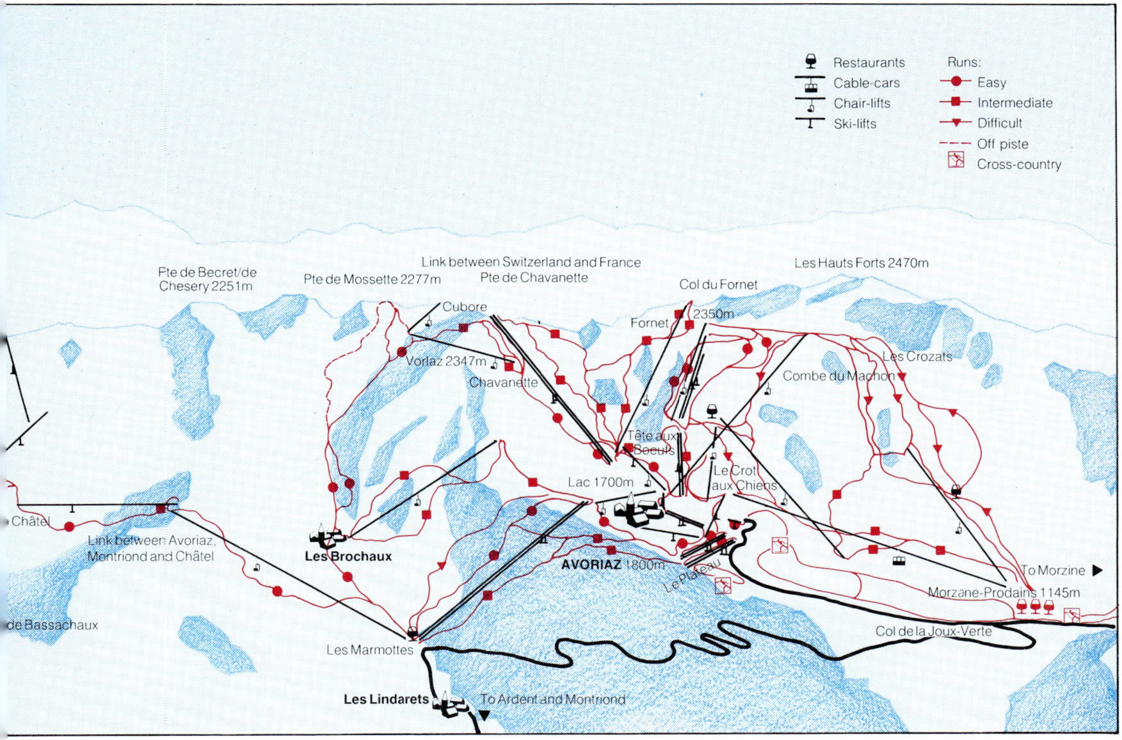
Restaurants
Cable-cars
Chair-lifts
Ski-lifts
Runs:
Easy
Intermediate
Difficult
Off piste
Cross-country
Pte de Becret/de Chesery 2251m
Pte de Mossette 2277m
Link between Switzerland and France
Pte de Chavanette
Les Hauts Forts 2470m
Col du Fornet
Cubore
Fornet
2350m
Vorlaz 2347m
Chavanette
Les Crozats
Combe du Machon
Tête aux Boeufs
Le Crot aux Chiens
Lac 1700m
Châtel
Link between Avoriaz, Montriond and Châtel
Les Brochaux
AVORIAZ 1800m
Le Plateau
To Morzine
Morzane-Prodains 1145m
de Bassachaux
Les Marmottes
Col de la Joux-Verte
Les Lindarets
To Ardent and Montriond

CHAMONIX AREA

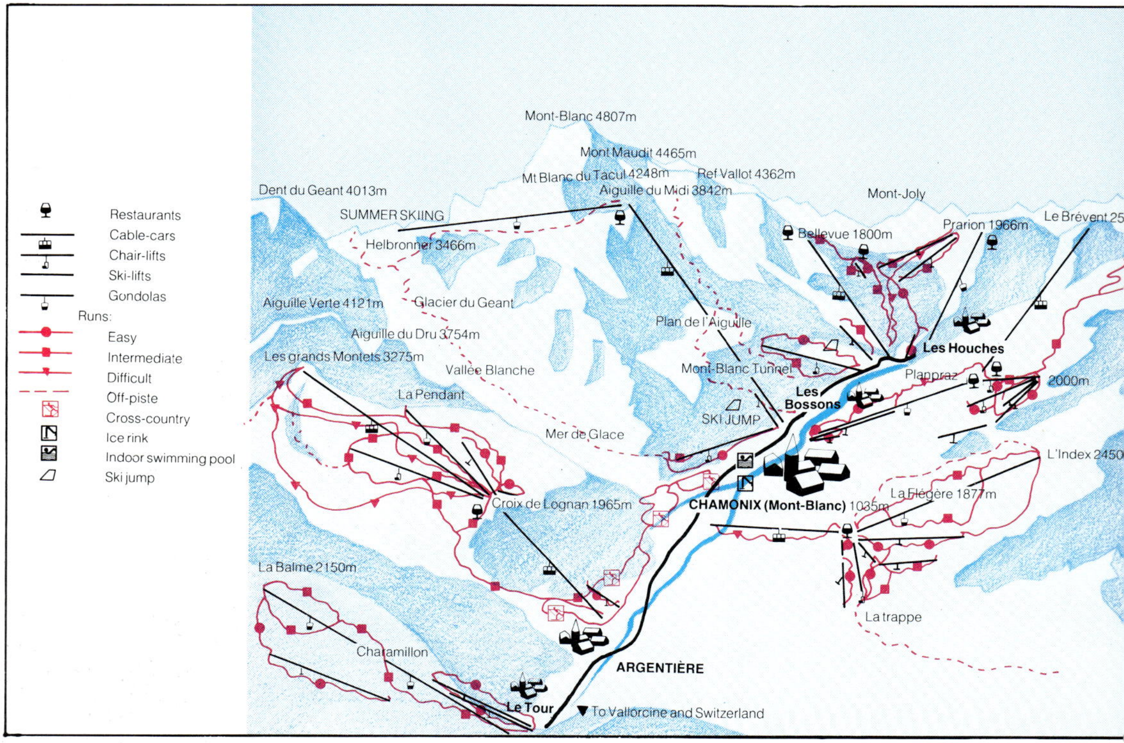

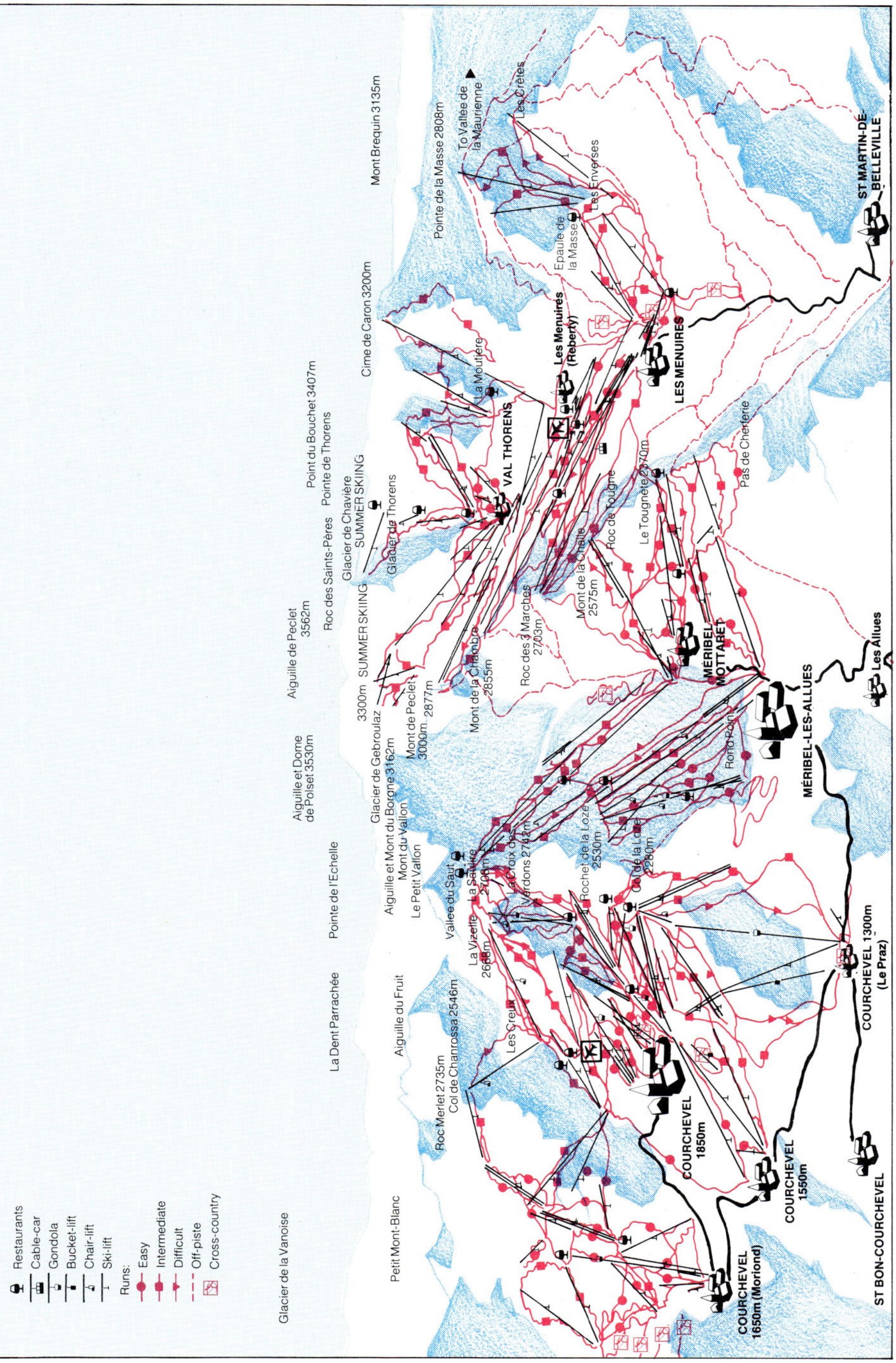
Restaurants
Cable-car
Gondola
Bucket-lift
Chair-lift
Ski-lift
Runs:
Easy
Intermediate
Difficult
Off-piste
Cross-country
Glacier de la Vanoise
Petit Mont-Blanc
La Dent Parrachée
Pointe de l'Echelle
Aiguille et Dome de Polset 3530m
Aiguille de Peclet 3562m
Roc des Saints-Peres
Point du Bouchet 3407m
Pointe de Thorens
Glacier de Chavière
SUMMER SKIING
Cime de Caron 3200m
Mont Brequin 3135m
Pointe de la Masse 2808m
To Vallée de la Maurienne
Les Crêtes
Les Enverses
Epaule de la Masse
Les Menuires (Reberty)
LES MENUIRES
ST MARTIN-DE-BELLEVILLE
La Moutière
VAL THORENS
Glacier de Thorens
Roc de Fougne
Le Tougnete 2470m
Pas de Cherferie
Mont de la Challe 2575m
Roc des 3 Marches 2703m
MERIBEL MOTTARET
Les Allues
MÉRIBEL-LES-ALLUES
Rond Point
3300m
Glacier de Gebroulaz
Mont de Peclet 3000m
2877m
Mont de la Chambre 2855m
Aiguille et Mont du Borgne 3162m
Mont du Vallon
Le Petit Vallon
Vallee du Saut
La Saulire 2708m
La Croix des Verdons 2742m
Rochet de la Loze 2530m
Col de la Loze 2280m
La Vizelle 2668m
Aiguille du Fruit
Les Creux
Roc Merlet 2735m
Col de Chanrossa 2546m
COURCHEVEL 1300m (Le Praz)
COURCHEVEL 1850m
COURCHEVEL 1550m
COURCHEVEL 1650m (Moriond)
ST BON-COURCHEVEL

COURMAYEUR AREA

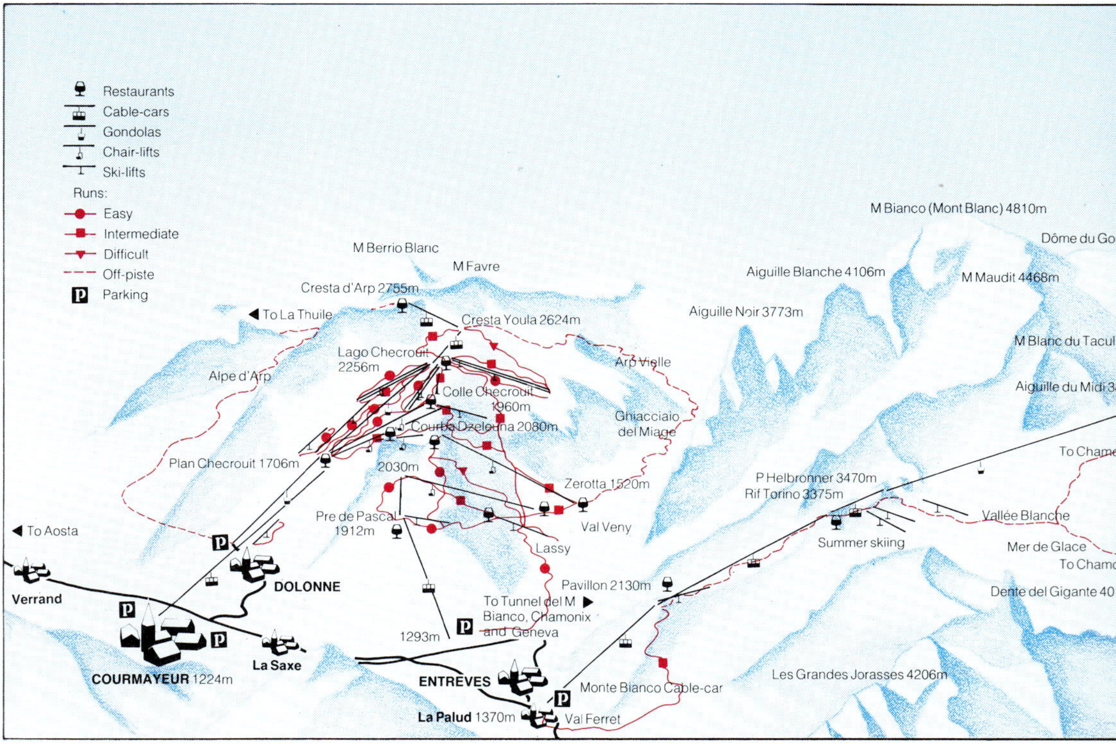

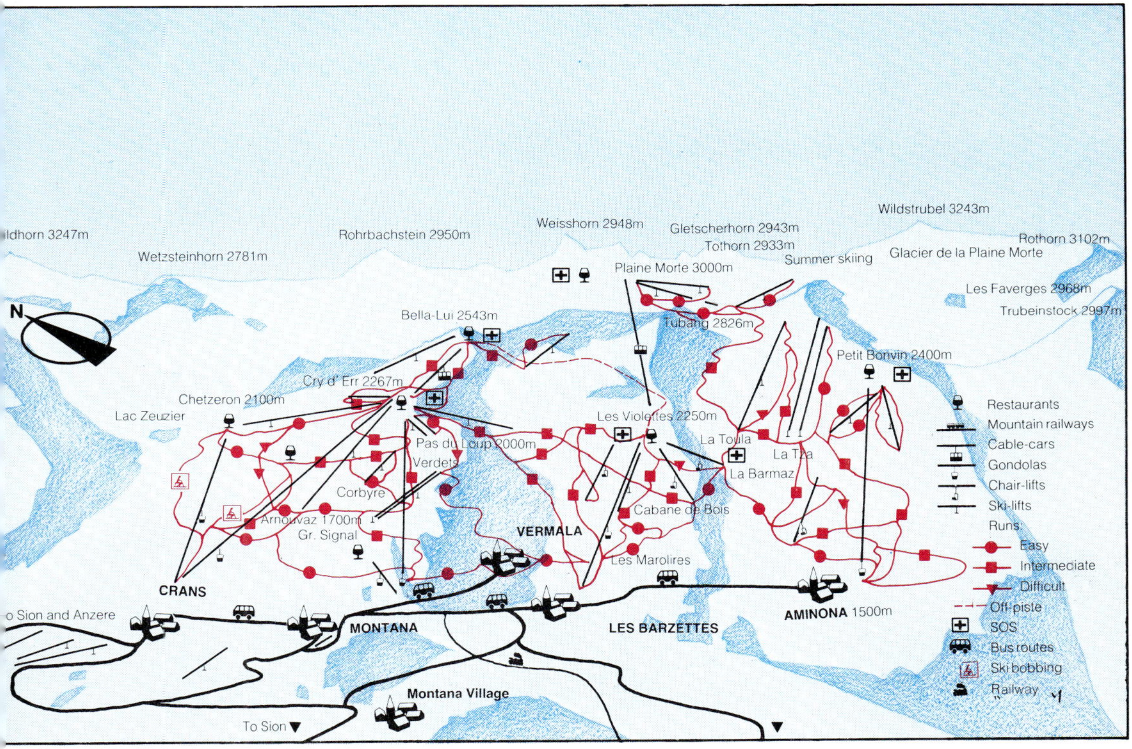

ldhorn 3247m
Wetzsteinhorn 2781m
Rohrbachstein 2950m
Weisshorn 2948m
Gletscherhorn 2943m
Tothorn 2933m
Wildstrubel 3243m
Rothorn 3102m
Glacier de la Plaine Morte
Summer skiing
Plaine Morte 3000m
Les Faverges 2968m
Trubeinstock 2997m
N
Bella-Lui 2543m
Tubang 2826m
Petit Bonvin 2400m
Cry d' Err 2267m
Chetzeron 2100m
Lac Zeuzier
Les Violettes 2250m
Pas du Loup 2000m
Verdets
La Toula
La Tza
La Barmaz
Corbyre
Cabane de Bois
Arnouvaz 1700m
Gr. Signal
VERMALA
Les Marolires
CRANS
o Sion and Anzere
MONTANA
LES BARZETTES
AMINONA 1500m
Montana Village
To Sion
Restaurants
Mountain railways
Cable-cars
Gondolas
Chair-lifts
Ski-lifts
Runs:
Easy
Intermediate
Difficult
Off-piste
SOS
Bus routes
Ski bobbing
Railway

DAVOS (PISCHA/JACOBSHORN/RINERHORN AREA)

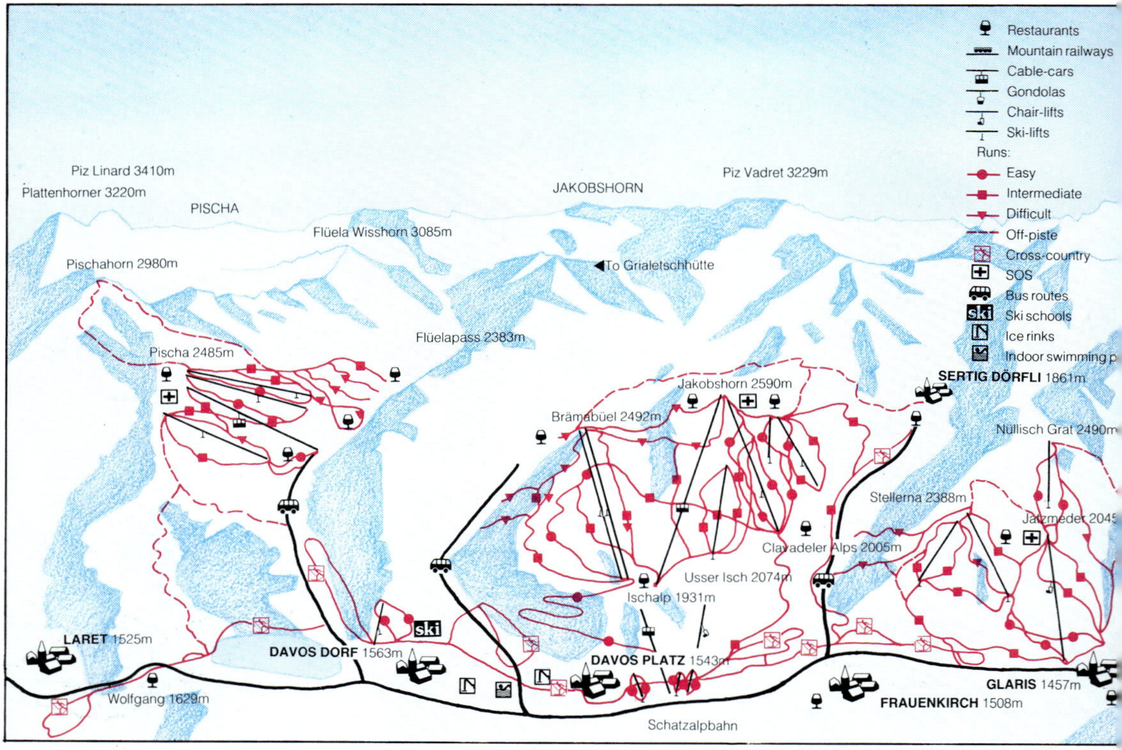

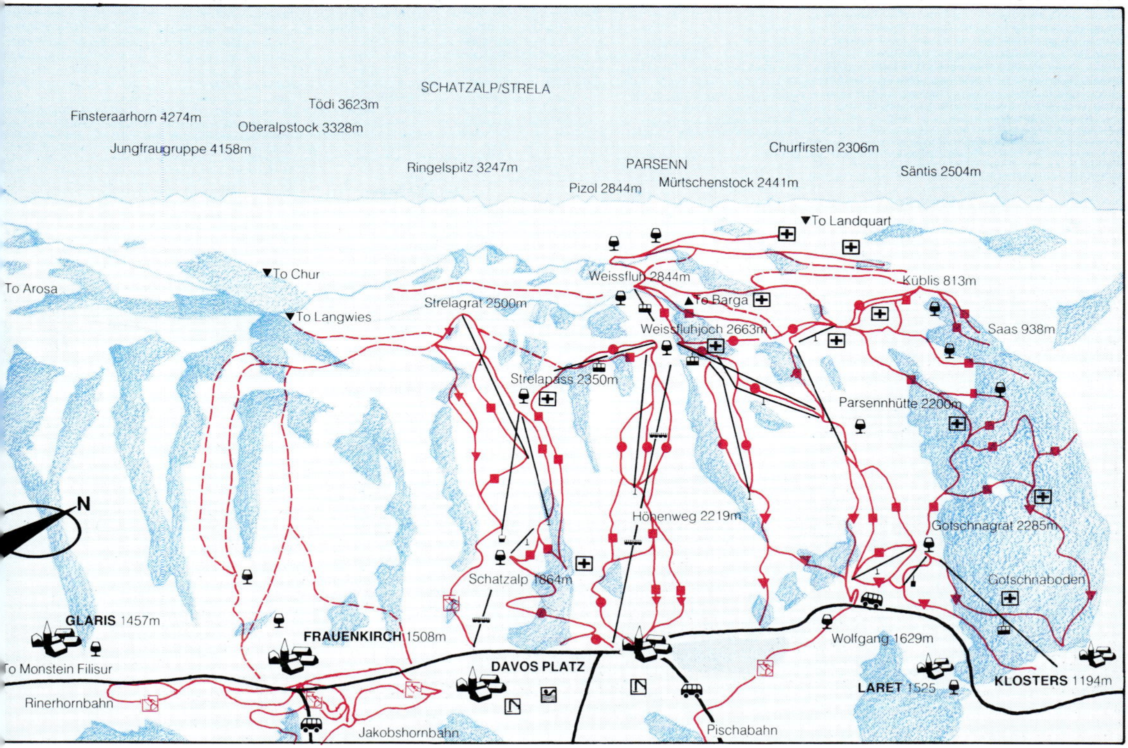
SCHATZALP/STRELA
Tödi 3623m
Finsteraarhorn 4274m
Oberalpstock 3328m
Jungfraugruppe 4158m
Churfirsten 2306m
Ringelspitz 3247m
PARSENN
Säntis 2504m
Pizol 2844m
Mürtschenstock 2441m
To Landquart
To Chur
Weissfluh 2844m
Küblis 813m
To Arosa
To Barga
Strelagrat 2500m
To Langwies
Weissfluhjoch 2663m
Saas 938m
Strelapass 2350m
Parsennhütte 2200m
N
Höhenweg 2219m
Gotschnagrat 2285m
Schatzalp 1864m
Gotschnaboden
GLARIS 1457m
FRAUENKIRCH 1508m
Wolfgang 1629m
To Monstein Filisur
DAVOS PLATZ
LARET 1525
KLOSTERS 1194m
Rinerhornbahn
Jakobshornbahn
Pischabahn

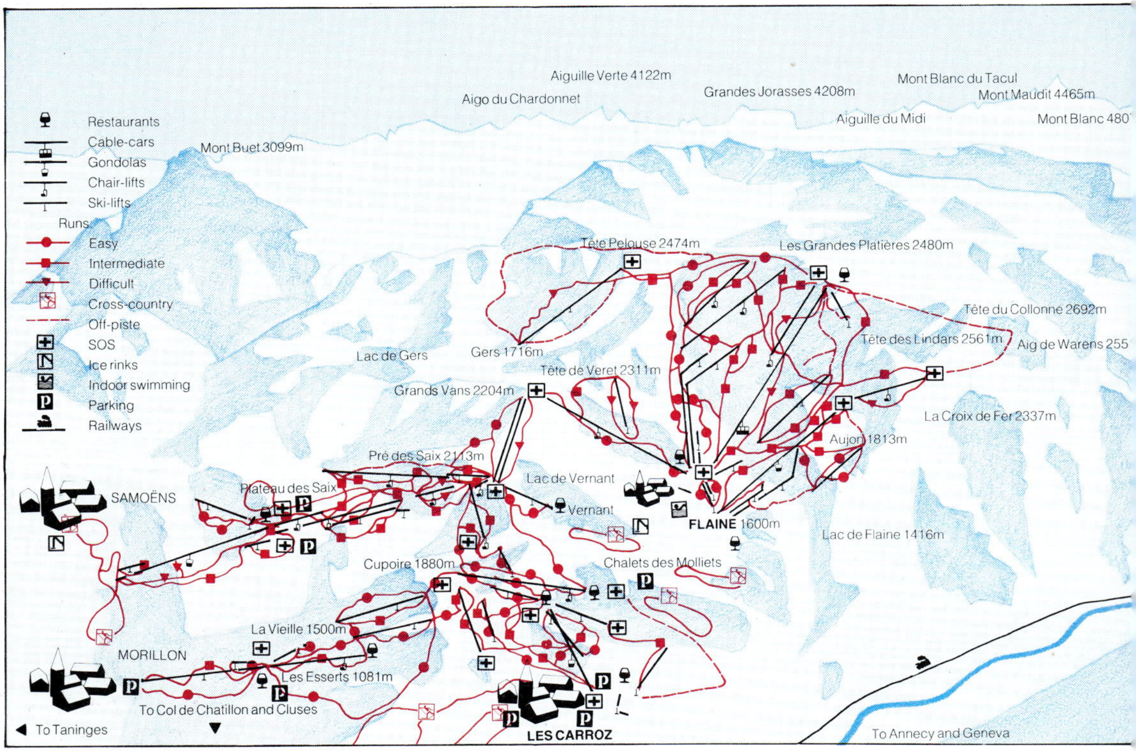
Aiguille Verte 4122m
Aigo du Chardonnet
Grandes Jorasses 4208m
Mont Blanc du Tacul
Mont Maudit 4465m
Aiguille du Midi
Mont Blanc 480
Restaurants
Cable-cars
Gondolas
Chair-lifts
Ski-lifts
Runs:
Easy
Intermediate
Difficult
Cross-country
Off-piste
SOS
Ice rinks
Indoor swimming
Parking
Railways
Mont Buet 3099m
Tête Pelouse 2474m
Les Grandes Platières 2480m
Tête du Collonne 2692m
Tête des Lindars 2561m
Aig de Warens 255
Lac de Gers
Gers 1716m
Tête de Veret 2311m
Grands Vans 2204m
La Croix de Fer 2337m
Aujon 1813m
Pré des Saix 2113m
Lac de Vernant
Vernant
SAMOËNS
Plateau des Saix
FLAINE 1600m
Lac de Flaine 1416m
Cupoire 1880m
Chalets des Molliets
La Vieille 1500m
MORILLON
Les Esserts 1081m
To Col de Chatillon and Cluses
To Taninges
LES CARROZ
To Annecy and Geneva

Restaurants
Cable-cars
Mountain railways
Chair-lifts
Gondolas
Ski-lifts
Runs:
Easy
Intermediate
Difficult
Cross-country
Bus routes
Wildhorn 3264m
Arpelistock 3035m
Gstellihorn 2817m
Oldenhorn 3126m
Les Diablerets 3243m
Mont Blanc 4810m
Dents du Midi 3263m
Giferhorn 2543m
Cabane des Diablerets
Oldenegg
Reusch
Gsteig
Wispile
Lauenen
Wasserngrat
Gandlouenegrat
Saanerslochgrat
Rinderberg
Hornberg
Horneggli
Lochstafel
Oeschseite
Rellerligrat 1834m
Hugeligrat 1901m
La Videmanette
La Braye
Rocher du Midi 2097m
Col des Mosses
Monts Chevreuils
Les Moulins
Rossinière
To Montreux and Genève
CHÂTEAU D'OEUX
ROUGEMONT
SAANEN
GSTAAD SCHÖNRIED
SAANENMÖSER
ZWEISIMMEN
St Stephan
To Lenk
To Interlaken and Bern

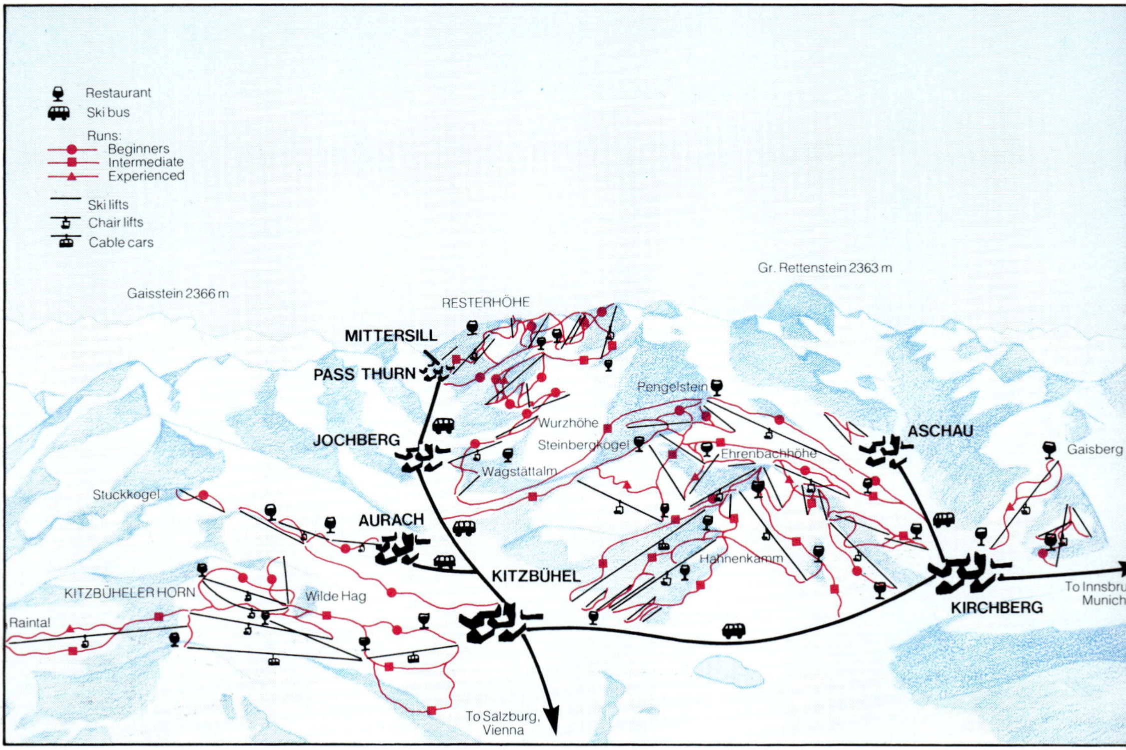
Restaurant
Ski bus
Runs:
Beginners
Intermediate
Experienced
Ski lifts
Chair lifts
Cable cars
Gaisstein 2366 m
Gr. Rettenstein 2363 m
RESTERHÖHE
MITTERSILL
PASS THURN
Pengelstein
Wurzhöhe
JOCHBERG
Steinbergkogel
Ehrenbachhöhe
ASCHAU
Gaisberg
Wagstättalm
Stuckkogel
AURACH
Hahnenkamm
KITZBÜHEL
KITZBÜHELER HORN
Wilde Hag
Raintal
KIRCHBERG
To Salzburg, Vienna

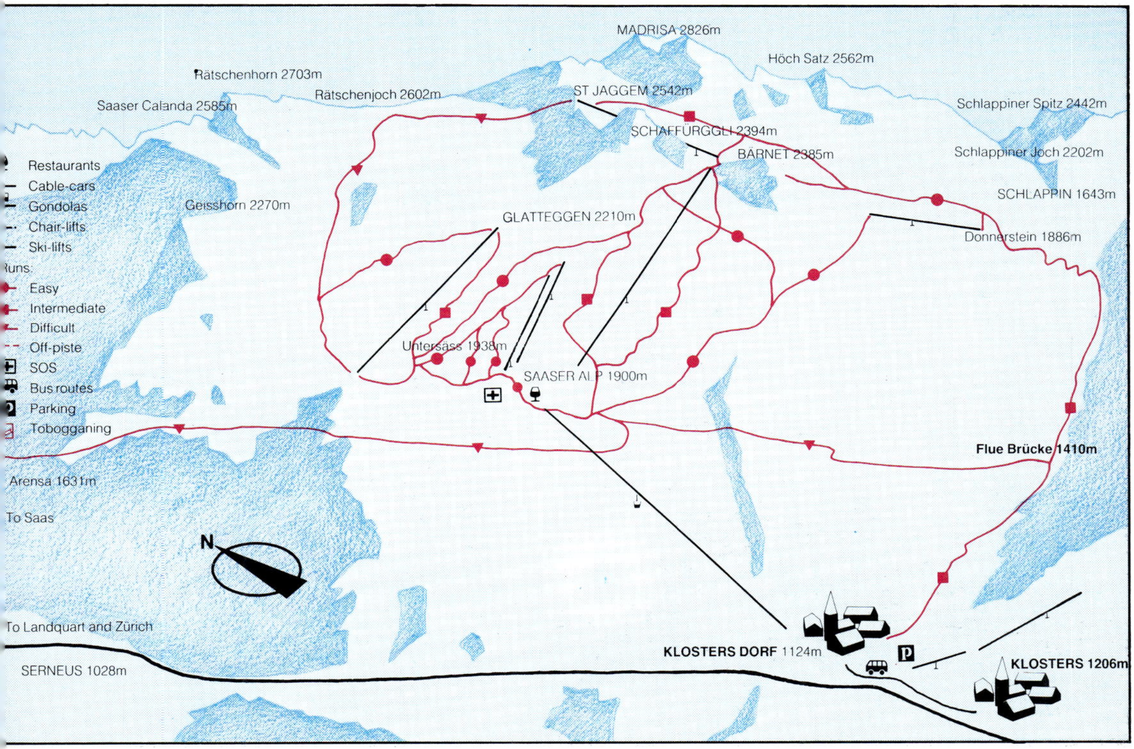
MADRISA 2826m
Höch Satz 2562m
Rätschenhorn 2703m
Rätschenjoch 2602m
ST JAGGEM 2542m
Saaser Calanda 2585m
Schlappiner Spitz 2442m
SCHAFFÜRGGLI 2394m
BÄRNET 2385m
Schlappiner Joch 2202m
Restaurants
Cable-cars
Gondolas
Chair-lifts
Ski-lifts
Runs:
Easy
Intermediate
Difficult
Off-piste
SOS
Bus routes
Parking
Tobogganing
Geisshorn 2270m
SCHLAPPIN 1643m
GLATTEGGEN 2210m
Donnerstein 1886m
Untersäss 1938m
SAASER ALP 1900m
Flue Brücke 1410m
Arensa 1631m
To Saas
N
To Landquart and Zürich
KLOSTERS DORF 1124m
P
KLOSTERS 1206m
SERNEUS 1028m

KLOSTERS AREA (SOUTH)

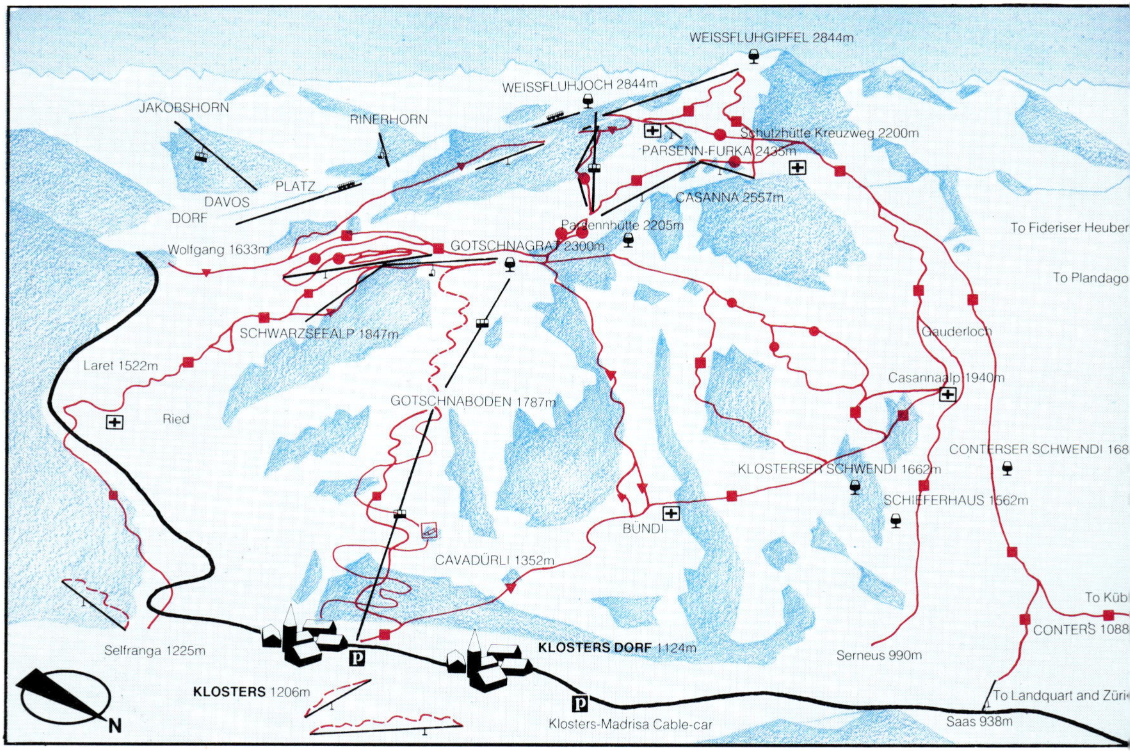

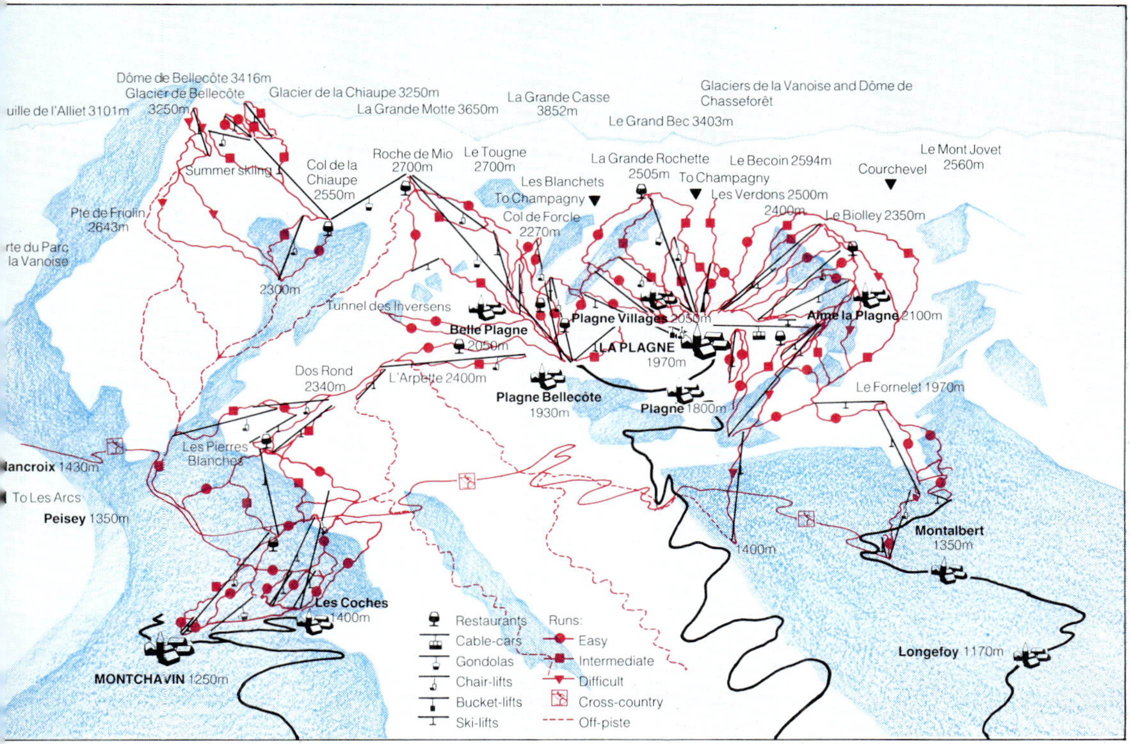
Dôme de Bellecôte 3416m
Glacier de Bellecôte 3250m
Glacier de la Chiaupe 3250m
La Grande Motte 3650m
La Grande Casse 3852m
Glaciers de la Vanoise and Dôme de Chasseforêt
Le Grand Bec 3403m
uille de l'Alliet 3101m
Summer skiing
Col de la Chiaupe 2550m
Roche de Mio 2700m
Le Tougne 2700m
La Grande Rochette 2505m
Le Becoin 2594m
Le Mont Jovet 2560m
Courchevel
Les Blanchets
To Champagny
To Champagny
Les Verdons 2500m
2400m
Le Biolley 2350m
Col de Forcle 2270m
Pte de Friolin 2643m
rte du Parc la Vanoise
2300m
Tunnel des Inversens
Belle Plagne 2050m
Plagne Villages 2050m
Aime la Plagne 2100m
LA PLAGNE 1970m
Dos Rond 2340m
L'Arpette 2400m
Plagne Bellecôte 1930m
Plagne 1800m
Le Fornelet 1970m
Les Pierres Blanches
lancroix 1430m
To Les Arcs
Peisey 1350m
1400m
Montalbert 1350m
Les Coches 1400m
Longefoy 1170m
MONTCHAVIN 1250m
Restaurants
Cable-cars
Gondolas
Chair-lifts
Bucket-lifts
Ski-lifts
Runs:
Easy
Intermediate
Difficult
Cross-country
Off-piste

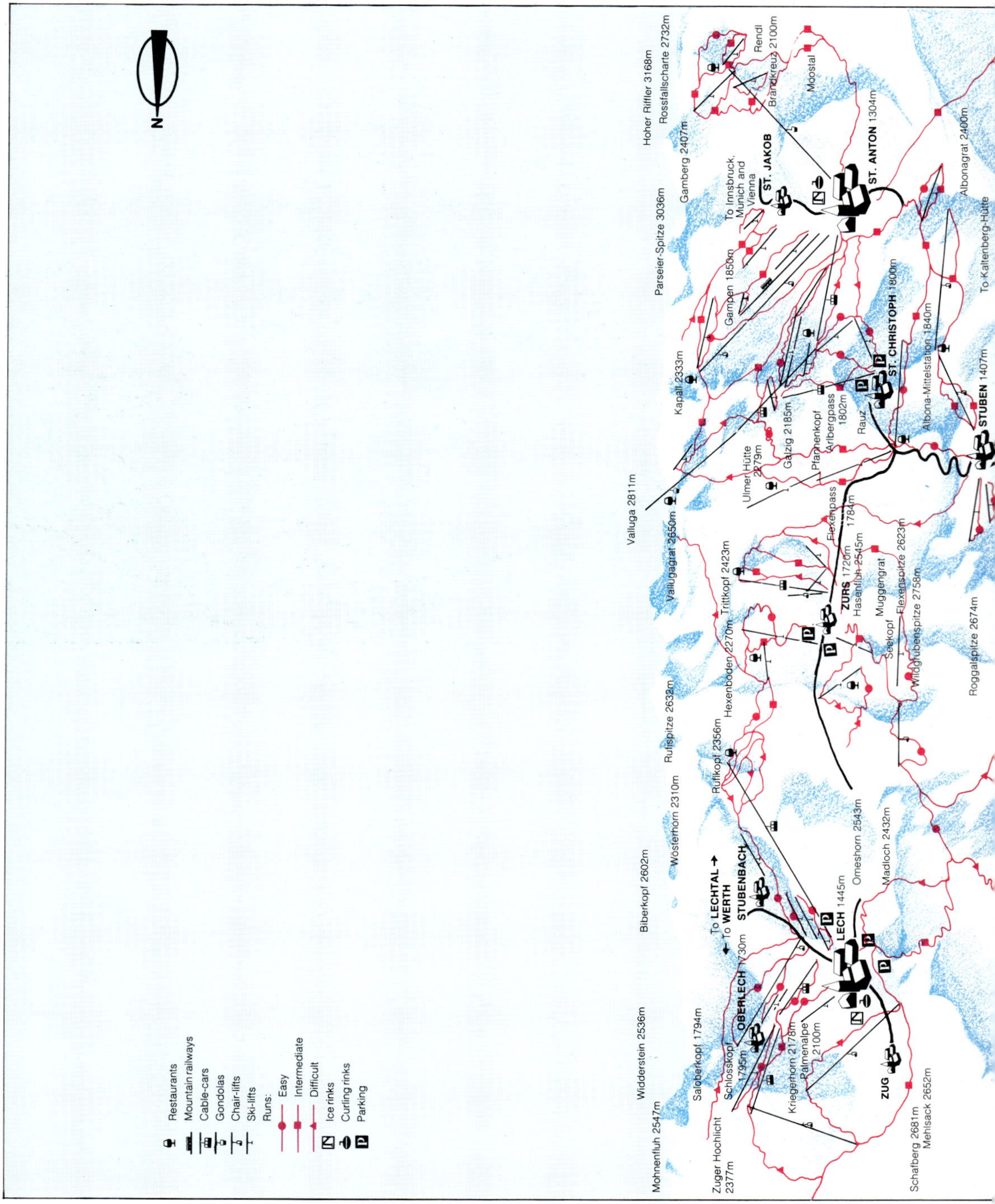
N
Restaurants
Mountain railways
Cable-cars
Gondolas
Chair-lifts
Ski-lifts
Runs:
Easy
Intermediate
Difficult
Ice rinks
Curling rinks
Parking
Mohnenfluh 2547m
Widderstein 2536m
Biberkopf 2602m
Wösterhorn 2310m
Rüfispitze 2632m
Vallugagrat 2650m
Valluga 2811m
Kapall 2333m
Parseier-Spitze 3036m
Gamberg 2407m
Hoher Riffler 3168m
Rossfallscharte 2732m
Rendl
Brandkreuz 2100m
Moostal
ST. JAKOB
To Innsbruck, Munich and Vienna
ST. ANTON 1304m
Albonagrat 2400m
To Kaltenberg-Hütte
Gampen 1850m
ST. CHRISTOPH 1800m
Albona-Mittelstation 1840m
STUBEN 1407m
Galzig 2185m
Pfannenkopf
Arlbergpass 1802m
Rauz
Ulmer Hütte 2279m
Flexenpass 1784m
Trittkopf 2423m
ZURS 1720m
Hasenfluh 2545m
Muggengrat
Flexenspitze 2623m
Seekopf
Wildgrubenspitze 2758m
Roggalspitze 2674m
Hexenboden 2270m
Rüfikopf 2356m
To LECHTAL →
← To WERTH
STUBENBACH
LECH 1445m
Omeshorn 2543m
Madloch 2432m
OBERLECH 1730m
Saloberkopf 1794m
Schlosskopf 1795m
Kriegerhorn 2178m
Palmenalpe 2100m
ZUG
Zuger Hochlicht 2377m
Schafberg 2681m
Mehlsack 2652m

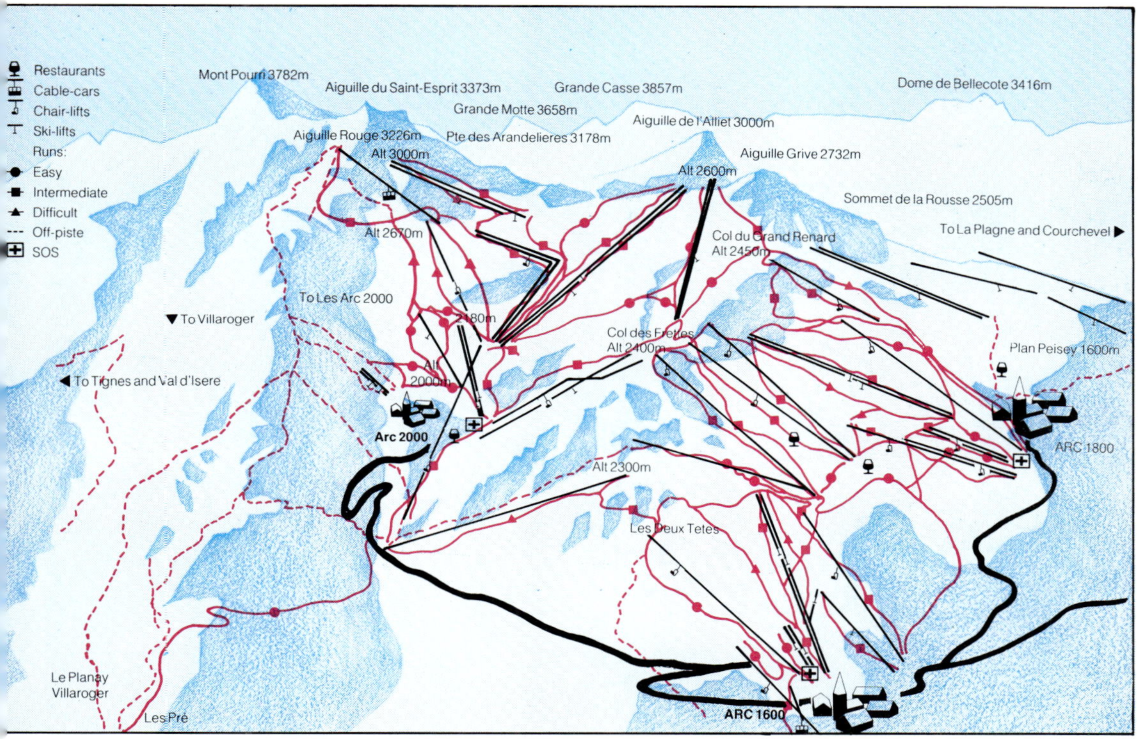
Restaurants
Cable-cars
Chair-lifts
Ski-lifts
Runs:
Easy
Intermediate
Difficult
Off-piste
SOS
Mont Pourri 3782m
Aiguille du Saint-Esprit 3373m
Grande Casse 3857m
Dome de Bellecote 3416m
Grande Motte 3658m
Aiguille de l'Alliet 3000m
Aiguille Rouge 3226m
Pte des Arandelieres 3178m
Alt 3000m
Aiguille Grive 2732m
Alt 2600m
Sommet de la Rousse 2505m
Alt 2670m
Col du Grand Renard
Alt 2450m
To La Plagne and Courchevel
To Les Arc 2000
To Villaroger
2180m
Col des Frettes
Alt 2400m
Plan Peisey 1600m
To Tignes and Val d'Isere
Alt
2000m
Arc 2000
ARC 1800
Alt 2300m
Les Deux Tetes
Le Planay
Villaroger
Les Pré
ARC 1600

LES DEUX-ALPES AREA

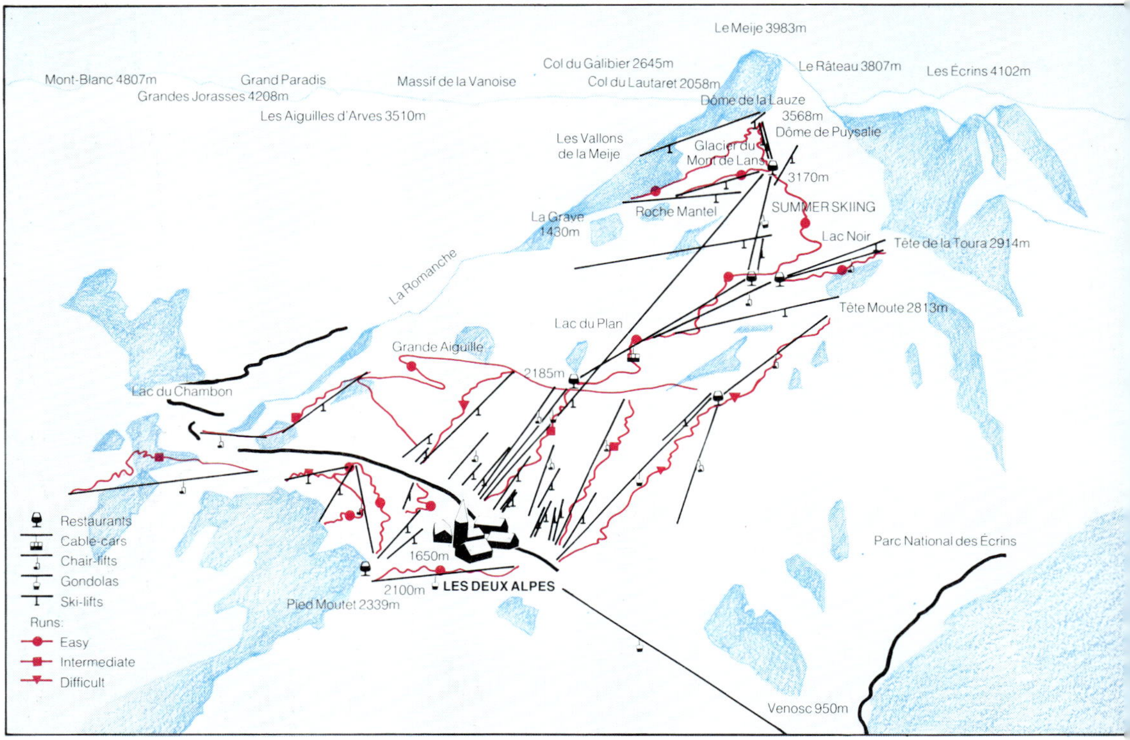

Schwarzhorn 2928m
Oberjoch 2468m
Krinnenboden 2250m
Grosse Scheidegg 2006m
Wetterhorn 3701m
Schreckhorn 4078m
Eiger 3970m
Mönch 4099m
Jungfrau 4158m
Ebnefluh 3960m
Grosshorn 3762m
Breithorn 3782m
Tschingelhorn 3577m
Gspaltenhorn 3437m
Schilthorn 2971m
Birg 2676m
Engetal
Schiltgrat 2145m
Allmendhubel 1912m
Maulerhubel
MÜRREN 1634m
LAUTERBRUNNEN 796m
Grütschalp 1487m
Gimmelwald 1390m
Stechelberg 922m
Wengernalp 1873m
Innerwengen
WENGEN
WILDERSWIL
INTERLAKEN
BEATENBERG
Wixi
Kleine Scheidegg 2061m
Lauberhorn 2472m
Eigergletscher 2320m
Jungfraujoch 3454m
Eismeer 3160m
Underground mountain railway to observation point only (no skiing from top)
Salzegg 1990m
Tschuggen 2520m
Honegg
Männlichen Station 2235m
Männlichen 2343m
Sattelegg
Läger
Brandegg
Alpiglen 1615m
Pfingstegg 1391m (summer only)
GRINDELWALD 1034m
Grund 943m
Schwendi
Oberhaus
Bort 1570m
Egg
First 2168m
N
Restaurants
Mountain railway
Railway
Observation point
Cable-cars
Gondolas
Chair-lifts
Ski-lifts
Runs:
Easy
Intermediate
Difficult
Cross-country
Parking
Bus routes

ST MORITZ AREA

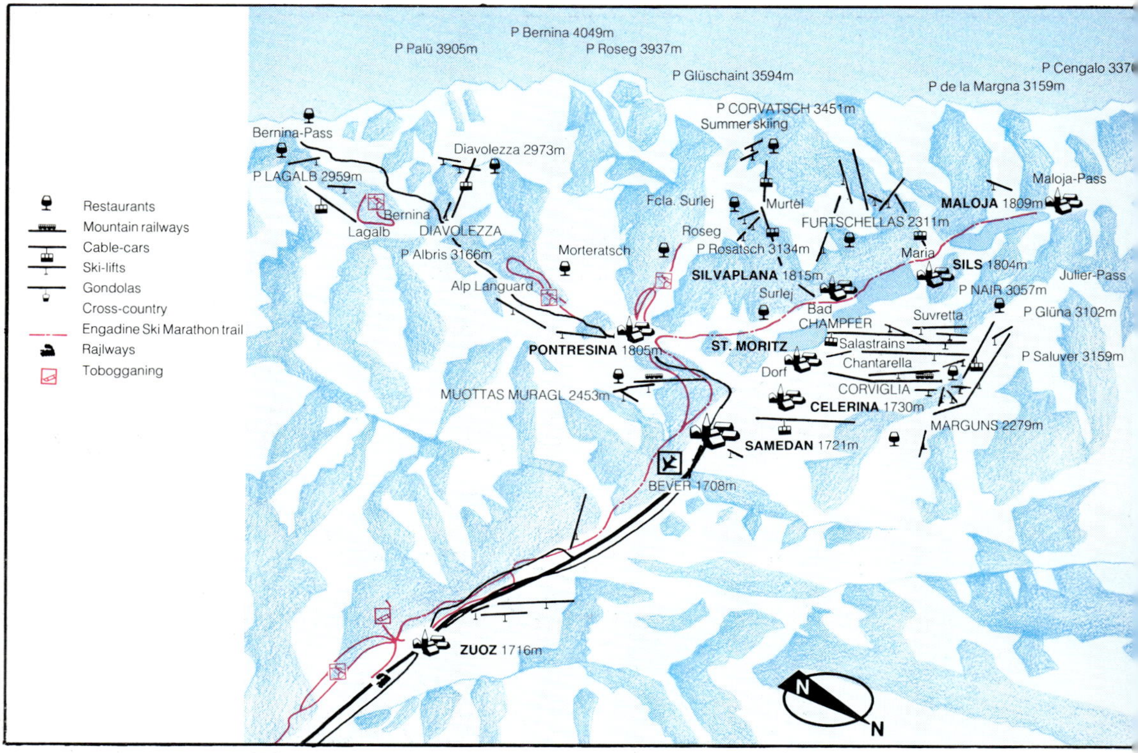

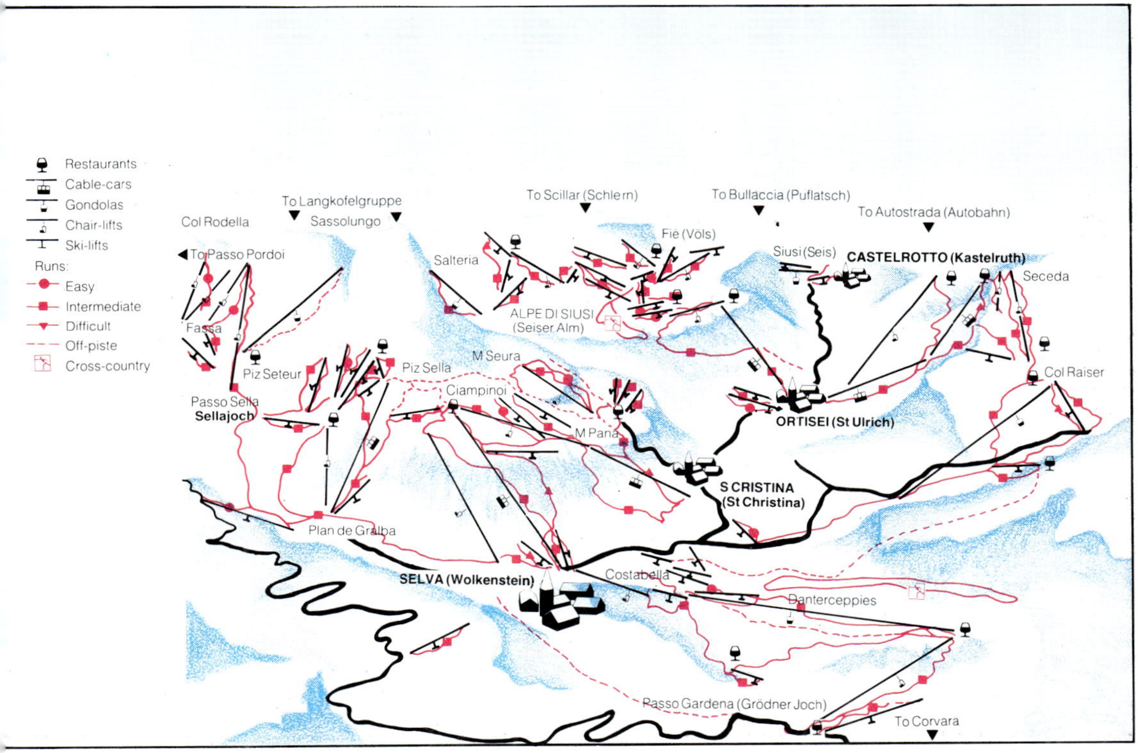
Restaurants
Cable-cars
Gondolas
Chair-lifts
Ski-lifts
Runs:
Easy
Intermediate
Difficult
Off-piste
Cross-country
Col Rodella
To Langkofelgruppe
Sassolungo
To Scillar (Schlern)
To Bullaccia (Puflatsch)
To Autostrada (Autobahn)
Fiè (Völs)
Siusi (Seis)
CASTELROTTO (Kastelruth)
Seceda
To Passo Pordoi
Salteria
ALPE DI SIUSI
(Seiser Alm)
Fassa
Piz Seteur
M Seura
Piz Sella
Ciampinoi
Col Raiser
Passo Sella
Sellajoch
M Pana
ORTISEI (St Ulrich)
S CRISTINA
(St Christina)
Plan de Gralba
SELVA (Wolkenstein)
Costabella
Danterceppies
Passo Gardena (Grödner Joch)
To Corvara

TIGNES/VAL D'ISERE AREA

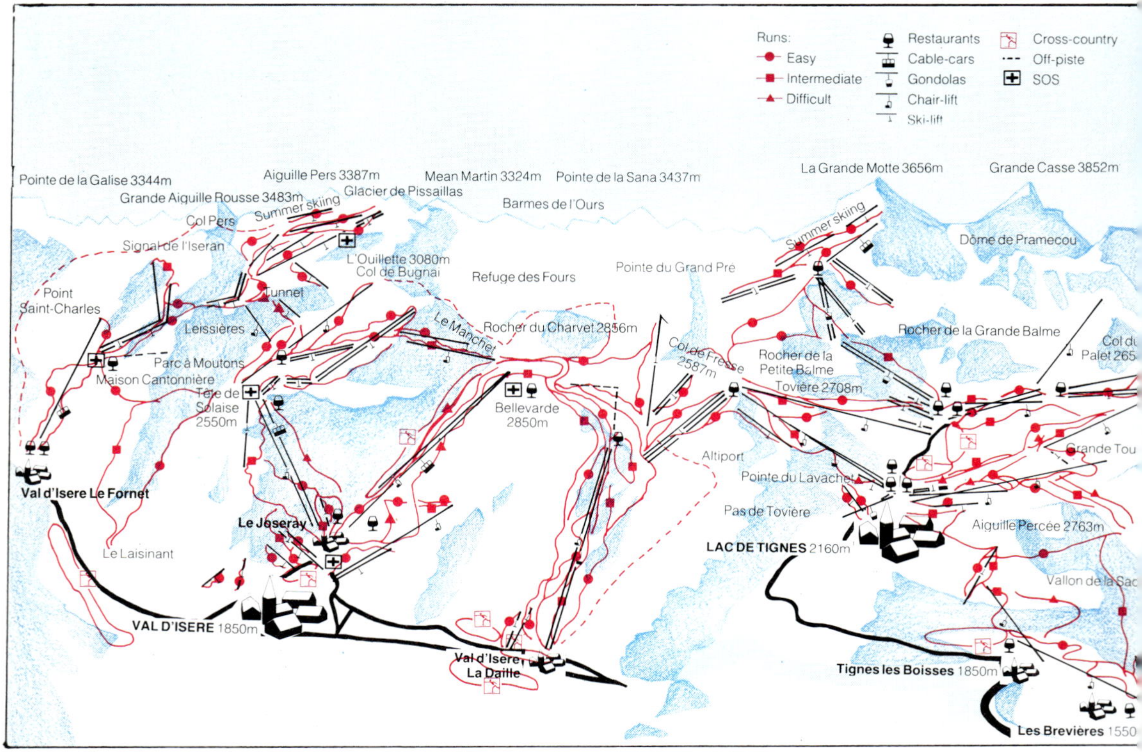

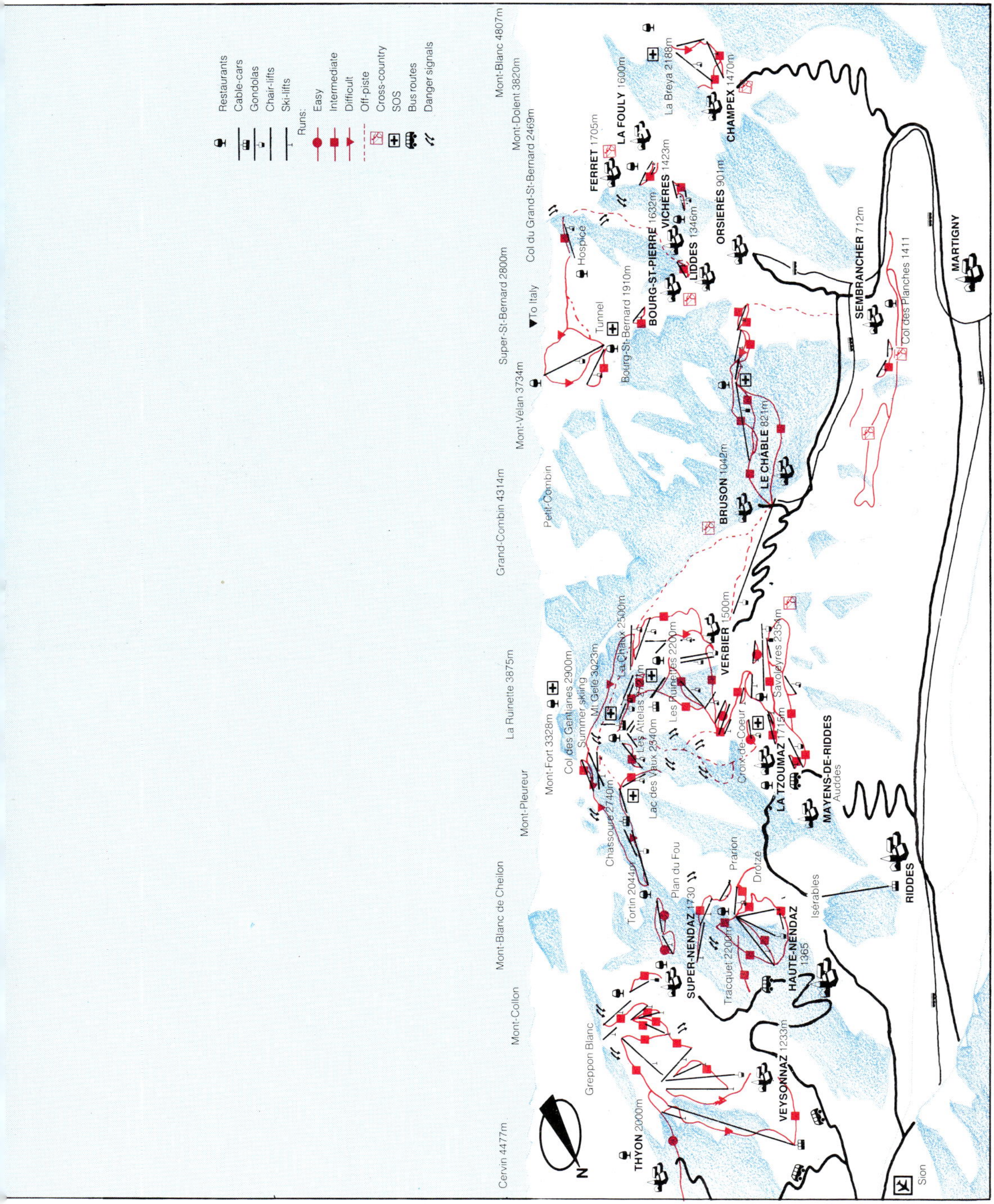
Restaurants
Cable-cars
Gondolas
Chair-lifts
Ski-lifts
Runs:
Easy
Intermediate
Difficult
Off-piste
Cross-country
SOS
Bus routes
Danger signals
Mont-Blanc 4807m
Mont-Dolent 3820m
Col du Grand-St-Bernard 2469m
Super-St-Bernard 2800m
To Italy
Mont-Vélan 3734m
Grand-Combin 4314m
Petit-Combin
La Ruinette 3875m
Mont-Pleureur
Mont-Blanc de Cheilon
Mont-Collon
Cervin 4477m
FERRET 1705m
LA FOULY 1600m
La Breya 2188m
CHAMPEX 1470m
VICHÈRES 1423m
BOURG-ST-PIERRE 1632m
LIDDES 1346m
ORSIÈRES 901m
Hospice
Tunnel
Bourg-St-Bernard 1910m
SEMBRANCHER 712m
MARTIGNY
Col des Planches 1411
BRUSON 1042m
LE CHÂBLE 821m
VERBIER 1500m
Mont-Fort 3328m
Col des Gentianes 2900m
Summer skiing
Mt Gelé 3023m
La Chaux 2500m
Les Attelas
Les Ruinettes 2200m
Lac des Vaux 2540m
Savoleyres 2354m
Croix-de-Coeur
LA TZOUMAZ 1715m
MAYENS-DE-RIDDES
Auddes
Chassoure 2740m
Tortin 2044m
Plan du Fou
Prarion
Drotzé
Isérables
RIDDES
SUPER-NENDAZ 1730
Tracouet 2200m
HAUTE-NENDAZ 1365
VEYSONNAZ 1233m
Greppon Blanc
THYON 2000m
Sion
N

ZERMATT AREA

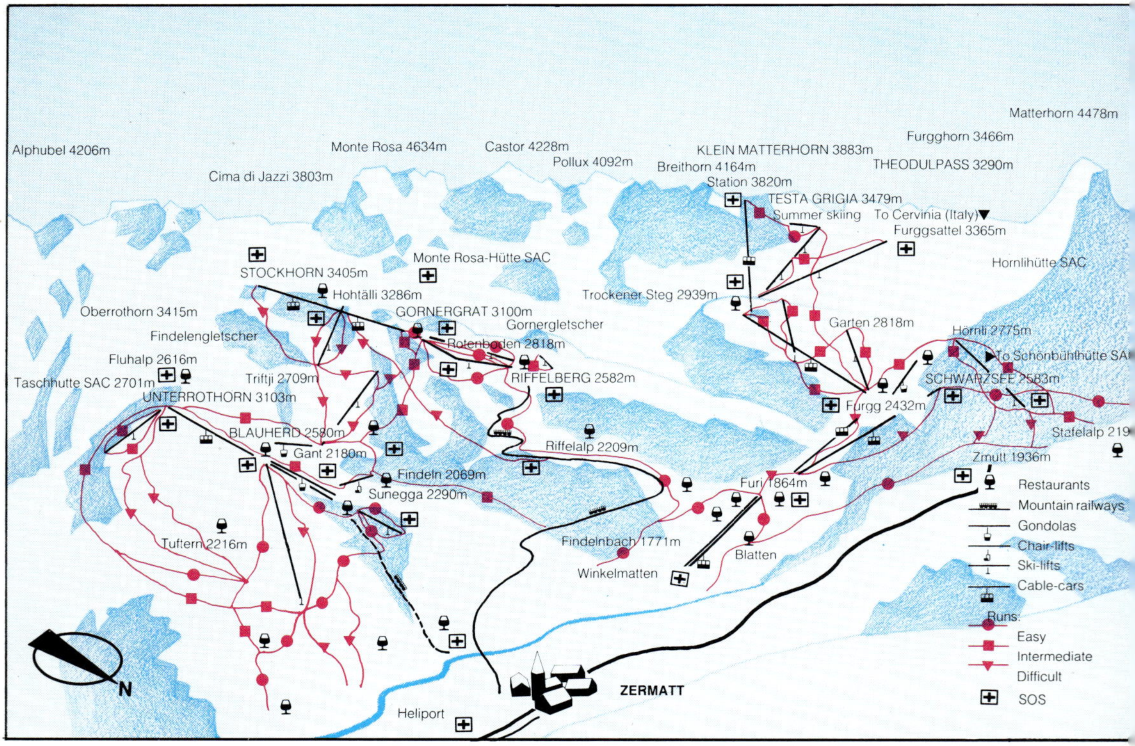